ALLIANCE FOR PROGRESS:

A Social Invention in the Making

ALLIANCE
for PROGRESS

*A Social Invention
in the Making*

HARVEY S. PERLOFF

PUBLISHED FOR Resources for the Future, Inc.
BY The Johns Hopkins Press, BALTIMORE AND LONDON

338.91
P 422
37567

RESOURCES FOR THE FUTURE, INC.
1755 Massachusetts Avenue, N.W., Washington, D.C.   20036

Resources for the Future is a non-profit corporation for research and
education in the development, conservation, and use of natural resources. It was established in 1952 with the co-operation of the Ford
Foundation and its activities since then have been financed by grants
from that Foundation. Part of the work of Resources for the Future is
carried out by its resident staff; part is supported by grants to universities
and other non-profit organizations. Unless otherwise stated, interpreta-
tions and conclusions in RFF publications are those of the authors; the
organization takes responsibility for the selection of significant subjects
for study, the competence of the researchers, and their freedom of
inquiry.

Harvey S. Perloff is Dean of the School of Architecture and Urban
Planning, University of California, Los Angeles. From 1955 until 1968
he was director of RFF's urban and regional studies, and is still associated with RFF as a consultant. The charts were drawn by Clare and
Frank Ford. The index was prepared by Margaret Stanley.

RFF editors: Henry Jarrett, Vera W. Dodds, Nora E. Roots, Sheila
M. Ekers.

Copyright © 1969 by The Johns Hopkins Press
All rights reserved
Manufactured in the United States of America

The Johns Hopkins Press, Baltimore, Maryland 21218
The Johns Hopkins Press, Ltd., London

Library of Congress Catalog Card Number 70-94826

Standard Book Number 8018-1102-3

CONTENTS

LIST OF TABLES

APPENDIX TABLES

LIST OF FIGURES

PREFACE AND ACKNOWLEDGMENTS

THIS long memo — addressed to those who care about the future of our international relations and actions — was prompted by a unique experience. Between April of 1961 and the beginning of 1965, I served first on a committee that was given the responsibility by the Organization of American States of preparing the groundwork for the meeting at Punta del Este which drew up the charter of the Alliance for Progress, and then for some three years was a member of the Alliance's Committee of Nine. This latter organization, which is no longer in existence in its original form, was set up to evaluate plans of the Latin American countries that wanted financial and technical assistance through the Alliance machinery.

As members of the Committee, my colleagues and I, seven of them Latin Americans, had a remarkable vantage point from which to view the problems and efforts of the Latin American nations on the one side and the working of the "donor" mechanism on the other, that is, the activities not only of the U.S. Alliance vehicle — the Agency for International Development (AID) — but the international banks and other organizations dedicated to the job of helping the poorer countries of the world. From this vantage point it was almost impossible not to be saddened by the opportunities being lost because a truly magnificent concept was being carried out in a halfhearted manner and with a weak, underfinanced, and poorly designed mechanism.

Great tasks remain on both sides. The Latin American nations must do very much more for themselves; the donors can help them at many critical points.

As a North American, I have felt that I could not properly or effectively address myself to the job ahead for the Latin Americans. It seemed more appropriate for my Latin American colleagues to do so if they felt so inclined. There were some lessons, however, for the donor group that emerged from my experience and from detailed study of the operations of the Alliance mechanism. These, I felt, might direct some discussion to the question, "What of the future?" And they might raise the challenge of how best to fulfill the objectives that we set for ourselves in 1961 when we undertook to help the Latin Americans.

This book looks ahead to the tenth anniversary of the Alliance and even farther beyond, all the way to the year 2000. For we have to learn to think in terms of decades, and not from year to year and crisis to crisis. While the book concerns itself with all sorts of details of the inevitably technical business of helping to generate development, it raises, I hope, a more critical issue: Can we do anything else but try to perfect a social invention dedicated to one of the most critical tasks of our day — helping the three-quarters of the world that is poor to achieve decent levels of living?

If we succeed with the Alliance for Progress in Latin America, we may develop a pattern that will permit us to do an equally effective job in the other poor regions of the world. The alternative could be a chaos which could engulf all of the rich nations, and certainly the richest nation of all.

Many persons helped me with this book and my debt is very large. First and foremost, I want to express my gratitude to two unselfish collaborators: to Roberto Gonzalez Cofiño, who developed much of the data and provided many valuable suggestions incorporated in the volume, and to Jack Heller, who thoroughly reviewed an earlier version of the book and furnished a host of ideas and materials that are included in chapters throughout the book.

Antonio Casas and Roger Fontaine brought together background materials on the Alliance for Progress which appear particularly in the first three chapters of the book and the chronology in the Appendix.

I must single out four friends and colleagues who reviewed the entire book with care and provided many valuable suggestions for revisions: Luis Escobar Cerda (of the World Bank, formerly Chilean Minister of Development and member of CIAP); Joseph Grunwald (of The Brookings Institution); Felipe Pazos (of the Inter-American Development Bank, formerly President, Central Bank of Cuba); and Ben S. Stephansky (of the Ford Foundation and Twentieth Century Fund, formerly, U.S. Ambassador to Bolivia).

The following, who have expert knowledge on various phases of development and international agency operations, reviewed different parts of the book, ranging from one to eight chapters; their comments played a large part in the extensive revisions I have made in the various versions of the study: Romulo Almeida (Brazil), Robert T. Brown (ECLA), Gerardo A. Canet (Pan American Union), Pierre R. Crosson

(RFF), Isaiah Frank (Johns Hopkins University School of Advanced International Studies), H. Field Haviland (Tufts University), Frederick Harbison (Princeton University), Ann Keiswetter, Charles Montrie, and Donald K. Palmer (U.S. Agency for International Development), John Planck (The Brookings Institution), Alan M. Strout (U.S. Agency for International Development), Luis M. Szekely (Pan American Union), Richard Thorn (University of Pittsburgh, formerly staff member of IMF), and Lowdon Wingo (RFF).

The Pan American Union and the Agency for International Development have been more than generous in providing information and statistical assistance.

The study was carried out at Resources for the Future, whose support I gratefully acknowledge. The study could not have been carried out under more favorable and personally satisfying conditions.

My thanks are also due to Henry Jarrett, for his invaluable editorial guidance, and to Edward O'Neill and Nora E. Roots for their expert editing of the entire volume.

I owe a different and even larger debt to my wife, Mimi, who encouraged me to continue to make the many, many revisions required in writing history in the making and in groping toward new solutions to old and complex problems.

January 1969   Harvey S. Perloff

ABBREVIATIONS

AID........... Agency for International Development
CECIC......... Comisión Ejecutiva del Comité Interamericano Cultural (Executive Commission of the Inter-American Cultural Council)
CIAP.......... Comité Interamericano de la Alianza para el Progreso (Inter-American Committee for the Alliance for Progress)
CIDA.......... Comité Interamericano de Desarrollo Agrícola (Inter-American Committee on Agricultural Development)
ECLA.......... United Nations Economic Commission for Latin America
Eximbank...... U.S. Export-Import Bank
IA-ECOSOC.... Inter-American Economic and Social Council
IBRD.......... International Bank for Reconstruction and Development
IDA........... International Development Association
IDB........... Inter-American Development Bank
IFC........... International Finance Corporation
ILPES......... Instituto Latinoamericano de Planificación Económica y Social (Latin American Institute for Economic and Social Planning)
IMF........... International Monetary Fund
OAS........... Organization of American States
OECD......... Organization for Economic Co-operation and Development
SPTF.......... Social Progress Trust Fund

INTRODUCTION

The future cannot be predicted, but it can be invented. . . .

Dennis Gabor*

NORMALLY we make our great moves forward through social inventions. The Marshall Plan was such an invention. It not only prevented postwar political upheaval, but gave birth to the European Coal and Steel Community and the European Common Market. The machinery set up in the United States by the Full Employment Act of 1946 was another such social invention. It took away the fear of depression, a blessing that can be appreciated only by those who lived through the 1930's.

The Alliance for Progress is still another such social invention. It has created an approach through which nations of a vast continent can be helped to modernize themselves, and to achieve decent levels of living.

The Alliance is as yet a very imperfect mechanism, but that is the way with social inventions. A de Gaulle can hold back progress in the European Common Market. After more than twenty years, our full employment machinery is still weak in handling inflation. And some eight years — and $8 billion — after the Alliance came into being, the situation of the majority of the more than 250 million Latin Americans is still unhappy and hazardous.

The Alliance for Progress is at a crossroads. Much has been accomplished and much has been learned, but, as might be expected following the first phases of so sweeping a social invention, major adjustments in concept and structure are now essential. The question today is whether the Alliance can adapt and innovate flexibly and promptly enough. An implacable rule of nature is that those who do not adapt do not survive.

The Charter of Punta del Este which set up the Alliance in 1961 as a joint Latin American-U.S. enterprise, had a ring of certainty about it and established specific targets to be reached at a terminal date, 1971. Almost from the first, it was recognized that the Alliance, like any effort of its kind, had to tread new ground, and its goals were very long range

* Dennis Gabor, *Inventing the Future* (New York: Alfred A. Knopf, 1964).

indeed — past 1971 at any rate. The terminal date was removed in April 1967 when President Johnson told the Latin American leaders that the United States considered the Alliance's period of existence to be as long as was needed for accomplishment.

Properly seen, the Alliance is a program in the making. It could hardly have been expected that fully effective operating concepts and ideal mechanisms for moving this complex undertaking to large achievement would be found immediately. Indeed, its concepts and mechanisms still require continued testing, adjustment, and development. Nevertheless, the Alliance represents one of the most ambitious concepts in the history of international relations, involving a cooperative effort of twenty countries in this hemisphere.

This book looks back at the historical, economic, and social conditions that brought the Alliance into being, and at the eight years of the Alliance's existence. It also looks forward — to 1971, and beyond to the end of the century.

The purpose of looking backward is to find better means of achieving the goals of the future. An attempt is made to appraise the Alliance from three broad points of view: (1) as a mechanism for transferring resources; (2) its impact on the economies of Latin American countries and the lives of their peoples; (3) as an ideological and political instrument. The discussion inevitably will rely on certain subjective judgments.

In large part, looking ahead means discussing the possibilities of solving the still unresolved problems of the near and the long past and anticipating the problems of the future. These problems are many. With only a few exceptions, the Latin American countries still face serious deficiencies in human resources, serious weaknesses in social and political institutions, and cannot earn enough from their exports to pay for the things they need from abroad to support extensive development programs. In addition, there is no strong technical and institutional base on which rational development policies can depend. Latin America is not Europe before the Marshall Plan needing only a transfusion of dollars to revive basically strong economies and provide jobs for a cadre of skilled technicians waiting to get back to their machines.

Of course a transfusion of dollars, and other foreign currencies, is needed by Latin America, and a major theme of this book is the best use of such foreign assistance. But there are barriers to be hurdled before outside assistance can work as effectively as it should within the Alliance for Progress.

The Alliance came into being in August 1961. Its beginnings were rhetorical, emotional, and practical: rhetorical, in that it was, and is, based on high-sounding but still meaningful words; emotional, in that it was a warm Latin reaction to John F. Kennedy's proffered hand of friendship and assistance; practical, in that it looked coolly and hard at the large and mounting problems of a continent, and suggested ways of overcoming them.

In the main, the aims of the Alliance were not vainglorious. The Charter called for modest but significant economic growth rates in all the nineteen Latin American member countries,[1] for improvements in health, agriculture, education, manufacturing, and exports, for internal savings, and tax and fiscal reforms, and for broad social change — the last a difficult goal in some of the traditional societies of Latin America. In addition, each nation was to prepare a national development program; the Charter laid great stress on the need for planning.

The role of the United States was to support the efforts of the Alliance with money and technical assistance. At Punta del Este — and later — the United States pledged such support and in large measure. (One can only hope that the failure of the Congress in 1968 to continue this support at an adequate level was a temporary aberration.)

Little organizational structure for carrying out the aims of the Charter was provided by those who met at Punta del Este, and organizational support is still weak. The Alliance came into being under the general framework of the Organization of American States, and was to rely on other existing agencies as well. At first the only new unit was a "Panel of Experts" whose job was to study national development plans when submitted, and to make recommendations on them. However, two years after the organization of the Alliance, the CIAP (*Comité Interamericano de la Alianza para el Progreso*) came into being, with much broader powers than those given to the "experts." The existing arrangements have many evident weaknesses.

The accomplishments of the Alliance since 1961 have been poor indeed. So far in the 1960's, the rates of growth of the gross domestic product (GDP) of many of the countries have been lower than in the 1950's. Other goals have not been attained. Also, those working with the Alliance have found many countries to be woefully lacking in the

---

[1] Argentina, Bolivia, Brazil, Chile, Colombia, Costa Rica, Dominican Republic, Ecuador, El Salvador, Guatemala, Haiti, Honduras, Mexico, Nicaragua, Panama, Paraguay, Peru, Uruguay, and Venezuela. Trinidad-Tobago and Barbados joined the OAS in 1967, and presumably are now eligible for Alliance assistance even though not signatories of the Charter.

ability to develop sensible national development plans, although there have been notable exceptions and some overall improvement in recent years. There is a pressing need for a multilateral approach to the area's problems, and one of the goals that should be established is rationalized region-wide development. Finally, a new approach to the use of international assistance needs to be found. There is today no overall coherence in this important component of the Alliance. To overcome these listed problems, revision of the Alliance's Charter will be necessary.

Despite its shortcomings and failures, the Alliance for Progress has enormous potential. If we turn away from it because we are impatient with our imperfectly working model, we will lose one of the truly great opportunities for forward movement in modern times.

This book concerns itself with ways through which the Alliance might be brought up to a plane of excellence and effectiveness. The first stage of the Alliance has shown what it can do, and what its weaknesses are. We need to bring it to the next stage as soon as possible. The tenth anniversary in 1971 might be a symbolically useful time for a major reorganization.

ALLIANCE FOR PROGRESS:
A Social Invention in the Making

Chapter 1

BACKGROUND OF THE ALLIANCE

THE problems of the countries of Latin America are both old and complex. Some of them originated in the long period of Spanish and Portuguese colonial rule that started in the early sixteenth century; certainly, most of them can be traced to the period of the wars of liberation in the early nineteenth century.

It is against this backdrop that the Alliance for Progress must be viewed. But it also must be viewed in terms of the long-standing and shifting relationships of the United States with Latin America.

Relations between the United States and the nations of Latin America, in broad terms, have been characterized by three great themes: (1) domination and intervention, (2) neighborliness and mutuality, and (3) "a helping hand." The temper of these relations has largely been determined by the theme or themes at the forefront at a given time. The third theme is of relatively recent vintage, emerging in a small way in the 1930's and not achieving importance until the maturing of the Alliance for Progress. The two other themes, often in uncomfortable juxtaposition, have colored United States-Latin American relations from the early nineteenth century to the present.

Almost from the beginning of the United States as an independent nation, American leaders recognized the influence of developments in Latin America on the security and well-being of this country, particularly when world powers were involved. Whatever other considerations may have been involved — economic, cultural, moral, or other — the security interest was the dominant one. And so it is today.

A spirit of neighborliness and mutuality dominated the earliest relations. The United States officially, though erratically, and the U.S. people emotionally backed the Latin American revolutions that broke the rule of Spain and Portugal in the first part of the nineteenth century, and ended a French attempt at domination of Mexico at the time of our Civil War. The earlier U.S. revolution had been an inspiration to Latin America. Washington was the first capital to recognize the new regimes. The U.S. Constitution was the model for many of the post-revolutionary constitutions in Latin America.

The new and weak nations of Latin America came into being at a time when European imperialism was flagrant and unashamed. A mere declaration of independence by a new nation was no defense against imperialistic designs. The U.S. government felt it necessary to assert its own interest and this President Monroe did in a message to Congress late in 1823.[1] Of European designs against America, he said: "We should consider any attempt on their part to extend their system to any portion of this hemisphere as dangerous to our peace and safety." The nations of the new world formed a political system distinct from the old, and its integrity had to be guarded. "The American continents, by the free and independent condition which they have assumed and maintain, are henceforth not to be considered as subjects for future colonization by any European power." This was the beginning of a political policy toward Latin America that was a direct corollary of an isolationist policy toward Europe that lasted for almost a century until World War I.

Latin American views in regard to European intervention in the Western Hemisphere coincided with those of the United States, and Monroe's words were well received by the new nations. Actually, the United States then was not strong enough to enforce the doctrine. But it demonstrated its ability to make good its promise after the middle of the nineteenth century in tests of will in the Caribbean and Mexico. And as United States wealth and strength grew toward the end of the nineteenth century, there was still greater disposition to enforce the Monroe Doctrine, and to diminish European leverage in the Western Hemisphere.

The years 1895 to 1933 marked what historian Hubert Herring has called "the rise and fall of American imperialism." These were years strongly characterized by U.S. domination of or intervention in Latin America, particularly in the Caribbean area. It began in 1895 with the issuance of a U.S. ultimatum to England during a Venezuelan-British Guiana dispute, when Secretary of State Richard Olney declared: "Today the United States is practically sovereign on this continent, and its fiat is law upon the subjects to which it confines its interposition." The British, occupied with the Boer issue in South Africa, yielded.

The war of 1898 removed the last vestiges of the Spanish Empire

---

[1] James Monroe, Seventh Annual Message to the Senate and House of Representatives, Washington, December 2, 1823, in Robert N. Burr and Roland D. Hussey, *Documents on Inter-American Cooperation* (Philadelphia: University of Pennsylvania Press, 1955), vol. 1, *1810–1881*, pp. 32–33.

in the New World. The Pan American movement was begun with a major objective of maintaining hemispheric peace, thus removing any possible justification for any European nation's intervention in the protection of its interests. When the United States wanted to build a canal, essential to expanding trade and to a two-ocean navy, the province of Panama was encouraged to separate from Colombia when the national government resisted Washington's canal proposal.

When chaos and bankruptcy threatened to bring armed intervention to several Caribbean countries by the governments of European creditors, President Theodore Roosevelt in 1904 announced a "corollary" to the Monroe Doctrine which justified, not merely the isolation of the Americas under the protective cover of the United States, but the right of intervention in the event of "wrongdoing, or an impotence which results in a general lessening of the ties of civilized society...." ("These wretched republics cause me a great deal of trouble," Roosevelt is reported to have complained.) What followed left an indelible mark on United States-Latin American relations. It made the words "U.S. Marines" invidious ones in Latin America, and they are to this day. By the time the United States entered World War I, it had implemented the Roosevelt "corollary" by landing Marines in Nicaragua, Haiti, and the Dominican Republic, converting all three to virtual protectorates. There were repeated diplomatic and military abrogations of the independence of Cuba, interpositions by U.S. armed forces in Panama, and threats and armed interventions in Mexico in the name of border security and the sanctity of the American flag.

These acts enraged Latin Americans everywhere, not alone in the Caribbean area. The Peruvian writer García Calderón was to exclaim in 1911: "To save themselves from Yankee imperialism the Latin-American democracies would almost accept a German alliance, or the aid of Japanese arms. Everywhere the Americans of the North are feared."[2]

By the end of World War I, an exhausted Europe openly recognized the Monroe Doctrine — referring to it in the League of Nations Charter as "a regional understanding" — and accepted the right of the United States to maintain its dominant position in the hemisphere. In the century following the proclamation of Monroe's doctrine, the United States had achieved its Western Hemisphere objective. But it had also gleaned a harvest of jealousy, irritation and hatred.

[2] As quoted in John A. Crow, *The Epic of Latin America* (New York: Doubleday, 1946), p. 691.

As Robert Burr points out in his perceptive analysis, when "European exclusion" turned out to mean unchallenged hemispheric domination by the United States, the Latin Americans changed their minds about a coincidence of interest with Washington. He wrote, "For they found themselves confronting the new and potentially more dangerous threat of a far stronger, geographically closer, politically more unified and expansive people than any who now menaced them from across the Atlantic."[3]

The first formal machinery designed to bring Latin America together was the Pan American Union (first known as the Bureau of American Republics), organized more than three-quarters of a century ago. (On the agenda of the conference of 1889–1890 at which the Bureau was set up was the formation of an American customs union with a uniform system of customs regulations.[4] The Pan American Union provided a framework for cooperation on some economic and social matters of mutual interest, including international highways and other transportation, telecommunications, patents, trademarks and copyrights, commercial law, interchange of professors and students, and trade.

The Pan American movement did not dissolve the differences between the North and the South. During the 1920's fear of the United States became widespread and intense. Not only were the Latin Americans faced by the political and military power of Washington, but by growing domination of U.S. capital. During and after World War I, the United States had displaced the European nations as Latin America's main trading partner. Throughout the 1920's Latin American trade with the United States was considerably greater than the combined total of that with Britain, France, and Germany.[5] U.S. investments spread rapidly into all parts of Latin America. At the end of 1929, direct investments in Latin America, according to the Department of Commerce, amounted to more than $3.5 billion, more than twice the value of U.S. investments in any other geographic region of the world.

Latin Americans after World War I found themselves increasingly dependent on the United States for needed capital as their traditional European bankers were unable to undertake the financing of major

---

[3] Robert N. Burr, *Our Troubled Hemisphere: Perspectives on United States-Latin American Relations* (Washington: The Brookings Institution, 1967), p. 5.

[4] Some 75 years later, Senator Jacob Javits (R., N.Y.) was to make a similar proposal.

[5] Donald W. Baerresen, Martin Carnoy, and Joseph Grunwald, *Latin American Trade Patterns* (Washington: The Brookings Institution, 1965), pp. 19–21.

development projects. In the Caribbean region, U.S. loans and investments and political interference became inseparable. During the 1920's
Haiti, Cuba, Panama, and the Dominican Republic practically were
being governed by directives from Washington. The major countries of
South America, as well as Mexico, however, were determined that there
would be no U.S. infringement of their sovereignty and independence.

But efforts to bring the Latin American nations into some sort of
political union or to develop other forms of countervailing power came
to naught. Latin American leaders then attempted to secure from the
United States a nonintervention commitment. Washington, throughout
the period, refused to relinquish the unilateral right of intervention. It
appeared to Latin Americans that the United States was bent upon the
political domination of the entire Western Hemisphere.[6]

Good Neighbor Policy

The U.S. government elected in 1932 was determined to bring a
New Deal to inter-American affairs as well as to national affairs. In his
inaugural address of 1933, President Franklin D. Roosevelt declared:

> I would dedicate this nation to the policy of the good neighbor — the
> neighbor who resolutely respects himself, and because he does so, respects
> the rights of others — the neighbor who respects his obligations and
> respects the sanctity of agreements in and with a world of neighbors.

These words — which are as meaningful today as when first spoken —
were to be made good. The Roosevelt Administration immediately
began to liquidate all vestiges of U.S. intervention, and at the seventh
inter-American conference in Montevideo in 1933 renounced the right
of intervention itself. By agreeing to nonintervention and consultation,
the United States accepted the Latin American nations as juridically
equal, and they in turn responded warmly and positively to the "good
neighbor" policy. The extent to which Latin American-U.S. relations
had been colored by the intervention issue was demonstrated by the
remarkably good relations that characterized the Roosevelt period,
despite the lack of any material aid in the 1930's and minuscule aid
during World War II.

The general atmosphere of sympathy and mutuality was maintained, and even strengthened, during World War II when the United
States bent every effort to keep the Western Hemisphere as a secure

[6] Burr, *Our Troubled Hemisphere*, pp. 6–11.

bastion for the Allies. The view of Latin America as an essential part of any U.S. security arrangement gained an additional dimension.[7] Disruptive and threatening activities of various Fascist groups suggested that satisfactory relations among governments were not enough, and that elements alien to U.S. security interests could be introduced into Latin America. The threat of subversion and insurgency increasingly became a matter of concern.

The period was marked by important beginnings in economic as well as in political and military concepts and activities. In Latin America, the Great Depression dealt a severe blow to the major export industries upon which the nations' economies had become largely dependent.[8] There was a clamor for positive governmental action, and many of the governments reacted with measures they hoped would make their nations less reliant on external demand in the future. They tried to turn their economies inward by encouraging import-substituting industries, and they adopted many measures to maintain the prices of basic commodities. (In Brazil, for example, coffee in excess of the amount that could be sold at a fixed price was burned.) A new concern for the health of national economies began to emerge, and a new view was taken of the responsibility of government in economic affairs.

This period also marked a small beginning in the provision of technical and financial assistance. First, there was a limited but highly useful U.S. program of technical assistance in agriculture to a number of Latin American countries, and then the concept of external assistance was expanded and broadened with the establishment of the position of Coordinator of Inter-American Affairs. (Nelson A. Rockefeller held this post during most of the war period.) This office originally was set up to help create an atmosphere of cooperation in Allied efforts by strengthening U.S.-Latin American relations in cultural and economic matters. During the period 1941–45, some $263 million in "Lend-Lease" funds were granted to Latin American countries.

---

[7] The Acts of Chapultepec and Rio (1945 and 1947), providing for joint defense against aggression, were of great importance in the evolution of the inter-American system.

[8] Both the quantity and prices of raw materials exported fell dramatically with the sharp curtailment of aggregate demand in the industrial economies. An index of export prices shows a drop from 113 in 1929 (with 1937 as 100) to 53 in 1932. Even by the end of the decade export prices were still well below the 1929 level. The decline of import prices was not so great, and the terms of trade worsened. United Nations Economic Commission for Latin America, *Economic Survey of Latin America, 1949* (1951), p. 17.

The Postwar Lull

After World War II, events in Europe and the Far East demanded urgent U.S. attention. The threat of Communist penetration in Western Europe produced the Marshall Plan response. The Cold War dominated the international scene. U.S. foreign policy increasingly was formulated on immediate and direct strategic considerations. This condition hardened with the outbreak of the Korean War and with active Communist challenges in other Asian countries such as the Philippines. The apparent quiet in Latin America was a welcome relief. It was assumed in the United States that the political situation in that part of the world was relatively static, and that all was well with Latin American relations. This was a dangerous misconception.

The stirrings in Latin America that had become noticeable in the 1930's all the while were gathering momentum. The "revolution of rising expectations" swept across Latin America with as much impact as was felt anywhere in the less developed world. And new problems had arisen, one of the most difficult being the rapid increase in population.

The introduction of modern public health measures and other improvements in Latin America, as elsewhere, had a tremendous impact on death rates. Between 1935–39 and 1955–59, crude death rates in Mexico dropped from 23.3 to 12.5 and in Costa Rica from 20.0 to 9.6. The population of Latin America increased from 124 million in 1940 to 206 million in 1960. Life in the countryside, which in most places offered very little at best, became intolerable for many, and great numbers moved to the cities in the hope of jobs or at least better public services and better opportunities for their children. In the extreme case, between 1950 and 1960 Venezuela's urban population increased at an annual rate of 6.3 per cent while the rural population increased at only 0.7 per cent. The country's overall population increase was a startling 3.9 per cent. In Brazil, the urban figure was 5.2 per cent and the rural, 1.6 per cent, with an overall increase of 3.1 per cent.

Substantial industrial enterprises were being set up in Brazil, Argentina, Mexico, Cuba, Chile, and elsewhere. Steel, electric power, petroleum, chemicals, pulp and paper, and many other industries were being established through governmental as well as private auspices. New skills were being learned, and a large urban labor force was in formation. But the number of new jobs fell far short of the population increase, and sizable unemployment became almost endemic, reaching rates of

12 and 15 per cent in some countries. In some cases, national attempts to speed industrialization through high tariffs and various kinds of subsidies contributed to inflation and to pressure on limited import capacity, and helped to create economic imbalances that inflicted additional hardships on the classes least able to bear them.

New social groups were achieving importance — industrial entrepreneurs, merchants, bureaucrats, labor union officials, intellectuals. Many of them spoke a relatively new language of nationalism. The new middle and working classes were much more conscious of their membership in a distinctive national group than was the old landowning aristocracy that had dominated life in the nineteenth century and had tended to feel more akin to European elites than to the masses of their own countries. While these new groupings differed in many ways, they had a common bond in their search for a national identity and their deep resentment of foreign domination. They tended to feel that their nations had for far too long been under the political and economic domination of the richer and stronger countries, particularly the United States.

At the same time, the basic demand of the poor for land, food, and jobs generated growing political pressures. In desperately poor Bolivia this pressure exploded in violent revolution in 1952. Elsewhere its form ranged from the invasion of farmland by small bands of landless workers and the organization of Peasant Leagues to quiet and sullen anger in much of the countryside and in the growing slums of the large cities· The dissatisfaction of the less skilled workers increased because, no matter how hard they worked, they could never quite catch up. The general alienation fed movements like Peronismo in Argentina and radical parties[9] elsewhere.

The sources of dissatisfaction and the outlets for it were many, and they were potent enough to force political response. In the few instances in which relatively progressive governments were in office, efforts to launch economic development programs were undertaken. And even where entrenched elites were determined to resist any substantial changes in the status quo, it was found convenient to use the language of economic development and social reform to get and hold political power.

Latin America was looking for new answers to the long-standing

[9] It should be noted that there are political parties in Latin America (e.g., in Chile) bearing the name Radical which in fact are not radical but middle-of-the-road groups. The above refers to extreme leftist political groupings.

problems of poverty and dependence, and the striking imbalance of wealth and power in the hemisphere. There also was growing dissatisfaction with the existing machinery of inter-American cooperation.[10] The Pan American Union was totally under U.S. control, so much so that some Latin Americans referred to it as the "American Ministry of Colonies." However, at the ninth conference in 1948 in Bogotá, the Pan American Union Board was supplanted by the Organization of American States, with the Union put into a subordinate secretariat position. But the OAS was to be concerned principally with political and security affairs. To take care of the social and economic side, a special OAS agency, the Inter-American Economic and Social Council, was established. This turned out to be an organization of low-ranking diplomats, who had no power to make policy.

Also in 1948, the United Nations Economic Commission for Latin America (ECLA) was formed, designed to be a center of economic and social research, education, and service to the area. Under the strong leadership of Dr. Raúl Prebisch, it was to have a profound influence on Latin American thought.[11]

ECLA saw much Latin American economic trouble as inherent in the international trading system. Caught in their dependence on a few basic commodities in order to be able to import the many products they themselves could not produce but wanted, the Latin American countries were doubly disadvantaged. The income elasticity of demand (that is, the rates at which purchases increased as incomes went up) of their raw material exports was not very high. They could not look forward to greatly expanding markets for their traditional exports. On the other hand, the income elasticity of demand of the manufactured goods they imported tended to be very much higher. Thus, for example, people in the United States did not drink more coffee as their incomes rose, but Latin Americans wanted more cars and machinery and appliances

[10] Hubert Herring, *A History of Latin America* (New York: Alfred A. Knopf, 1965), pp. 810–13.

[11] In addition to the extremely influential Raúl Prebisch, a number of outstanding Latin American economists, some directly associated with ECLA and others independently working at universities and in government posts, probed the problems of Latin America during the 1950's and suggested possible approaches to their solution. Included in this group are Víctor L. Urquidi, Roberto de Oliveira Campos, Celso Furtado, Luis Escobar Cerda, Jorge Ahumada, Anibal Pinto, Osvaldo Sunkel, Javier Márquez, Edmundo Flores, and Felipe Pazos. Urquidi's book, *The Challenge of Development in Latin America* (New York: Frederick A. Praeger, 1964), based on a series of lectures given in Mexico City in October 1961, is an excellent summary of the basic ideas evolving out of ECLA studies at the time of the Charter of Punta del Este.

whenever their incomes increased. As a consequence, Latin American countries tended to suffer deteriorating terms of trade over time (i.e., the price of imports increased more than the prices of their exports). In addition to enjoying a more favorable demand situation, the economically more advanced countries had a greater capacity to control the prices of their products and trading conditions.

To correct the situation and promote rapid development, not only would efforts have to be directed to stabilizing prices of basic export commodities and to diversifying exports, but governments would have to take a key role in pressing internal development. Principally, they would have to promote rapid industrialization, starting with the substitution of domestic production for imports. This would not only help overcome the balance-of-payments problem but would provide jobs for the rapidly expanding population. Central government planning was a critical ingredient in such an effort.

The limited internal savings of Latin American countries that could be directed to capital investment made development in Latin America inevitably dependent on external public capital in substantial amounts. The cooperation of the United States, the only industrialized country that emerged from World War II in a position to provide large-scale external assistance, was indispensable.

Latin Americans watched with growing resentment the outpouring of U.S. assistance to Europe and Asia while their own requests for assistance were being rejected. U.S. statements, particularly during World War II, of the special fraternal relationship with Latin America seemed like a mockery in the 1950's. The Latin Americans had reason to believe that the U.S. interest in Latin America was limited to immediate security considerations. In 1954 there was open U.S. support of the forceful overthrow of a Guatemalan government that had been infiltrated by Communists, and at an OAS meeting in Caracas in the same year Secretary of State John Foster Dulles insisted on passage of a resolution calling for "consultation to consider the adoption of appropriate action" in the case of a threatened takeover of any American state. Latin American requests at the Caracas meeting for U.S. assistance to stabilize export prices and to finance development programs received little attention from the U.S. delegation.

Still, the Latin Americans had nowhere else to turn, so they kept trying. At the fourth meeting of the Inter-American Economic and Social Council in Quitandinha, Brazil, several months after Caracas, they presented a thoughtful case for U.S. financial and technical assistance, incorporating in their presentation many of the basic ideas that were later to be included in the Alliance for Progress. A report prepared by ECLA brought together figures on past and projected economic development in the Latin American countries to demonstrate the urgency of the need for outside public funds if levels of living were to be raised. The report emphasized the need for stabilizing the prices of basic commodities, for promoting rapid industrialization planned and supervised by governments, and for freer trade among the Latin American countries. In an accompanying document, a "Preparatory Group" composed of prominent Latin Americans emphasized the need for external public capital.[12] They estimated that, at least for a "transitional period," over one billion dollars of external funds annually would be required for Latin America. In a pointed summary comment, they wrote:

> Our people will find this meeting the best occasion to discover whether it is possible to extend the Good Neighbor Policy to the field of economics as well as politics.... The cooperation of the United States is a basic condition upon which not only the success of this effort depends, but also the possibility of undertaking it in our time.... Cooperation alone can create the possibility of an America whose fundamental unity is based on a firm dedication to its democratic way of life.[13]

The U.S. response was negative. Apparently the Good Neighbor Policy was a thing of the past. The old theme of domination and intervention, even though a pale shadow of what it had been in the early part of the century, came again to the forefront. Anti-Americanism became very fashionable throughout the continent.[14]

The U.S. position was not just a matter of resisting requests for large-scale aid to Latin America because of heavy Cold War obligations. There was strong U.S. resistance to the view that economic developments must be centrally planned and directed by government, to external funds coming largely from government sources rather than from private enterprise, to stabilizing prices of primary commodities through com-

---

[12] The group was composed of Eduardo Frei (Chile), Evaristo Araiza (Mexico), Cleantho de Paiva Leite (Brazil), Carlos Lleras Restrepo (Colombia), Rodrigo Facio (Costa Rica), and Francisco García Olano (Argentina). The group had the technical advisory services of Jorge Sol Castellanos and Paul Rosenstein-Rodan.

[13] United Nations, "International Cooperation in Latin American Development Policy," Doc. E/CN.12/359 (New York, 1954).

[14] For extensive documentation on the growing anti-American feelings in Latin America during the postwar 1940's and the 1950's, see Donald Marquand Dozer, *Are We Good Neighbors: Three Decades of Inter-American Relations, 1930–1960* (Gainesville: University of Florida Press, 1959), chap. 6–9.

modity agreements and other collective action, and to regional economic integration in Latin America. The popular Latin American position, many U.S. government leaders felt, overemphasized the role of the state, was prejudiced against private enterprise, would progressively socialize Latin American economies and create a vast bureaucracy, and would adversely affect U.S. business interests in Latin America.

This theme, which was to dominate the official United States position on aid to Latin American countries until the end of the 1950's, was explicitly stated by the U.S. delegation at the ninth inter-American conference at Bogotá in 1948:

> There was and is a strong feeling in a number of other American republics that their economic development should be carried forward and given its principal impetus, not by private initiative as it is known in the U.S., but through government development corporations financed by foreign and local government capital, or, at the most, mixed government and private financing, with a considerable degree of governmental influence and control in planning and operations.... The United States delegation took the position that we strongly favored sound economic development, that we believed that private capital, whether domestic or foreign, would have to be counted upon and should be allowed to do the main part of the job, that only through private capital channels could an adequate volume of foreign capital be furnished, and that the United States Government itself had no interest or desire to force private American capital into any country where it was not welcomed.

A decade later, at a meeting of the OAS Committee of Twenty-one in 1958, Douglas C. Dillon, the U.S. representative, was to make the same point: "Public lending...can never substitute for private initiative and private capital.... We need to clear away the obstacles to the entry of private capital into the countries desiring investment, and provide, in greater degree, positive incentives to increased investment."[15]

Officials were not the only ones to express this view. The Latin American doctrines, and more specifically the concepts of Raúl Prebisch and of ECLA, again and again were challenged by U.S. scholars and writers.

---

[15] Alberto Lleras Camargo, a moderate in Latin American politics, commented on this position in a speech at Georgetown University in 1964: "The policy of inter-American cooperation before the Alliance for Progress was conceived upon another philosophy: the underdeveloped countries of Latin America should develop in the same manner on which the prosperity of the United States was achieved, in other words, by the action of the private entrepreneur, free, or more than free, in the vast solitude of a new and savage continent. Our people were invited, one might say with impertinence, to realize similar great achievements, when all the conditions in the world had changed."

However, the 1950's provided some chastening experiences with regard to the limitations of development solely through the efforts of private enterprise and financial assistance solely through the existing international mechanisms. American social scientists began to note the need for new approaches to help poor countries.

It became apparent that in many of the underdeveloped countries private enterprise was often far from enterprising, limiting itself to the exploitation of small high-income markets and seeking, frequently with success, monopoly or near-monopoly positions. At the same time, foreign private capital tended to be interested in limited areas of investment, particularly in the exploitation of mineral resources (petroleum, copper, etc.), and showed much less interest in undertaking risky new manufacturing enterprises that might open up new export markets overseas and broaden national markets. There were of course brilliant exceptions, companies that opened up new opportunities and brought both capital and know-how to the underdeveloped countries, but they were relatively few. At the same time, the limitations of reliance on funds cautiously channeled through the Export-Import Bank, largely to encourage the import of U.S. goods, and through the World Bank, for a limited number of infrastructure and industrial projects, became increasingly apparent.

But the change in the U.S. view of Latin America did not come from logic. It came as a result of the shock that followed the hostile and violent reaction to Vice President Richard M. Nixon's so-called "goodwill tour" of South America in the spring of 1958. The fact that a Vice President of the United States could be spat upon, insulted, and his life threatened, focused U.S. attention forcefully on the disintegration of its Latin American policy.

While some in the United States saw the Nixon incident as a Communist plot, the Vice President himself, as well as many thoughtful officials in Washington, saw it as a reaction to U.S. policy and an indication of the need for a new U.S. approach to Latin America. The President sent his brother, Dr. Milton Eisenhower, a man already familiar with Latin American affairs, on a tour of Latin America. Dr. Eisenhower presented a forceful report in January 1959 (when Fidel Castro was marching into Havana) warning the United States: "Latin America is a continent in ferment. The people generally, including the most humble of them, now know that low living standards are neither universal nor inevitable, and they are therefore impatiently insistent that remedial action be taken." The reaction throughout Latin

America to Castro's victory placed a large exclamation point after the warning voiced by the President's brother. Vice President Nixon joined Dr. Eisenhower in suggesting the key ingredients of a new approach to Latin America. The United States must stand ready to provide expanded aid to meet the development needs of the Latin American nations, and it must differentiate its treatment of democratic and dictatorial governments: an *abrazo*, a warm embrace, for democratic rulers; a cold handshake for dictators. Only the recommendation on aid was to be implemented, and then only halfheartedly.

The question of how the United States should act toward various kinds of governments, whether democratic or dictatorial, was a difficult one. While the Latin American countries, upon achieving independence, wrote democratic principles into their constitutions, in practice — excepting only Chile, Costa Rica, and Uruguay — they were neither democratic nor representative, except for brief periods. Until well into the twentieth century, the political system of Latin America, comfortably adapted to an old social system, was centralized, paternalistic, and personalistic. It was based on three dominant institutions, the Army, the Catholic Church, and the landlords, which provided a framework of stability even while governments came and went in an endless succession of palace revolutions. Although democratic forces, led by the great leaders who inspired the wars of independence, at first held power, the movements were soon captured by predatory *caudillos* or died with the leaders. Political parties were generally tied to a dominant personality or were merely vehicles for the personal ambitions of party leaders.[16] The democratic movements really began to come into their own after World War II. But the building of a broad base of popular support was a difficult task. For centuries the masses of people had been disenfranchised by various practices and by their own indifference and isolation. Hardly had the *Acción Democrática* party, under the inspired leadership of Rómulo Betancourt, come into office in Venezuela and begun the long delayed task of social change while broadening its own base of support, than the Army took over in a military coup. At almost the same time in Peru, General Manuel Odría overthrew the democratic but chaotic regime of José Luis Bustamente y Rivera.[17] A little later, in June 1953, General Gustavo Rojas Pinilla made himself dictator of

---

[16] Pat M. Holt, *Survey of the Alliance for Progress: The Political Aspects*, prepared for the Subcommittee on American Republics Affairs of the Committee on Foreign Relations, U.S. Senate (Washington, D.C.: U.S. Government Printing Office, 1967).

[17] In October, 1968, Peru experienced another military usurpation of power.

Colombia, joining a long list of dictators then in power — Perón in Argentina, Batista in Cuba, Magloire in Haiti, Stroessner in Paraguay, Trujillo in the Dominican Republic, and Somoza in Nicaragua.

Washington's warmth toward the dictators — displayed through the granting of loans (as readily as to democratic regimes) and the award of honors to such exemplars as Perón, Odría, and Pérez Jimenez — was clearly based on the assumption that such actions were needed to prevent Communist inroads in the hemisphere. As Tad Szulc pointed out in his book, *The Winds of Revolution:*

> Although no Latin American liberals seriously expected the United States to oust the dictatorships forcibly, they bitterly resented the policies that resulted in political as well as economic strengthening of the dictatorships. The whole exercise, conducted by a nation that loudly preached democracy's superiority over totalitarianisms like Communism, did little to enhance the democratic cause or to awaken faith in it. Yet, common sense and a show of sympathy for the democratic forces, fully in line with the great American tradition, could have been a sound, practical investment for the immediate future.[18]

Juscelino Kubitschek, then President of Brazil, saw in the Nixon incident a propitious time to urge once again upon the United States the need for substantial financial assistance if Latin American nations were to modernize themselves. He did this in the form of a dramatic proposal for the launching of an Operation Pan America. This was to promote an inter-American, government-sponsored crash program of development based on massive U.S. economic aid. In both its objectives and sweep, Kubitschek's Operation Pan America anticipated the Alliance for Progress.

While the U.S. government was wary of the vagueness of the plan and its implications of a huge U.S. financial commitment, it agreed to the establishment of a Committee of Twenty-one of the OAS (i.e., representatives of the twenty-one members) to formulate new measures for economic cooperation based on the ideas embodied in Operation Pan America.

Also in 1958, the Latin Americans took the occasion of a meeting of foreign ministers to stress the desirability of creating a regional bank which could facilitate the channeling of more capital for the development of the Latin American nations. The Latin Americans again emphasized their view that neither private foreign investment, nor

---

[18] New York: Frederick A. Praeger, rev. ed., 1965, pp. 82–83.

the existing lending institutions, such as the Export-Import Bank and the World Bank, were adequate for the task.

The Committee of Twenty-one met a number of times during the winter of 1958–59 and made the establishment of a regional lending agency the first order of business. By April of 1959 the Committee had drafted provisions for the Inter-American Development Bank, and the United States had agreed to provide $350 million out of an anticipated $850 million of initial capital. The United States also would provide the largest part of another $150 million to be set aside in a Fund for Special Operations for making "soft" loans (i.e., loans at a zero or low rate of interest and with long repayment periods). The establishment of the IDB after a long period of resistance to a regional bank for Latin America was a significant step toward a new U.S. policy toward Latin America.

The need for a new policy had been given urgency by the Castro victory in Cuba. As his government and the Cuban press became increasingly anti-American and pro-Communist in tone during 1959 and 1960, U.S. policy shifted from a position of patience and tolerance. In March, 1960, President Eisenhower approved initial work on a contingency plan to overthrow the Castro regime. Four months later, while U.S. embassies were reporting from all parts of Latin America that the Castro victory was exciting interest in a revolutionary approach to winning long-denied reforms from the ruling elites, President Eisenhower said the United States would support sweeping reforms in Latin America with financial assistance. The Latin Americans were quick to respond.

The third meeting of the Committee of Twenty-one in September, 1960, held in Bogotá, Colombia, focused on the social aspects of development and on the righting of the many social wrongs that had so long existed in most of Latin America. This meeting was given encouragement and substance by the fact that, at the request of the President, Congress had authorized a general commitment of $500 million in advance of the meeting. The U.S. emphasis on "social" matters was a reaction to fear that violent revolution might sweep across Latin America.

Alberto Lleras Camargo, then President of Colombia, was later to write (in a 1963 article in *Foreign Affairs*): "The Act of Bogotá was, among documents of its kind, the first to proclaim the need for structural reforms — above all in the systems governing taxes, tenure and use of land, and education — in order to set on foot a great effort directed toward endowing the population of Latin America with shelter, schooling, employment and health, by means of the wholehearted mobilization of domestic resources and a considerable contingent of foreign aid."

To help finance this undertaking, the United States promised to set up a special fund for social development, using $394 million of the $500 million voted by Congress.[19] The United States had been won over to a positive approach to social development that had been pressed for a long time by a number of the more progressive Latin American leaders.

In contrast to the enthusiasm of these leaders who mostly came from smaller and more progressive countries, representatives of two large Latin American nations, Brazil and Argentina, expressed impatience and some irritation at proposals made by the United States. They were quite capable of taking care of the social problems themselves, they said. What they needed was enough aid to enable them to undertake their own programs of economic development.

This opposition was a compound of several factors: (1) Nationalism — a focus on the need for social reforms emphasizes inadequacies and backwardness while economic development efforts suggest national vigor and forward movement; (2) Class interest — concern for the views of the landholding classes and other conservative interests dictated a go-slow policy in social reform measures such as land and tax reform, and even in education and other social developments that could drastically change the status quo; (3) An unresolved issue in developmental theory — certain business groups and economists leaned strongly to the view that economic growth was essential to all other improvements and therefore the focus should be on production and productivity.

But even the largest Latin American countries, with their urgent need for foreign exchange, would not turn down an offer of hundreds of millions of dollars, even if intended for schools, health facilities, and housing. Facilities like schools would have to be built anyway, and budgetary savings on these items would permit the transfer of funds to other expenditures considered more appropriate. So the Act of Bogotá was signed by all members of the OAS. Behind the facade of unanimity, however, lay a real resistance to social development and especially

---

[19] $100 million was given for earthquake relief in Chile and $6 million was given to the Pan American Union to support its reorganized economic and social development staff.

social reform, a resistance that was to plague the Alliance for Progress when it was brought into being.

Thoughtful persons on both sides, while elated at the beginning of a new spirit of cooperation between the United States and Latin America, had few illusions about the practical impact of the specific measures that were to be taken. It would be some time before the regional bank could be organized, and years before the volume of its loans could reach significant levels.

As concerned persons began to take a closer look at conditions in the Latin American countries, bubbling with revolutionary ferment, there was no avoiding the seriousness of the situation — the legacy of centuries of colonial exploitation, a religion biased against change, one hundred and fifty years of governments principally concerned with the interests of a tiny landholding elite, and economic development narrowly based on a few raw material exports. Far-reaching changes were called for.

Chapter 2

ORGANIZING AN ALLIANCE
FOR REGIONAL PROGRESS

BY the time of the U.S. presidential campaign of 1960, it had become evident that Communism had established its first national base in the Western Hemisphere in Cuba. Cuban Communism had a homegrown flavor that could be expected to have a special appeal to the disaffected of other Latin American lands. And it was ready to challenge U.S. leadership in Latin America. The spread of Communism to the Western Hemisphere, a possibility long feared by the United States, had become a reality.

Much concerned with the immediate threat posed by the Castro regime, and at the same time strongly critical of the Eisenhower Administration for its vacillating policy toward Castro, the campaigning Senator John F. Kennedy was even more concerned with the prevention of other Castro-like revolutions in Latin America. The United States, he said, had to take its position on the side of revolutionary change in the interest of the masses of Latin Americans. As summed up by Arthur M. Schlesinger, Jr.: "He [Kennedy] had no illusions about the difficulty of maintaining the position of the United States in the midst of a social revolution in Latin America, but, as revolution seemed inevitable, he clearly believed that we had no choice but to do our best, partly because the loss of Latin America would damage our own security, but even more because we had a particular, almost familial, responsibility to help these peoples in their battle for democracy."[1]

Kennedy was convinced that it was necessary to move ahead on several fronts. Immediate security considerations, he said, must not be overlooked and Communism must be contained, but it also was essential to launch an economic program capable of raising the living standards of the masses. It was equally important to speed social reforms, and to support political leaders and parties committed to democratic objectives.

[1] *A Thousand Days: John F. Kennedy in the White House* (Boston: Houghton Mifflin, 1965). Schlesinger provides a detailed and extremely thoughtful account of the events and thinking leading up to the development of the Alliance for Progress.

He pressed these views in a speech at Tampa, Florida, in October, 1960. It was in this speech that he first referred to an "alliance for progress." He was looking forward to a Western Hemisphere "where all people — the Americans of the South and the Americans of the North — the United States and the nations of Latin America — are joined together in an alliance for progress — *alianza para progreso.*"[2]

To help him develop the policy outlined in his Tampa speech, Kennedy set up a task force on Latin America under the chairmanship of Adolf Berle, who had worked for President Roosevelt in the creation of the Good Neighbor Policy.[3] The task force urged a long-range program of national and continental development to lead Latin America to self-sustaining economic growth and to encourage democratic political institutions.

Shortly after Kennedy's inauguration a group of Latin Americans, headed by the leaders of the major agencies concerned with development in the area, presented their views in a memorandum to the White House about the kind of inter-American cooperation that the urgency of the situation called for. This document was signed by Raúl Prebisch of the UN Economic Commission for Latin America, Felipe Herrera of the Inter-American Development Bank, José A. Mora of OAS, and Jorge Sol of the Inter-American Economic and Social Council.

On March 13, 1961, John F. Kennedy, before a group of Latin American diplomats at the White House, formally launched his new program of inter-American cooperation, a program broader in scope and grander in purpose than anything tried before in the hemisphere:

> Our unfulfilled task is to demonstrate to the entire world that man's unsatisfied aspiration for economic progress and social justice can best be achieved by free men working within a framework of democratic institutions. . . .

[2] The phrase, according to Schlesinger, was coined jointly by Richard Goodwin (who, as Kennedy's assistant, had prepared a first draft of the speech) and Ernesto Betancourt, a Cuban who had broken with Castro and was working with the Pan American Union. Goodwin had dropped the "el" from the Spanish version suggested by Betancourt — *Alianza para el Progreso* — "in the interest of euphony." Eventually it was restored in the interest of good grammar.

[3] Other members of the task force were: Richard Goodwin, Arturo Morales-Carrión, Teodoro Moscoso (who had helped to develop the highly successful "Operation Bootstrap" in Puerto Rico), Lincoln Gordon, of Harvard University, Robert Alexander, of Rutgers, and Arthur Whitaker, of the University of Pennsylvania. Earlier, in December 1960, Gordon had brought a group together at Harvard University to discuss positive measures towards Latin America. They issued a report entitled: *Alliance for Progress: A Program of Inter-American Partnership.* A Statement Developed at a Conference on December 19, 1960, Faculty Club of Harvard University, Cambridge, Massachusetts.

I have called on all people of the Hemisphere to join in a new Alliance for Progress — *Alianza para Progreso* — a vast cooperative effort, unparalleled in magnitude and nobility of purpose, to satisfy the basic needs of the American people for homes, work and land, health and schools — *techo, trabajo y tierra, salud y escuela.*[4]

To achieve the goal set, the President suggested the preparation of a ten-year development program based on a maximum effort within each country and on substantial U.S. financial and technical aid. He stressed the need for self-help, for regional markets, for stabilization of commodity prices, and for hemispheric cooperation in education, technical training, and research. Sound plans, he urged, were essential. "For if our alliance is to succeed," he said, "each Latin nation must formulate long-range plans for its own development — plans which establish targets and priorities, insure monetary stability, establish the machinery for vital social change, stimulate private activity and initiative, and provide for a maximum national effort. These plans will be the foundation of our development effort and the basis for the allocation of outside resources."

He called for a ministerial meeting of the Inter-American Economic and Social Council of the OAS to draw up a program of inter-American cooperation within the framework he had suggested. Preparation for such a meeting was made at once. A meeting of the Council was scheduled for late summer, to be held at the Uruguayan resort town of Punta del Este.

To define more precisely the ends and means of the new Alliance, the OAS Secretariat formed four task forces. Three of the task forces were concerned with the specific questions of commodity exports, regional economic integration, and public information. The fourth was to deal more broadly with questions of goals, national planning, and organization of the new effort. This task force, under the chairmanship of Felipe Pazos, former president of the Central Bank of Cuba, recommended a series of specific targets for the Alliance, a main goal being a minimum 2.5 per cent per capita growth rate in national income for each country.[5] It suggested that while each nation would be free to define its own objectives in its planning, Alliance aid should be channeled to those countries meeting minimum requirements of self-help, social reform, and economic policy.

[4] Address by President John F. Kennedy to the Latin American diplomatic corps, March 13, 1961. U.S. Department of State, *Bulletin* 44, no. 1136 (April 3, 1961).

[5] U.S. members of this task force were Gerhard Colm, Albert O. Hirschman, and the author.

The Inter-American Economic and Social Council convened August 5, 1961. Its main task was to work out an agreement each of the nations could sign. The conferees prepared a lofty "Declaration to the Peoples of America" and a Charter. The Alliance for Progress came into being with the signing of the Charter on August 17, 1961.[6] The meeting was given drama by the persistent and powerful opposition of the Cuban delegation, led by the late Che Guevara. The solution to the problems of Latin America, he declared, was to be found not in loans but in bayonets. The proposed Alliance was nothing but a hoax, a device to continue U.S. imperialism in Latin America. But Cuba found no allies. All of the other Latin American nations voted for the Charter.

The Alliance for Progress program hammered out at Punta del Este was essentially a pragmatic and eclectic one. Previous studies by ECLA and others were useful, but new answers had to be worked out through the process of trial and error. The Marshall Plan experience, unfortunately, did not provide much guidance because it was concerned with revitalizing economic growth rather than initiating it.

The Alliance was experimental in nature, and provisions should have been made for evaluation and periodic revision. However, political considerations prompted the setting of impossible objectives, and much of what went into the Charter — the targets set, the proposals stressed, and even the rhetoric — was a direct reflection of the economic difficulties then facing the Latin American countries.

At the time of the meeting in Punta del Este, most of the Latin American economies had been depressed for several years. During the late 1950's, the rate of growth in most of the countries was lower than it had been in the earlier part of the decade. For Latin America as a whole the rate of growth of per capita gross domestic product (GDP) declined from an annual average of 2.4 per cent for 1950–55 to only 1.8 per cent for 1955–60.[7] Some of the countries — Argentina, Colombia, Ecuador, Uruguay, and Costa Rica — had experienced quite substantial declines; others, like Paraguay and Bolivia, were stagnating. With the economic decline came high unemployment, low agricultural prices, and a limited government expenditure for social services.

---

[6] OAS, *Alliance for Progress. Official Documents Emanating from the Special Meeting of the Inter-American Economic and Social Council at the Ministerial Level*, Punta del Este, August 5–17, 1961, OAS/Ser. H/X.1, Doc. 145 (August 16, 1961).

[7] Gross domestic product is equal to gross national product plus (or minus) net payments abroad. The numerical difference in the rates of growth of the two tends to be rather small.

The first objective of the Charter of Punta del Este was, therefore, to reverse the downward trend in the growth rate. An annual increase in per capita product in every Latin American country of not less than 2.5 per cent, roughly the average for Latin America during the relatively good years of the early 1950's, was set as a goal. It did not seem possible that self-sustaining development, the major objective, could be achieved with a lower rate of annual growth. The increases in income, the Charter suggested, should be employed to raise the relative levels of living of the needier sectors of the population, and at the same time to increase the proportion of the national product devoted to investment. In this way, the major goals of income equalization and self-sustaining economic growth might be attained.

Exports earnings during the late 1950's and early 1960's indicated clearly that the export of primary products alone could not provide the required thrust for the Latin American economies. Prices had improved from the low of the 1930's because of the high demand generated by the Second World War and the Korean conflict, but after hostilities ended a downward trend began again. The index of unit value of exports, which in 1951 and 1954 had reached 117 (1958 = 100) declined to slightly more than 93 for the 1959–61 period. And, in some countries, the roller-coaster trend reached disturbing proportions. For instance, coffee exports from Colombia, which were $589 million in the peak year of 1954, were only $308 million in 1961. (The price of Manizales coffee fell from $0.88 per pound to $0.436 during this period.) At the same time, there was a slackening of industrial expansion as the more obvious import-substitution possibilities were becoming exhausted.

It was necessary to find new avenues for development if the target growth rate of 2.5 per cent was to be achieved. The Charter recognized that need, aiming some of its provisions at the betterment of the conditions in the traditional export markets (seeking new ways to stabilize commodity prices) and at wider opportunities for new exports, as well as increased possibilities of import substitution regionally through the integration of the Latin American economies. The strengthening of the Latin American Free Trade Area that had already been established and movement toward a genuine common market were needed in order to provide a broad enough base for the establishment of intermediate and capital goods industries, and for greatly expanded general trade among the Latin American countries.

The pressing social situation at the beginning of the 1960's suggested that total reliance could not be placed on long-term economic expansion. Efforts had to be made to improve the immediate situation in matters about which people cared most, particularly education, health, and housing.

Education was of great importance. Illiteracy was shamefully high in many of the countries. As shown in Table 1, in the majority of the countries nearly half or more of the adult population was illiterate. Obviously, such a condition seriously handicaps a nation's capacity to pull itself out of poverty through a developmental effort. The Charter included among its objectives the elimination of adult illiteracy and the provision of six years of primary education to all children within a decade, that is, by 1971. While it set completely unrealistic goals, the

Table 1.   Illiteracy in Latin America circa 1950

Region and country	Est. adult population (15 years and over)	Extent of illiteracy (est.)	
		Number of adult illiterates	Percentage of adult population illiterate*
	thousand	*thousand*	*per cent*
Northern and Central:			
Costa Rica	460	92–115	20–25
Cuba	3,400	680–850	20–25
Dominican Republic	1,200	660–720	55–60
El Salvador	1,100	660–720	60–65*
Guatemala	1,600	1,100–1,200	70–75
Haiti	1,900	1,600–1,700	85–90
Honduras	890	530–580	60–65
Mexico	15,000	5,300–6,000	35–40*
Nicaragua	600	360–390	60–65
Panama	470	140–160	30–35
South:			
Argentina	11,900	1,200–1,800	10–15
Bolivia	1,800	1,200–1,300	65–70
Brazil	30,300	15,200–16,700	50–55
Chile	3,700	740–930	20–25*
Colombia	6,600	3,000–3,300	45–50
Ecuador	1,850	740–830	40–45
Paraguay	810	240–280	30–35
Peru	4,900	2,500–2,700	50–55*
Uruguay	1,650	250–330	15–20
Venezuela	2,900	1,300–1,500	45–50

   * In general, the percentages reported in the UN *Demographic Yearbook* (1960) correspond to the ranges estimated by UNESCO; however, there are some discrepancies. The *Yearbook* reports higher percentages than UNESCO for Peru (57.6) and Mexico (42.5) and lower percentages for El Salvador (59) and Chile (19.6).
   Source: United Nations Educational, Scientific and Cultural Organization, *World Illiteracy at Midcentury* (1957), pp. 38, 40, 42, 43.

Charter did at least underline a truly serious problem and an urgent need — to quickly improve the capacity of available human resources.

Health conditions were deplorable in a majority of countries. There was an immediate need for a greatly increased professional staff, for the construction of hospitals and clinics, and for a whole range of urban and rural sanitation services. The Charter set as a goal the increase of life expectancy at birth by a minimum of five years within a decade; mortality rates of children were to be reduced by at least one-half; medical and other health services were to be substantially improved; potable water supply and sewage disposal were to be provided to not less than 70 per cent of the urban and 50 per cent of the rural population.

At the beginning of the 1960's, according to a United Nations housing report, about 40 per cent of the urban population and about 50 per cent of the rural population of Latin America lived in unhealthy, crowded homes and communities.[8] The Charter proposed that low-cost housing for low-income families be increased substantially both in urban and rural areas.

The same hesitancy that had marked the incorporation of social reforms in the Act of Bogotá characterized the discussions of these questions at Punta del Este. But those who wanted a strong reform plank in the Charter had impressive data to bring to bear on the question.

The great wealth and power of the large landowners, they showed, contrasted sharply with the near-desperate situation of the very small farmers, the masses of landless peasants, and the agricultural workers. The land tenure situation in Latin America in the 1950's is broadly suggested by the data in Table 2, which shows the vast domain of the large farms (over 1,000 hectares) and the remarkably small holdings of the great majority of farmers. In Argentina some 5 per cent of the farms represented three-quarters of the area in agriculture; in Paraguay roughly the same proportion of farms covered almost 94 per cent. In seven of the countries, more than three-quarters of all farms were less than ten hectares in size.

The Charter stressed the need for carrying out land reform with a double objective: to change the unjust distribution of wealth and income in the rural sector; and to accelerate the growth of agricultural production in order to improve conditions of rural living and increase demand

[8] United Nations, *Report of the Ad Hoc Group of Experts on Housing and Urban Development*, Department of Economic and Social Affairs, ST/SOA/50, E/CN.5/367/Rev. 1 (New York, 1962).

Table 2.   Number and Size of Latifundia and Minifundia in Some Latin American Countries in the 1950's*

Country	Latifundia		Minifundia	
	Per cent of the total no. of farms	Per cent of the total area in farms	Per cent of the total no. of farms	Per cent of the total area in farms
Argentina	5.1	74.8	n.a.	n.a.
Bolivia**	6.3	91.9	69.4	0.4
Brazil	1.6	50.9	84.4	1.3
Chile	2.2	73.2	n.a.	n.a.
Colombia	0.4	26.7	70.5	6.9
Costa Rica	0.2	34.7	76.0	5.2
Cuba	0.5	36.1	n.a.	n.a.
Dominican Republic	1.9	53.3	87.5	23.3
Ecuador	0.2	37.4	83.6	11.7
El Salvador	0.1	19.9	88.7	18.9
Guatemala	0.2	40.8	88.3	14.3
Honduras	0.1	20.6	75.0	16.1
Nicaragua	0.7	32.8	34.8	2.3
Panama	0.1	12.2	71.7	17.4
Paraguay	5.2	93.8	n.a.	n.a.
Peru	4.6	66.5	n.a.	n.a.
Uruguay	4.2	56.4	25.9	0.6

n.a.—Not available.

* Latifundia include all farms over 2,470 acres (1,000 hectares) and Minifundia, farms of less than 24.7 acres (10 hectares).

** Before the Revolution of 1952.

Sources: Sociedad Interamericana de Planificación, News Letter No. 23, San Juan, Puerto Rico, July 1962; and Harry Kantor, "Agrarismo y Tierra en Latinoamérica," *Combate* (Enero-Febrero 1961), quoted by Rafael Pico, "Problems of Land Tenure Reform in Latin America," *Journal of Inter-American Studies*, 6:2 (April 1964), p. 143.

for the nation's industrial output. An increase in agricultural production through agrarian reform was possible since in most of the countries many of the very large farms were cultivated in a haphazard manner and production was far below their potential. While the hard problems involved in successful land reform were well known to most of the delegates, an unambiguous statement about the desirability of land reform seemed appropriate to a document essentially devoted to intentions. The U.S. delegates joined forces with enough liberal Latin American leaders to write such a statement.

The Charter also dealt with the need to increase the efficiency of the public sector, and to strengthen the capacity of the various nations to mobilize their own resources for development through better administrative practices and improved tax collection procedures. In signing the Charter, the Latin American countries agreed to the need for tax reform, not only for revenue purposes but also to make the tax systems more equitable. In most cases the tax structures reflected the traditional society, with its limited popular base and its special privileges. Thoroughgoing reforms were needed in almost all of the countries if they were to approximate the tax patterns achieved decades earlier by the modern progressive nations.

The Charter envisaged that the needed economic and social development efforts of the Latin American countries would be carried out "within the framework of personal dignity and political liberty...in democratic societies adapted to their own needs and desires." Throughout the Declaration and the Charter, stress was laid on the achievement of democratic institutions as central to the whole Alliance effort. Even if one doubted the sincerity of some who signed the Charter, particularly those representing military dictatorships, the commitment to democracy by all the Latin American countries, excepting Cuba, was significant. Joined with the then clear U.S. backing of democratic forces throughout the hemisphere, the commitment gave new hope to those who dreamed of a whole continent developing economically and achieving social justice in a political framework of personal freedom and representative government.

The establishment of social and political, as well as economic, objectives was a highly significant feature of the Alliance design. This was something new in the realm of external assistance and in relations among sovereign nations. It was an acceptance of the idea that economic progress was not enough. Political freedom and social justice were to be considered equally important goals. More specifically, the basis for substantial external assistance was to be not only sound economic policies and self-help measures but social and political progress. And sovereign nations were to submit their projected policies and programs to outside scrutiny.

How simultaneous advances on all fronts were to be achieved or judged was another matter, and the Charter provided only ambiguous answers. In retrospect, it is clear that those preparing the Charter were handicapped by lack of knowledge of how economic progress was or was not related to social and political development, and by lack of consensus on the relative importance and desirability of advances on the various fronts. The Charter was inevitably a compromise document that attempted to include as many of the diverse points of view concerning Latin American development as possible.

The economic and social changes within the Latin American countries envisaged at Punta del Este included a wide range of policy decisions that were to be adopted throughout the hemisphere, ranging from substantial structural reforms to proper stabilization policies in fiscal and monetary fields. To a large extent, changes were to be achieved through *national development programs.*

A large part of the Charter is devoted to describing what a national development program should include. Implicit throughout is the concept that to achieve the ambitious goals of the Alliance each nation must have a fully articulated plan of action involving both the private and public sectors of the economy.

The national development plans were to include the following: (1) establishment of mutually consistent targets in expanding productive capacity in industry, agriculture, and other fields and in improving conditions of urban and rural life; (2) specifications of methods to achieve the targets, the assignment of priorities, and justification of development projects in terms of relative costs and benefits; (3) estimation of cost in national and foreign currencies of major projects and of the development program as a whole; (4) estimation of the internal resources, public and private, available for the execution of the program; (5) estimation of the direct and indirect effects of the program on the nation's balance of payments; (6) recommendation of fiscal and monetary policies to be followed in order to make the program work within the framework of price stability; and (7) the selection of machinery of public administration to be used in carrying out the program.

In order to achieve the agreed-upon developmental objectives, a mammoth effort was required in terms of increased savings and investments, both public and private. A sudden increase in the use of national resources for long-term investments would mean a lowering of the already low levels of living of the masses of people. External assistance in large quantities would be required to launch a developmental thrust. The United States government made a commitment to provide most of the external assistance needed to complement Latin American self-help efforts. The Declaration stated:

> The United States, for its part, pledges its efforts to supply financial and technical cooperation in order to achieve the aims of the Alliance for Progress. To this end, the United States will provide a major part of the minimum of twenty billion dollars, principally in public funds, which Latin America will require over the next ten years from all external sources in order to supplement its own efforts.[9]

[9] Pan American Union, *Alliance for Progress*, Doc. OEA/Ser. H/XII.1, Rev. 2 (1961), p. 4.

The Charter stated:

> The United States will assist those participating countries whose develop-
> ment programs establish self-help measures, economic and social policies
> and programs consistent with the goals and principles of this Charter.
> To supplement the domestic efforts of such countries, the United States is
> prepared to allocate resources which, along with those anticipated from
> other external sources, will be of a scope and magnitude adequate to
> realize the goals envisaged in this Charter. Such assistance will be allo-
> cated to both social and economic development and, where appropriate,
> will take the form of grants or loans on flexible terms and conditions. The
> participating countries will request the support of other capital-exporting
> countries and appropriate institutions so that they may provide assistance
> for the attainment of these objectives.[10]

Left essentially unresolved were the organizational means by which
the ten-year program of inter-American cooperation was to be carried
out. There were only general references to loans, grants, and technical
assistance to be provided by such institutions as the Inter-American
Development Bank, the U.S. Agency for International Development,
OAS, and ECLA. The signing of the Charter only marked the beginning
of the search for effective tools of implementation and coordination.
The Alliance was given no organizational machinery at the start other
than a "Panel of Experts," later to be known as the "Committee of
Nine," set up to evaluate national development plans when submitted.
The continuing quest for such machinery, and the effort to move toward
multilateral action are the theme of the next chapter.

[10] *Ibid.*, p. 14.

Chapter 3

MULTILATERAL MACHINERY:
CREATING A COOPERATIVE ENTERPRISE

THE OAS task force that prepared the groundwork for the meeting at Punta del Este had assumed that the Alliance for Progress would have the greatest chance of success if it was established within a multilateral framework instead of as a series of uncoordinated bilateral aid programs. But, fully aware of the probable resistance to strong centralized controls over projected programs of international cooperation, the task force had proposed an organizational structure with "minimal" authority, given the ambitious goals to be achieved. It proposed the establishment of a permanent committee of high political stature to evaluate development plans and to report its findings to the Inter-American Economic and Social Council, the Inter-American Development Bank, and the applicant country. The committee also would review implementation of national plans each year, and make appraisals of performance. Finally, the committee would recommend improvements either in the plans themselves or in their execution.[1]

Even this minimal authority failed to win acceptance at Punta del Este. The larger countries — Brazil, Argentina, and Mexico — considered this "multilateralism" as an abridgement of sovereignty. Moreover, they judged that more financial aid could be obtained by direct bilateral negotiations with Washington, and with the international lending organizations than through what seemed to be a complicated maze of multilateral procedures. Their opposition, coupled with a noncommittal attitude toward such a committee on the part of the United States, was enough to defeat the task force proposal.

The defeat of this minimal proposal reflected the ambivalence of both the United States and the Latin American countries toward multilateralism, an ambivalence that still complicates inter-American relations.

The U.S. government wanted to make the Alliance as much of a

[1] Pan American Union, *Planning for Economic and Social Development for Latin America: Report of the Group of Experts*, OAS Official Records, OEA/Ser. H/X. 1, ES-RE-Doc. 4 (English), Rev. (June 29, 1961).

cooperative effort as possible, but it was extremely reluctant to reduce the U.S. capacity to decide which countries were to get how much aid, partly because the question of whether or not it was wise to employ development assistance for security purposes and immediate political objectives was still unresolved and partly because there was some doubt about the capacity of multilateral agencies to channel aid effectively.

The attitude of the Latin Americans toward multilateralism was even more complicated. The bases for cooperation were extremely weak. Both geography and economics presented great barriers to multilateral action. Until recently the area had little common development of resources, little shared power, and few transportation and communication links. (Even now, telephone calls between most Latin American countries must go by way of New York or Miami.) Intraregional trade was no more than 9 per cent of total Latin American trade at the time of Punta del Este, and is not much more now. Relatively non-complementary economies, with little trade among them, precluded extensive economic ties.

The compromise solution worked out at Punta del Este was the creation of a new inter-American body with some resemblance to the one proposed by the OAS task force, but differing in both function and membership. It was to be a Panel of Nine Experts chosen for their expertise, and not for what they represented politically. The panel initially was not a cohesive standing committee, but was called upon by the OAS Secretary General to supply two or three members at a time to form half the membership of ad hoc committees (the other members being experts from outside). Such ad hoc committees carried little political weight. Although empowered to review national plans and make recommendations, and although their recommendations were to be of "great importance in determining the distribution of public funds," these bodies did not have the power to encourage change and reform in a substantial manner. As they had no permanent status, they could not confront each Latin American country each year with its record of accomplishments and failures.[2]

[2] The Panel requested and achieved Committee standing — that is, existence as a permanent collective body — after a year, but its suggestion that the Ad Hoc Committee arrangement be reconstituted did not receive serious consideration. Despite the inherent limitations of the Committee of Nine structure, the high standing and personal contacts in their own countries of the seven Latin American members of the Committee often exerted influence on national plans and associated policy. At the time the Panel became a Committee, the members, and their former positions, were: Hernando Agudelo Villa, former Finance Minister of Colombia; Romulo Almeida, former Executive Secretary, Latin American Free Trade Association; Jorge Grieve,

Other multilateral ventures were approved at Punta del Este, the most ambitious of which was a scheme to coordinate the technical assistance efforts of the OAS, ECLA, and the Inter-American Development Bank. It was hoped that such collaboration would eliminate duplication and pool talents from the various agencies. Another coordination effort was the Inter-American Committee on Agricultural Development (CIDA), which was to help the Latin American countries learn how to cope more effectively with their difficult agricultural problems.[3]

From the beginning it was evident that the efforts at multilateralization were essentially makeshift. The principal multilateral organ — a permanent, politically respected committee to evaluate and guide the Alliance efforts — was still missing, and that gap became the center of the controversy regarding the Alliance as a multilateral development effort.

Provision of Loans and Grants

The sources of funds available to Latin American countries had been substantially enlarged by the early 1960's. As in the past, they could still turn to the International Bank for Reconstruction and Development (the World Bank) mainly for loans for specific infrastructure projects, to the U.S.-sponsored Export-Import Bank for loans to assist in the import of U.S. products, and to the United Nations family of agencies for small grants and technical assistance in a wide variety of fields. In addition, the Inter-American Development Bank was now ready to make loans for projects in any category that advanced economic or social development. However, in the first stage of the Alliance, the funds available from these sources were relatively small and closely tied to well-defined "bankable" projects. The largest source of funds was the U.S. Agency for International Development. This

former Minister of Public Works, Peru; Ernesto Malaccorto, former Minister of Agriculture, Argentina; Manuel Noriega Morales, former Minister of Economy and head of Central Bank, Guatemala; Felipe Pazos, former President, Central Bank of Cuba; and Raúl Saez, former President, Electricity Company of Chile. Also a member, in addition to the author, was Professor Paul Rosenstein-Rodan, a brilliant scholar in the field of economic development and a true citizen of the world. During most of the life of the Committee, its Secretary was Gerardo Canet.

[3] Since CIDA's birth, an immense amount of research has been carried out on Latin America's long-neglected agricultural problems. Much less successful has been its effort to coordinate technical assistance among the various agencies, due in no small part to the tendency for interagency infighting.

agency was not only in a position to make loans at more attractive terms than the banks, but could make them for any reasonable purpose and in very flexible ways. It could supply "program loans," not limited to any specific project but available to help finance a broad government program of development, as it did for Chile shortly after the Alliance came into being. It could help finance a broad regional development program, as it did for Brazil to help develop the poverty-stricken northeast region of the country. It could provide loans for specific projects which, for one reason or another, were not appropriate for financing by the international banks. Finally, it could furnish grants when the purpose was important but did not qualify as a loan project, or when the country's loan-repayment capacity was being strained.

AID loans and grants are made through direct negotiations with the applicant countries and without any intermediaries. The Charter of Punta del Este had specified that Latin American countries were to apply for loans and grants within the context of their comprehensive national development plans, that the plans were to be evaluated by an inter-American committee of experts before applications were considered by the lending agencies, and that the lending agencies should weigh heavily the recommendations of the expert evaluating group. However, there were many elements that tended to minimize the "multilateral" aspect of loans and to strengthen the "bilateral" aspect. National development plans were hurriedly pieced together and had serious limitations as guides for making loans or grants. The evaluations by the ad hoc committees tended to be general in nature, concerned with economic policy, social reforms, and the like rather than with the quality of individual projects. The great majority of loans, however, was made on a project basis. Even more important was the fact that it was U.S. policy to control internally the aid apparatus. Thus, while they sometimes found it difficult to disregard findings by the ad hoc committees, AID officials essentially relied on their own evaluation and judgment in making loans and grants, with political considerations often involved. The organization of AID itself contributed to a bilateral, essentially piecemeal approach to implementation of Alliance objectives.

Adolf Berle, when he was chairman of the Task Force on Latin America advising President Kennedy about the organization of the Alliance, very strongly stressed the need of giving the Latin American program special standing within the Department of State. Berle, who was knowledgeable about both Latin American affairs and the State Department, having previously served in the department, urged that the head of the Latin American program should have the rank of Undersecretary with extra powers to implement the Alliance that such a position would provide. The President did not accept Berle's recommendation. Instead the office of the Assistant Administrator of AID working on Latin America was combined with a newly created office of the U.S. Coordinator of the Alliance for Progress. While the latter position provided some scope for bringing together the U.S. governmental agencies concerned with Latin America, it carried very little actual authority. At the same time, pouring the Latin American aid apparatus into the State-AID mold, designed for providing project aid to countries in all parts of the world in support of U.S. foreign policy, weakened the whole effort. The product had too many characteristics of traditional U.S. foreign assistance, and Alliance objectives were lost.

President Kennedy had appointed an unusual man to serve as the leader of the U.S. Alliance effort, Teodoro Moscoso. He had been a key member of the group, under the leadership of Governor Luis Muñoz Marín, that had brought about a near-miracle in the development of Puerto Rico. Moscoso had created the most successful government development corporation in the Western Hemisphere, an agency that had a great deal to do with changing the economic condition of Puerto Rico in less than two decades. A man far different in background and personality from the U.S. Foreign Service officer, Moscoso had trouble with the State Department. Devoted to the bold objectives of the Alliance for Progress and aware of the great changes in approach and technique they demanded, Moscoso sought to endow the whole U.S. effort with a strong development-and-reform spirit. It soon became evident that he would not succeed. The forces of inertia and traditionalism were strong, and the position of the office of the Coordinator was inherently weak.

Moscoso, however, tried to keep alive at least the spirit of the Alliance goals and patterns. He stressed social reforms when he could. He pressed for greater efforts in the preparation of plans so that individual projects made sense. He tried to follow the suggestions of the ad hoc committees wherever he could, but he was unhappy that so little true multilateralism could be obtained.

The divergence between new things that needed to be done — and done in new ways — and the bureaucratic mechanisms available for the task made administrative and organizational untidiness inevitable. It became evident that the Latin American program either had to be fitted more smoothly into the State-AID mold or an entirely new approach had to be invented. President Lyndon B. Johnson chose the former course. To head the Latin American program, he brought in Thomas Mann who had been Assistant Secretary of Latin American Affairs under Eisenhower and was very much in the Foreign Service tradition. Mann was to head both the State and AID Latin American programs, combining what formerly had been two jobs. Mann, who had outstanding administrative capacity, was able to eliminate much of the confusion and crossed lines of authority, but in the process of reorganization much of the original spirit of the Alliance, which Moscoso had tried so hard to keep alive, inevitably disappeared, and aid to Latin America settled increasingly into the traditional country-by-country, project-by-project approach.[4]

Panel of Nine and Plan Evaluation

The Charter of Punta del Este had specified that national plans were to be evaluated for their soundness to clear the way for foreign aid, and this was to be done by a multilateral instrumentality — the Panel of Nine Experts, whose members (two or three at a time) along with two or three outside experts would sit as ad hoc committees and evaluate national plans submitted to them.

In evaluating plans the ad hoc committees were guided by several criteria established by the panel, based on its interpretation of the major provisions in the Charter. First, the plan's objectives had to conform to the goals described in the Act of Bogotá and the Charter, especially in matters of reform and self-help such as mobilizing more internal capital resources through more efficient tax collection. Second, the plan had to outline effective means to achieve these goals; it could not resort to vague formulas but had to spell out in precise terms how they were to be implemented. Third, the foreign exchange estimates, including how much external financial assistance was required, had to be consistent with sound policies with regard to exports and imports, national savings, and monetary stability.

These rather stringent standards were to be applied by the ad hoc committees without interfering "with the right of each government to

---

[4] Although program loans continued to be granted, mainly to three countries — Brazil, Chile, and Colombia.

formulate its own goals, priorities and reforms in its national development program," as the Charter delicately phrased it. Despite this restriction, when an ad hoc committee made its preliminary report to the applicant nation, the committee did not hesitate to point out shortcomings (though accomplishments were always generously noted) and to urge greater efforts at internal reform. There then followed discussions between the ad hoc committee and the government, including a trip to the host country by the entire committee for direct talks with policy makers. The last step in the evaluation process was a final report with recommendations to the lending agencies. This report needed the approval of the host government before it could be distributed.

Despite their concern with such sensitive issues as domestic reform, sixteen countries asked the assistance of the ad hoc committees in the five years of their existence. The first plans were submitted by Bolivia, Colombia, and Chile in the early months of 1962. Other national plans came soon after. The quality of the plans varied considerably, and all were short of what would have been desirable. The committees discovered that some of the so-called "plans," although issued by a central planning agency, bore no resemblance to the plans of individual ministries. These plans were useless. Other country plans were characterized by careful analysis and a serious effort to incorporate sensible projects. The greatest difficulty in most cases was the lack of "bankable" projects, i.e., specific construction or other activities (such as land improvement) whose economic and financial feasibility had been "proved out" and which were suitable for bank or aid-agency funding.

The weakness of most of the plans showed not only inexperience in developmental planning and lack of capacity to speed good projects, but also, in most instances, the great gap between central planning and the actual policies of the government. The inability or unwillingness to face up to the Alliance commitments was demonstrated as well. Many of the countries were not yet ready to carry out genuine economic and social reforms; they were willing to "play the game," but only up to a point.

Other problems plagued this first effort at multilateral evaluation based on far-reaching objectives. In the first place, two major countries — Brazil and Argentina — never bothered to submit national plans while the Committee of Nine was in existence. Of the large countries, only Mexico did so. Secondly, a number of Latin American countries, including some that had submitted plans, sought and were granted bilateral aid without receiving approval of their plans from the ad hoc committees. For example, a mission headed by Moscoso and Richard Goodwin in 1962 promised aid to Chile before the ad hoc committee on the Chilean plan had been able to make its evaluation. Shortly thereafter the Frondizi government of Argentina received a substantial loan from the United States without having submitted a plan.

There was also a problem for the ad hoc committees in their incapacity, principally due to lack of staff, to evaluate project proposals. The committees had to depend for evaluation of projects on the two international banks. Even when one of the banks was actually in the process of evaluating a nation's projects while the ad hoc committee was in the midst of its deliberations (some of the countries submitted their plans to the banks at the same time as to the Committee of Nine), the problem of timing would arise. Even more serious, however, was the fact that, with the banks concerned with individual projects and with the ad hoc committees concerned with the broad issues of reform, general economic policies, and government administration, it was difficult to get coherence in the process of evaluation and aid-giving.

Despite the shortcomings of the ad hoc committees (which the Committee of Nine continuously stressed in its annual reports), the committees did contribute to the development of multilateral organization and to the operation of the Alliance. In regard to the latter, they remained the most consistent and official insistent spokesmen for the need to couple internal reform with external financial assistance for development. Their evaluations of country plans and the annual reviews of the Committee of Nine emphasized the themes of agrarian, tax, and other social reforms, thus helping to preserve the original philosophy of the Alliance. Moreover, by consistently advocating the need for reforms, they helped strengthen the position of progressive elements. A case in point was the submission of the Mexican plan for evaluation by an ad hoc committee, although it was evident that Mexico could receive only limited Alliance assistance given its capacity to borrow funds through the usual commercial channels. The submission followed an internal struggle among various groups in the Mexican government, with the group favoring submission seeing the occasion as an opportunity to bring additional pressure on the administration to make needed changes. Similar situations developed in other countries.

The Committee of Nine, in its annual reports to the Inter-American Economic and Social Council, pushed for better multilateral machinery, an effort that culminated in the creation of the Comité Interamericano de la Alianza para el Progreso (CIAP).

Birth of CIAP

As already said, the Punta del Este conference did not face up to the problem of making the new and ambitious program work. The result was a disorganized and badly-limping operation. Even before the first year of the Alliance came to a close, it was only too evident that the existing machinery was totally inadequate for the tasks it had set for itself.

The first year of the Alliance ended with few Latin American reforms effected, and few U.S. loans disbursed. Those who had hoped it would be a new and bold answer experienced an acute sense of frustration. Some of this was due to unrealistic expectations, but, even if the circumstances had been more favorable, the lack of coherence between goals and means inevitably would have doomed the effort.

The report by the Committee of Nine to the first meeting of the Inter-American Economic and Social Council (IA-ECOSOC) held in Mexico City in October of 1962 spelled out the deficiencies and recommended an immediate review of the whole situation. The Committee proposed that two prominent Latin Americans be selected to recommend measures to improve the Alliance. Former Presidents Alberto Lleras of Colombia and Kubitschek of Brazil were chosen. They worked for several months with the Committee of Nine and other interested Latin American groups, as well as with United States leaders. Lleras and Kubitschek prepared separate reports, which contained parallel recommendations but varied greatly in tone. Kubitschek, very much the practicing politician, found little good to be said about the Alliance's first two years, and placed special blame on the United States. Because anti-Americanism still won votes, he could not refrain from saying:

> My observations have led me to believe that the imperfect understanding prevalent in certain circles of the United States government in relation to the other countries of the hemisphere continues to limit its vision and to influence its conduct . . . I want to renew the assurances of my admiration to President Kennedy and to his great country. . . by stating that it is precisely the lack of boldness, an excessive fear of risk, timidity of action, perplexity, the clinging to outmoded approaches, the repetition of errors long since revealed, that is impeding the realization of what the President of the United States announced as a "vast cooperative effort, unparalleled in magnitude and in nobility of purpose."[5]

Lleras, who was not running for office but who was no happier about the Alliance's lack of progress, did not avoid mentioning Latin American

---

[5] Juscelino Kubitschek, "Report on the Alliance for Progress," Pan American Union Doc. CIES/350, mimeographed, 1963.

culpability as Kubitschek had so deftly done. Thus, according to Lleras:

> Certainly, as of today, the manner in which the Alliance has been administered by the United States is open to criticism, but it must be admitted that the countries of Latin America . . . have made a poor showing.

He also said:

> In truth, the President [of the United States] has been alone in defending, publicizing, and explaining the Alliance, in the face of the indifference of many of the peoples for whom this joint undertaking . . . will bring the most benefits.[6]

Despite their different targets for criticism, the two presidents' policy recommendations did coincide by endorsing stronger multilateralism. They urged the establishment of a permanent committee which would serve as "an active directive agency" for the Alliance, taking over many of the tasks involved in financing aid programs, including the power to determine the distribution of funds.

The Committee of Nine, in a second report to IA-ECOSOC, spelled out the proposed functions for a new multilateral agency in greater detail. The new committee would be *the* multilateral embodiment of the Alliance: It would act as the recognized source for new ideas to improve the Alliance; it would urge Latin American countries to make greater effort at reform; it would prepare an annual estimate of the available funds for Latin American programs; and, most importantly, it would make decisions on the distribution of Alliance funds after studying the evaluations of national plans made by ad hoc committees. Essentially, this was the kind of multilateral machinery the experts had recommended at Punta del Este.

Two years later at IA-ECOSOC's second annual meeting at São Paulo, Brazil, in October, 1963, the proposal received a kinder reception. A general feeling that something had to be done about the Alliance was nearly universal. The two presidents had pointed the way to a solution. In addition, several previously reluctant countries, like Mexico, now favored more multilateralism. Most importantly, the United States after two years of Latin American criticism of its aid policies began to welcome the idea of shifting some of the burden of judging plans and aid programs onto other shoulders.

The U.S. delegation finally took the position sponsored by the State Department, which favored setting up a group with a well-defined

---

[6] Alberto Lleras, "Report on the Alliance for Progress," Pan American Union Doc. CIES/351, mimeographed, 1963.

mandate and power to make recommendations on the distribution of Alliance funds. While final decisions on U.S. loans and grants could not be delegated to such a group, its recommendations would be given the most serious consideration possible in the allocation of funds. Writing about the U.S. position, William Rogers said:

> The strategy had its risks. In innumerable ways the organization might cause trouble, no matter how persuasive the U.S. delegate. The possibility of embarrassment with the Congress was real if, for example, the new entity were to condemn AID or the reform efforts of Latin America in ways which would strengthen the hands of the Passmans. The more the matter was discussed, however, the clearer it became that the national interest would indeed be served. Hopefully, the organization, by focusing on self-help in a multinational context, would add measurably to the external inducements to reform, and give those inducements a trademark other than "made in U.S.A."[7]

The new group, conveniently designated as CIAP in both Spanish and English, was given all the power and responsibility recommended by the Committee of Nine with one extremely important exception — it would not be allowed to make decisions as to the distribution of Alliance funds. The United States delegation argued that, even if the U.S. government were willing, there remained constitutional restrictions on the actual power to allocate. How giving CIAP the authority for allocations would differ from the distribution of blocks of capital to the Inter-American Development Bank for its decision on allocations was never clearly explained. It was clear that U.S. officials, although they might favor multilateralism, still did not want to give CIAP the power to distribute funds. They feared the almost certain outcries from the U.S. Congress and the danger that an organization like CIAP might not insist on internal reform. Nevertheless, the United States position had gone beyond its noncommittal attitude at Punta del Este. It was, in fact, symbolic of the whole shift in thinking on multilateralism.

Growth and Development of CIAP

CIAP was organized early in 1964 with seven members plus a chairman. Designated as chairman was Carlos Sanz de Santamaría, a respected Colombian diplomat who had distinguished himself both as ambassador to Washington and as minister of finance of his country. Each CIAP member, except the U.S. representative, is selected by a

[7] William D. Rogers, *The Twilight Struggle: The Alliance for Progress and the Politics of Development in Latin America* (New York: Random House, 1967), p. 270.

designated group of countries. In some cases the "representation" is rotated from country to country while in other instances the dominant state of the group supplies the delegate, as in the case of Brazil.[8] Members are elected by the Inter-American Economic and Social Council. Members are in a curious dual position, technical and political. They are supposed to have the capacity to contribute to CIAP's mostly technical tasks and yet have the political standing to "represent" a group of countries in matters of broad interest.[9]

Since 1964, the central task of CIAP has been an annual review of the economic and social development of each Latin American country. The CIAP secretariat prepares a detailed report which serves as a framework for the review of the nation's development, including consideration of growth, inflation, savings and investment, balance-of-payments problems, foreign exchange needs, reforms, government expenditures and revenues, and other pertinent matters. These are often probing documents and say a good bit about the course of Latin American development.[10] These reports are reviewed at a meeting at CIAP headquarters in Washington attended by high officials of the nation under review (usually including one Minister) and by representatives of all the donor agencies, including U.S. AID, the Inter-American Development Bank, the World Bank, IMF, the United Nations, and at times representatives of the Organization for Economic Co-operation and Development (OECD) countries.

The annual reviews have produced wide-ranging discussions of policies adopted or soon to be adopted by the various governments, and have disclosed some of the more serious shortcomings. However, most of the "review" function is carried out by members of CIAP's secretariat and representatives of the donor agencies. Normally only one CIAP representative is present; sometimes he views his role as only that of procedural chairman of the meeting, but in other instances the chairman has also become seriously involved in the review procedures.

[8] The question of just how CIAP members are supposed to represent the various countries is not at all clear.

[9] The first members of CIAP (in addition to Carlos Sanz de Santamaría) were Celso Furtado (Brazil, Ecuador, and Haiti); Emilio Castanon (Argentina and Peru); Luis Escobar Cerda (Colombia, Chile, and Venezuela); Rodrigo Gomez (Mexico, Panama, and Dominican Republic); Gervasio Posadas (Bolivia, Paraguay, and Uruguay); Jorge Sol Castellanos (Costa Rica, El Salvador, Guatemala, Honduras, and Nicaragua); and Teodoro Moscoso (United States).

[10] While the Committee of Nine was in existence, it, together with its technical staff, collaborated in the preparation of country reports and in the annual review in general. (That the awkward two-committee system worked at all, even for a time, was due to the dedicated efforts of the secretariat leadership including Walter Sedwitz, Germánico Salgado, Gerardo Canet, and Roberto Cofiño.)

In general, the reviews serve extremely useful purposes. They help to inform the various donor agencies of projects other agencies are planning to finance and to alert national officials to the reactions of the donor agencies to particular plans and policies. These reviews also provide the basis for estimating balance-of-payments gaps and total external resources needs. Finally, they provide the raw material for a broad-gauged analysis of the problems and progress of the Alliance each year. The latter is made in an annual report to the Inter-American Economic and Social Council of the OAS. CIAP annual reports have examined the troublesome debt burdens of Brazil, Argentina, Chile, and Colombia, difficulties with inflation, land reform and agricultural productivity, development of national markets, education, and income distribution.

The establishment of CIAP followed in many ways the 1961 recommendation of the original OAS task force to the conference at Punta del Este, but its creation after the Committee of Nine had been formed and was operating created an ambiguous situation for the Nine. At first it was assumed that the two groups could work together, with the Nine carrying out its evaluation function independent of CIAP, but this was not to be. The two groups, not surprisingly, had differing views on development and reform. Moreover, the Committee of Nine wanted major emphasis to be put on the preparation, evaluation, and close adherence to long-range national development plans while CIAP members, although in favor of long-range planning, felt that the process of annual review of overall national performance was a better basis for external assistance, at least for the time being.

Since neither "reform" nor insistence on sound long-range planning is particularly popular with national politicians, the Committee of Nine soon found itself with few defenders. In March of 1966 at the fourth meeting of the Inter-American Economic and Social Council in Buenos Aires, a resolution was passed that made the committee a strictly advisory body, subordinate to CIAP. In addition, the number of members was reduced from nine to five, largely for budgetary reasons.

This action brought about the collective resignation of the committee panel members a month after the Buenos Aires meeting, and for almost two years there was a gap in the evaluation machinery. Members of the new Committee of Five were not chosen until the end of 1967 (only three were appointed), and the committee did not begin to function until 1968.[11]

---

[11] When Uruguay submitted its plan for evaluation in 1967, CIAP, as a makeshift measure, created an ad hoc evaluating committee made up entirely of "outside" experts.

CIAP itself occupied an anomalous position organizationally, far down on the OAS hierarchical ladder. Technically it was merely a special committee of the Economic and Social Council, which in turn was distinctly subordinate to the OAS Permanent Council. The latter was concerned essentially with political and security matters and organized along diplomatic lines not well suited to provide development leadership. In February, 1967, the Organization of American States, through a Protocol to the OAS Charter, was restructured. The member states agreed to meet annually in an Assembly. The major subjects of concern to the inter-American system — political and security, economic and social, and cultural and educational — were to be the responsibility of three co-equal bodies each reporting directly to the Assembly: the Permanent Council, the Economic and Social Council, and the Cultural Council. CIAP would constitute the permanent executive committee of IA-ECOSOC, charged with considering all developmental issues, including aid, trade, integration, and internal reform. Furthermore, the new system, by providing for annual meetings of foreign ministers as a General Assembly, would encourage consideration at the ministerial level not only of the traditional political and security issues, but the developmental issues of the Alliance for Progress as well. "This strongly implies the need to include at the meetings not only ministers of foreign affairs but ministers of finance, economy and planning. Closer integration of the developers into diplomacy is desirable if the top OAS meeting each year is to consider the problems of Latin America in their broadest sense, and if it is to treat — as it should — the entire panoply of inter-related economic, political, psychological and social problems in a coherent fashion."[12]

In the meantime, with many of the Latin American countries suffering from relatively low prices of basic commodities and finding difficulties in developing new export industries, new initiatives in Latin American economic integration were taken. These efforts were neither instigated nor coordinated by CIAP. For example, it was the President of Chile, Eduardo Frei, who wrote to the heads of CIAP, ECLA, the Inter-American Development Bank, and the Institute of Economic and Social Planning (the last of these in order to involve Raúl Prebisch) asking their advice on the best method of stimulating further economic integration in Latin America. Then at the "little summit meeting" in Bogotá in August 1966, attended by Presidents Frei of Chile, Lleras Restrepo of Colombia, and Leoni of Venezuela, economic integration

---

[12] Rogers, *The Twilight Struggle*, pp. 275–76.

was again discussed and the pressure for it maintained. This meeting, in fact, stimulated the move for a sub-regional common market of the Andean countries and an Andean Development Corporation which are now being implemented.

The United States responded positively to the rising interest in regional economic integration on the part of the smaller countries, and President Johnson proposed a presidential summit meeting to consider this issue among other key questions. This meeting was held in April of 1967, once again at Punta del Este. This gathering of chief executives — the second in inter-American history, and the first since 1956 — was designed to revitalize the Alliance and to give new impetus to the economic integration effort at the highest level. The Latin American presidents agreed to the creation of a genuine common market, changes to start in 1970 with a 1985 goal of no internal tariffs and a common external tariff for the whole region. This common market was to embrace the countries within the existing Latin American Free Trade Area and the Central American Common Market as well as the Caribbean states that were not yet affiliated with either. There also was agreement on the desirability of sub-regional arrangements. In addition, in order to lay the groundwork for integration, the presidents pledged to develop international transportation and communications systems and to favor multinational infrastructure projects. The United States agreed to help financially with these efforts.

The resolutions, however, left much unsaid. The exact procedure by which integration was to be achieved was not spelled out, and there was a clear reluctance to go beyond the general commitment to a common market. The meeting, then, kept the Alliance idea alive but did not register substantive progress.

Beyond underlining the difficulties to be faced and overcome in achieving a regional common market, the presidential summit reminded those concerned with Latin American development that very little had yet been done to integrate progress on the trade front with progress on the aid front. It suggested the urgent need for strong leadership in these matters, a leadership that logically should rest with CIAP.

A development that could have significant results occurred in mid-1968 when U.S. AID granted CIAP the responsibility for reviewing all development loans and technical assistance requests submitted by Latin American countries *before* AID acted. Under this arrangement CIAP is to have the opportunity to discuss contemplated U.S. action with Latin American countries and to make its views known to both sides. If the CIAP review includes consideration of international or region-wide economic and political factors that would advance regional economic integration, it might well add a significant multilateral dimension to loan and technical assistance arrangements.

The creation and evolution of CIAP has clearly contributed to improving the multilateral character of the Alliance. However, the problem of finding effective means for achieving the goals set forth in the Charter of Punta del Este remains. Additional organizational changes are called for. These are discussed in the last chapter of this book. Meanwhile, the questions of just how much aid Latin America has received, and what the impact of the Alliance has been, deserve attention.

Chapter 4

THE FLOW OF FUNDS
TO LATIN AMERICA

ON the surface it would seem a simple matter to determine how much financial assistance has been provided under the Alliance for Progress and whether or not this amount has been in keeping with the promises made by the United States at Punta del Este.[1] Actually, such a determination turns out to be anything but a simple matter, full of all sorts of technical issues.

At Punta del Este, there was no adequate basis for determining how much Latin America as a whole would need annually in outside financing if the countries were to undertake a major developmental thrust. The amount would depend on how quickly and effectively total developmental investment could be increased, how much could be raised in national resources to finance the costs of development, how much had to be imported that could not be covered by the nations' export earnings, and how much of a debt burden the nations could carry. Data from the past were, however, broadly suggestive, and, on the basis of these, technical experts at the conference assumed that a total of some $10 billion in new investment annually would be needed to achieve the Alliance goal of an average 2.5 per cent per capita annual increase in GNP within each nation. It was assumed further that about $8 billion in new investment funds could be provided from internal sources, leaving an estimated $2 billion a year needed from outside sources, mainly to cover the costs of imports not covered by export earnings. The United States delegation did not know how much of the commitment would be acceptable to Congress over a number of years and preferred to keep the figures vague. The only certainty was that a commitment of about $1 billion for the next year was acceptable to top officials in the United States. It is not surprising, then, that it never became clear just what was promised at Punta del Este — whether

---

[1] Financial assistance, or aid, is defined here as all grants and those loans carrying rates of interest and repayment terms that are more favorable than loans obtainable commercially.

the United States merely undertook to provide about $1 billion a year in financial assistance or whether it had accepted a broader responsibility for underwriting all the financial assistance deemed necessary to achieve the goals of the Alliance.

The language of the Charter itself is ambiguous. The introduction to the Charter, in the "Declaration to the Peoples of America," states:

> The United States, for its part, pledges its efforts to supply financial and technical cooperation in order to achieve the aims of the Alliance for Progress. To this end the United States will provide a major part of the minimum of twenty billion dollars, principally in public funds, which Latin America requires over the next ten years from all external sources in order to supplement its own efforts.

> The United States will provide from public funds, as an immediate contribution to the economic and social progress of Latin America, more than one billion dollars during the twelve months which began on March 13, 1961, when the Alliance for Progress was announced.

> The United States intends to furnish development loans on a long-term basis, where appropriate running up to fifty years and in general at very low or zero rates of interest. . . .

In one of the titles of the Charter there is an additional reference to external assistance:

> The United States will assist those participating countries whose development programs establish self-help measures and economic and social policies and programs consistent with the goals and principles of this Charter. To supplement the domestic efforts of such countries, the United States is prepared to allocate resources which, along with those anticipated from other external sources, will be of a scope and magnitude adequate to realize the goals envisaged in this Charter.

While the first two references to U.S. government assistance suggest an amount in the vicinity of $1 billion a year, the third, within the body of the text itself, could well be construed as signifying the underwriting of "adequate" resources. Not surprisingly, it has been thus interpreted by Latin American commentators.

Whatever the figure used as a yardstick to measure the United States aid offer at Punta del Este, other definitions are not clear. For example, does the figure refer to the commitment of new funds each year, or to the actual delivery or *disbursement* of them to the recipient countries. From the internal U.S. government point of view, there is another and earlier stage in the process which adds to the confusion: the *appropriation* of funds by Congress. It is out of such appropriated funds that the Executive Branch makes commitments. The difference between appropriations and commitments is a domestic one, and only the latter is employed in any calculation of external assistance. The difference between commitments and disbursements is another matter, since it is only when funds are actually disbursed that they can be employed in a nation's development effort, and the time between commitment and disbursal can be substantial.

Also, in trying to grasp the meaning of the U.S. commitment at Punta del Este, one has to ask the question: Were the $2 billion a year indicated as required, and the U.S. share, *gross* or *net* figures? Since nations have to repay their loans, the actual *net* transfer of funds to Latin America can be small if the repayment schedule is stiff. There is, finally, the question of just what is meant by financial assistance. Should it include only long-term developmental loans and grants or should it include all types of assistance, including short-term loans, Food for Peace programs, Peace Corps assistance, and the rest?[2] These are all useful to recipients but in quite different ways, and they are not interchangeable.

What has been the actual performance? The key figures are set out in four tables that follow, showing commitments, disbursements, amortization of debt, and net flows to Latin America from the United States and international donor agencies. The importance of definitions of financial assistance becomes immediately apparent; the totals are substantially different depending on the category on which attention is focused.

Using the most generous possible interpretation of financial assistance (combined gross long-term and short-term commitments to Latin America), the average annually provided by the Washington-based agencies amounted to more than $2 billion for the period 1961–68 (see Table 3). The U.S. share amounted to nearly $1.2 billion, not

[2] In an address delivered before the World Affairs Council in Los Angeles shortly after the Charter was signed (on September 11, 1961), U.S. Secretary of the Treasury, Douglas Dillon, made it clear that the assistance contemplated under the $2 billion figure would cover a wide range of assistance from many sources. An approximate breakdown, he suggested, would include some $400 million from the U.S. Export-Import Bank, $250 million under the social development program outlined in the Act of Bogotá, $150 million through the Food for Peace program, $75 million by the Development Loan Fund, $75 million by technical assistance agencies; $750 million might be provided through loans by the international agencies, including Inter-American Development Bank, and through public loans and private investment by Western Europe, Canada, and Japan; the remaining $300 million might be expected to be furnished by U.S. private capital.

Table 3. Commitments of Financial Assistance by the United States and International Financial Institutions, 1961–68

(million dollars)

	1961	1962	1963	1964	1965	1966	1967	1968[a]	Average 1961–68
Long-Term Assistance	1,179.5	1,540.8	1,393.3	1,789.7	1,562.4	1,681.9	1,713.8	2,093.8	1,619.4
U.S. government grants and long-term loans[b]	728.6	1,066.7	872.2	1,439.5	857.2	944.0	1,054.0	1,088.3	1,006.3
AID	371.8	440.6	508.2	817.2	478.8	618.8	464.4	403.5	512.9
Food for Peace[c]	100.2	221.3	212.2	257.6	142.6	137.1	95.4	233.1[d]	174.9
Eximbank	139.4	183.9	86.4	239.1	160.8	150.7	470.5	428.2	232.4
Peace Corps[e]	1.6	16.0	18.3	39.7	23.8	37.4	23.7	23.5[d]	23.0
Social Progress Trust Fund	115.6	204.9	47.1	85.9	51.2	—	—	—	63.1
Inter-American Development Bank	174.4	125.3	213.9	214.8	321.2	395.8	493.3	427.0	295.7
International Bank for Reconstruction and Development, and affiliates	276.5	348.8	307.2	135.4	384.0	342.1	166.5	578.5	317.4
Short-Term Assistance	1,254.5	348.9	352.6	312.1	476.1	467.9	391.4	428.8	504.0
U.S. government	798.3	127.6	186.4	169.4	218.1	136.4	75.0	4.8	214.5
Eximbank[f]	651.3	2.6	126.4	73.1	148.3	123.9	—	—	140.7
U.S. Treasury	147.0	125.0	60.0	96.3	69.8	12.5	75.0	4.8	73.8
International Monetary Fund	456.2	221.3	166.2	142.7	258.0	331.5	316.4	424.0	289.5
Total	2,434.0	1,889.7	1,745.9	2,101.8	2,038.5	2,149.8	2,105.2	2,522.6	2,123.4

a Preliminary.

b Excludes U.S. contributions to international financial institutions except for the Social Progress Trust Fund; also excludes military assistance.

c Excludes Title I of P.L. 480 sales agreements for agricultural products intended for generation of local currency for "U.S. uses." The U.S. government considers as economic assistance only that portion of goods committed which will result in the generation of local currency for "country uses." Ocean freight is included for all Titles except III.

d Fiscal years.

e Includes funds for the Inter-American Highway.

f Includes reprograming of old debts as follow: 1961: $298.4 million (Brazil); 1962: $2.6 million (Costa Rica); 1963: $91.3 million (Argentina $72.0 and Brazil $19.3); 1964: $73.1 million (Brazil); 1965: $58.3 million (Argentina $15.4, Costa Rica $2.5, and Chile $40.4); 1966: $33.9 million (Bolivia).

Sources: Food for Peace and Peace Corps: "U.S. Report to the Inter-American Economic and Social Council, 1967" (Washington, D.C., April 1967), and data provided by AID to the Pan American Union. All other data: Pan American Union, "El Financiamiento Externo para el Desarrollo de la América Latina" (to be published for the 1969 CIES meeting).

counting the U.S. contributions to the Inter-American Development Bank (other than for the Social Progress Trust Fund) or to the World Bank. However, short-term commitments, largely compensatory financing by the U.S. Export-Import Bank, the U.S. Treasury, and the International Monetary Fund, while extremely helpful to countries in temporary financial difficulties, must be distinguished from "development aid." Most of these short-term loans have already been paid or will have to be repaid in the next few years; in addition, many of them carry fairly substantial interest charges.[3] Still, the yearly average figure for *long-term* aid alone is a substantial $1.6 billion. Fragmentary information about commitments of long-term, low-interest assistance from Europe and other sources suggest that about $150 million should be added to this figure, for an overall total in long-term commitments of about $1.75 billion on the average each year.

Actual *disbursements* to the Latin American countries were much lower, however, with grants and long-term loan disbursements from the Washington-based agencies averaging slightly above $1.1 billion annually for the period 1961–68 (see Table 4).

The European contribution would add some 10–15 per cent. U.S. long-term disbursements amounted to some $775 million a year.[4] Thus, disbursements of official long-term funds to Latin America have fallen short of expectations by a sizable margin and consequently have not filled the resources gap in Latin America as initially anticipated. Later, some of the causes of the shortfall will be discussed, but first let us note still another measure of foreign financial assistance: the *net* flows of official capital.

Table 5 shows the repayment of loans by the Latin American countries to the donor agencies for the period 1961–68. The figures represent actual repayments and are substantially lower than the amounts due during those years. A large part of the unpaid debt of several countries — especially Argentina, Brazil, Chile, and Colombia — was rescheduled, which increased the obligations to be paid in later years. This rolling-over of repayments and the accounting prac-

[3] Also, it is well to note that the eight-year average is greatly influenced by the substantial Eximbank and IMF commitments of 1961 when there was a large "rollover" of previous debt.

[4] It might be noted that U.S. disbursements have been much less erratic than commitments over the period, and have gained ground steadily. A relatively wide gap between commitments and disbursements has characterized operations of all the donor agencies. For example, by the end of 1967 the Inter-American Development Bank had committed $2.9 billion (counting the Social Progress Trust Fund which it administered) but had disbursed only $1.3 billion, or 44.8 per cent.

Table 4. Disbursements of Official Loans and Grants by the United States and International Financial Institutions, 1961–68

(million dollars)

	1961	1962	1963	1964	1965	1966	1967	1968[a]	Average 1961–68
Long-Term Assistance	676.5	794.7	1,054.8	1,136.5	1,107.3	1,351.5	1,242.7	1,487.9	1,106.5
U.S. government grants and long-term loans[b]	569.4	600.8	707.0	755.2	802.8	949.8	806.1	1,009.2	775.0
AID	201.5	277.9	347.3	360.5	455.7	578.5	426.6	466.2	389.3
Food for Peace	162.5	128.3	183.9	241.6	102.9	111.8	102.0	150.0[d]	147.9
Eximbank[c]	193.6	163.9	98.3	74.1	146.1	162.5	199.8	318.0	169.5
Peace Corps	0.9	8.6	11.7	12.2	27.7	26.8	17.7	20.0[d]	17.0
Social Progress Trust Fund		22.1	65.8	66.8	70.4	70.2	60.0	55.0	51.4
Inter-American Development Bank	5.9	36.6	75.5	130.8	111.6	143.2	180.9	235.0	114.9
International Bank for Reconstruction and Development, and affiliates	101.2	157.3	272.3	250.5	192.9	258.5	255.7	243.7	216.5
Short-Term Assistance	888.9	276.6	455.5	139.4	220.6	224.9	159.9	270.5	329.5
U.S. government	541.5	180.9	224.0	76.9	73.4	50.9	37.2	–	148.1
Eximbank[c]	476.5	146.4	133.5	58.6	60.0	37.4	37.2	–	118.7
U.S. Treasury	65.0	34.5	90.5	18.3	13.4	13.5	–	–	29.4
International Monetary Fund	347.4	95.7	231.5	62.5	147.2	174.0	122.7	270.5	18.1
Total	1,565.4	1,071.3	1,510.3	1,275.9	1,327.9	1,576.4	1,402.6	1,758.4	1,436.0

[a] Preliminary.

[b] Excludes U.S. contributions to international financial institutions, except for the Social Progress Trust Fund. U.S. contribution to IDB, in addition to SPTF, amounted to $970 million in 1961–1966. Excludes also military assistance.

[c] Eximbank official disbursement figures, as published in the annual U.S. Report to IA-ECOSOC, include short-term assistance (except reprograming of old debts) as well as long-term assistance. The figures for total disbursement shown in the 1967 report to IA-ECOSOC for the years 1961–1966 are as follows (in millions): $472.4, $271.2, $140.0, $65.4, $136.1, and $146.9. According to an estimate prepared by the Pan American Union, the reprogramed loan disbursements are as follows: 1961: $221.6 million; 1962: $38.6 million; 1963: $85.0 million; 1964: $58.5 million; 1965: $59.9 million; 1966: $37.3 million; 1967: $37.3 million.

[d] Fiscal years.

Sources: Food for Peace and Peace Corps: "U.S. Report to the Inter-American Economic and Social Council, 1967" (Washington, D.C., April 1967), and data provided by AID to the Pan American Union. All other data: Pan American Union, "El Financiamiento Externo para el Desarrollo de la América Latina" (to be published for the 1969 CIES meeting).

Table 5. Amortization of Long-Term and Short-Term Loans Granted by the United States and International Financial Institutions, 1961–68

(million dollars)

	1961	1962	1963	1964	1965	1966	1967	1968[a]	Average 1961–68
United States:									
AID	0.4	4.2	10.7	10.2	9.1	14.4	22.6	24.2	12.0
Eximbank	326.6	140.4	207.6	251.4	205.1	254.2	272.6	229.2	235.9
U.S. Treasury	47.0	7.1	64.8	48.3	31.2	41.4	6.8	10.0	32.1
Social Progress Trust Fund	–	0.4	1.3	3.0	4.3	6.2	10.3	13.8	4.9
U.S. total	374.0	152.1	284.4	312.9	249.7	316.2	312.3	277.2	284.9
Inter-American Development Bank	–	–	0.7	5.6	11.9	23.9	36.2	50.5	16.1
International Bank for Reconstruction and Development, and affiliates[b]	40.9	42.0	52.1	53.2	65.9	73.5	79.7	84.8	61.5
International Monetary Fund	60.8	164.2	118.1	133.3	170.0	215.2	146.0	221.5	153.6
Total	475.7	358.3	455.3	505.0	497.5	628.8	574.2	634.0	516.1

[a] Preliminary.
[b] Except IFC.

Source: Pan American Union, "El Financiamiento Externo para el Desarrollo de la América Latina" (to be published for the 1969 CIES meeting).

tices of some of the institutions involved make it impossible to distinguish the exact amount of the amortizations of loans in 1961–68 that correspond respectively to original long-term and short-term assistance. A rough estimate would suggest that the total repayments of the period are divided about evenly into the two categories. As shown in the table, total amortization of loans during 1961–68 averaged about $516 million a year. The amounts increased substantially during the period and averaged over $600 million for 1966–68.

It is only after debt repayment is accounted for that we get to *net* total official financial assistance. As can be seen from Table 6, total net disbursements of loans and grants during the 1961–68 period by the major donor agencies averaged about $920 million. (This compares with an average figure of just over $2 billion for total commitments made during the same period.) If we add to this a rough estimate of the financial assistance granted by other industrialized countries — for which no complete comparable data are available — we would reach a grand total of net official financial assistance in the vicinity of $1 billion per year.

Table 6 also highlights a striking fact about U.S. aid to Latin America: the actual net amount of U.S. public capital flows to the other Alliance members reached its highest level in its first year, 1961, when it amounted to $737 million.[5] The net amount was high again in 1968, but considerably less in the intervening years and averaged $638 million for the 1961–68 period.

The main point of the exercise is to establish the fact that the net flows of official financial assistance have been much smaller than was expected at Punta del Este, where the focus of attention was on anticipated shortfalls in foreign exchange availabilities.

Taken as an average for the whole region, the annual *net transfer* of resources to Latin America from the United States has amounted to about $3.00 per capita, while the total from all sources has amounted to slightly over $4.00 per capita. These amounts hardly seem enough to make a profound difference in the lives of the Latin Americans. The regional average is, however, misleading, since U.S. aid and total aid have been concentrated in a relatively small number of countries, and in certain strategic sectors.

Using the figures for total U.S. commitments to Latin America over the period 1961–66 (Table 7), it can be seen that in terms of dollar

[5] The 1961 figure is high because of the considerable short-term loans made by the Export-Import Bank in that year (see Table 4).

Table 6. Net Official (Long-Term and Short-Term) Capital Flows to Latin America from the United States and International Financial Institutions, 1961–68

(*million dollars*)

	1961	1962	1963	1964	1965	1966	1967	1968[a]	Average 1961–68
United States government[b]	736.9	629.6	646.6	519.2	626.5	684.5	531.0	732.0	638.3
Inter-American Development Bank[c]	5.9	36.6	74.8	125.2	99.7	119.3	144.7	184.5	98.8
International Bank for Reconstruction and Development, and affiliates[d]	60.3	115.3	220.2	197.3	127.0	185.0	176.0	158.9	155.0
International Monetary Fund	286.6	−68.5	113.4	−70.8	−22.8	−41.2	−23.3	49.0	27.8
Total	1,089.7	713.0	1,055.0	770.9	830.4	947.6	828.4	1,124.4	919.9

[a] Preliminary.
[b] Includes the Social Progress Trust Fund, administered by IDB.
[c] Excludes the Social Progress Trust Fund.
[d] Does not include International Finance Corporation amortization payments.

Sources: Tables 4 and 5.

54

Table 7.   Commitments of Financial Assistance to Latin American Countries by the United States, 1961–66

Country	1961	1962	1963	1964	1965	1966	Total 1961–66	Total 1961–66 per capita[b]
	(. . . . . *million dollars* . . . .)							*dollars*
Brazil	302.6	194.3	204.7	450.5	173.2	329.6	1,654.9	20.4
Chile	142.7	123.5	79.6	214.8	50.6	106.7	717.9	82.4
Colombia	89.1	120.0	60.6	143.8	88.9	43.4	545.8	29.2
Mexico	24.0	56.9	80.8	123.2	52.9	99.0	436.8	10.2
Dom. Rep.	0.1	53.4	40.7	25.3	107.8	73.6	300.9	82.0
Peru	39.7	50.5	31.9	96.8	25.2	38.0	282.1	29.2
Bolivia	30.5	52.5	60.3	66.0	19.1	37.2	265.6	64.2
Venezuela	70.1	76.3	29.5	36.9	30.0	18.2	261.0	28.6
Argentina	7.5	81.4	80.9	14.0	57.9	1.6	243.3	10.8
Ecuador	16.3	43.4	26.6	38.2	29.0	20.9	174.3	34.3
Panama	10.5	23.2	17.0	27.7	9.3	23.1	106.8	89.7
El Salvador	18.0	13.6	21.8	19.5	17.0	5.8	95.7	32.8
Nicaragua	10.3	13.1	6.7	15.1	18.0	15.3	78.5	44.9
Costa Rica	17.8	2.3	22.5	15.3	9.8	7.5	75.2	50.5
Paraguay	16.8	8.6	6.0	13.0	4.0	14.7	63.1	30.9
Guatemala	3.7	14.4	9.3	21.7	5.3	7.3	61.7	13.7
Honduras	5.2	7.9	10.6	11.6	9.7	7.6	52.6	24.1
Uruguay	4.7	16.4	8.5	7.6	1.9	6.9	46.0	16.9
Haiti	4.2	10.5	2.6	3.7	5.1	3.4	29.5	6.4
Regional	12.8	27.5	37.8	78.6	64.0	31.4	252.1	24.1
Total[a]	826.6	989.6	838.4	1,419.3	778.7	891.2	5,743.8	

[a] Totals include short-term Eximbank loans and differ from totals in Table 3 where such loans are treated differently.
[b] Employing estimated 1965 population data, Centro Latinoamericano de Demografía, *Boletín Demográfico*, Santiago, Chile, January 1969.
Source: AID Reports.

volume, aid to Brazil, Chile, Colombia, and Mexico amounted to almost 60 per cent of the total. In per capita terms, the picture is quite different, with Panama, the Dominican Republic, Chile, and Bolivia far ahead of the others. The very low per capita figure for Mexico is due to the fact that U.S. financial assistance has been influenced by the capacity of Latin American countries to earn foreign exchange and to tap the commercial financial markets, although the much higher Venezuelan figure suggests that these are not the only considerations involved.

Inter-American Development Bank loan commitments to the various Latin American countries do not follow the U.S. AID pattern (see

Table 8). For both the total and per capita commitments the range is much narrower, in part a product of the pressures that individual members can bring to bear on a regional institution, but also suggesting more of a commitment to typical bank (project) standards than to the rapid development-and-reform criteria suggested by the Charter of Punta del Este. This is evident in the fact that some of the highest loans per capita went to countries ruled by dictators or military juntas. Yet, overall, the Bank loans have been channeled into developmental purposes. To the extent that sector categories reveal general purposes, it would be difficult to fault IDB lending in this regard. A total of $2.4

Table 8.   Total Loans to Latin American Countries by the Inter-American Development Bank, 1961–68[a]

Country	From ordinary capital resources	From Fund for Special Operations	From Social Progress Trust Fund	Other[b]	Total	Per capita[c]
	(. . . . . *million dollars* . . . .)					*dollars*
Brazil	277.1	242.3	62.1	0.8	582.3	7.2
Argentina	192.7	128.1	43.5	0.7	365.0	16.2
Mexico	174.9	134.5	35.5	0.5	345.4	8.1
Chile	90.7	100.4	38.9	8.9	238.9	27.5
Colombia	136.7	95.4	49.9	16.5	298.5	16.0
Venezuela	85.6	24.2	73.0	–	182.8	20.1
Peru	37.4	75.8	45.3	1.4	159.9	13.8
Bolivia	–	68.5	14.6	5.6	88.7	21.6
Ecuador	10.8	26.0	27.8	1.2	65.8	12.9
Paraguay	6.1	53.9	7.8	0.7	68.5	34.2
Nicaragua	18.2	26.8	13.1	–	58.1	34.2
Uruguay	36.4	27.3	10.5	–	74.2	27.5
Guatemala	11.6	19.6	14.3	–	45.5	10.1
Honduras	0.5	40.0	7.6	–	48.1	21.9
Panama	10.0	22.9	12.8	–	45.7	38.1
Costa Rica	13.5	11.5	12.6	–	37.6	25.1
El Salvador	8.6	3.2	22.0	3.0	36.8	12.7
Dom. Rep.	6.0	33.4	10.3	–	49.7	13.4
Haiti	–	7.2	–	–	7.2	1.6
Trinidad-Tobago	–	5.3	–	–	5.3	5.5
Regional	20.0	28.7	2.9	3.5	55.1	–
Total	1,136.8	1,175.0	504.5	42.8	2,859.1	12.3

[a] Includes all approved loans, whether disbursed or not, to member governments, subdivisions of members, or private enterprises within these countries.
[b] Includes loans from the Canadian and United Kingdom funds.
[c] Population for 1965.
Source: Inter-American Development Bank, Statement of Approved Loans, December 1968.

billion in loans during the period 1961–67 went to the following sectors (in millions of dollars):

Agriculture	$578	24.2%
Industry and mining	488	20.4
Economic infrastructure	468	19.6
Water supply & sewerage	395	16.5
Housing	288	12.0
Education	102	4.3
Preinvestment	52	2.2
Export financing	20	0.8

In agriculture, for example, the following were among the purposes for which the loans were made: irrigation, farm credit, land settlement, improvement of grain elevator facilities at ports, food-processing industries, and farm mechanization.

The External Debt Problem

In the years immediately before the organization of the Alliance for Progress, several Latin American countries contracted substantial amounts of short-term and medium-term debt to cover the costs of imports. Part was contracted by the public sector, but an important proportion had its origin in suppliers' credit to private firms. When lack of foreign exchange prevented the firms from meeting their obligations, the loans had to be refinanced, with the government or monetary authorities underwriting them.

At the beginning of the Alliance, almost no one paid attention to the impact of this problem on the net flows of financial assistance to Latin America. In fact, it was not until the CIAP Secretariat and the Committee of Nine prepared an overall analysis of the external resource requirements in mid-1964 that the proportions of the problem began to be grasped.

Preliminary estimates were revised later that year in the light of the evaluation of development programs of eight countries completed by the Committee of Nine, and of the first round of country reviews conducted by CIAP, and the results were presented at the IA-ECOSOC annual meeting held in December 1964. The reports showed that to a large extent Alliance aid provided during 1961–64 (in gross terms) had been significantly offset by the repayment of previous debt of the public and private sectors. For 1965 and 1966 the situation was going to be even more serious, with total repayments of $1.9 billion and $1.4 billion falling due. Most of the debt was owed by four countries — Argentina, Brazil, Chile, and Colombia.[6] The revision of those estimates one year later, after the second round of annual country reviews, confirmed the $1.9 billion figure for 1965 and raised the 1966 projection to some $1.7 billion.[7]

Once the seriousness of the problem had been grasped, action was taken in 1965 and 1966 to solve it temporarily through refinancing agreements involving the U.S. government (particularly in reference to Eximbank credits), IMF, and European suppliers and banks, with U.S. banks also playing some role. The situation was eased somewhat by the improved export situation of most of the large debtor nations, which permitted them to repay part of their obligations that had come due in 1965 and 1966. Nevertheless, the problem remains serious. Hard currency obligations rose from $4.3 billion in 1955 to $12.6 billion at the end of 1966. The service on this indebtedness rose from 6 per cent of the region's export earnings in 1955 to 18 per cent in 1966. The repayment and interest burden on loans made available by the U.S. government and other donors, added to the already heavy debt burden, could put most of the larger Latin American countries (excepting only Mexico) on a debt treadmill, with a large part of Alliance loans being absorbed in repayment of previous loans. Clearly, the Alliance must find a solution to this problem.

The Pipeline Problem and Absorptive Capacity

Funds committed but as yet undisbursed are referred to as "being in the pipeline." A detailed study of the pipeline problem made by CIAP in 1964 showed that at that time total undisbursed long-term commitments made by the U.S. government, the World Bank group, and the IDB to all Latin American countries amounted to $2.5 billion. The total of undisbursed funds increased another $500 million in 1965.

---

[6] Pan American Union, *El Esfuerzo Interno y las Necesidades de Financiamiento Externo de América Latina*, Doc. CIAP/150, mimeographed (Washington, D.C., 1964), p. 58.

[7] Pan American Union, *El Futuro de Desarrollo de la América Latina y la Alianza para el Progreso*, 1966, p. 251. These figures refer to all debts falling due during these years whether actually repaid or not, and include obligations to governments other than the United States and to private creditors. They are, therefore, much higher than the figures shown in Table 5, which cover only obligations actually paid to the U.S. government and international financial institutions (not including the part of those obligations whose payment was rescheduled for later years).

By 1966 some progress was made in accelerating the use of committed funds.

The pipeline problem is not peculiar to Latin America but is a common feature of aid programs to all less-developed countries. Funds may be in the pipeline for good reasons, especially when they are intended for large and complex projects that stretch over a number of years. But, to some extent, a clogged pipeline reveals underlying problems in the external financing of development efforts. These include the "absorptive capacity" of the recipient countries and certain practices and constraints in the process of granting aid.

The limits to absorptive capacity in Latin America have received a substantial amount of attention and are now fairly well understood. Particularly important is the lack of enough organizational and management skills in both government and private enterprise. In almost every country in Latin America there is a shortage of trained personnel in government with the capacity to develop "bankable" projects and attractive governmental investment programs, although, of course, the variations among the countries in this respect are very great. Furthermore, even in countries where private enterprise is both important and flourishing, starting modern industries has been found to be a very slow process. There simply are not enough people with management capacity to set up modern manufacturing and service industries at a rapid rate. Other factors add to the difficulties. Delays at the legislative level in final approval of projects are extremely common, particularly if the majority is of a party in opposition to the president. Some projects take several years to go through the required approval stages. In some cases, restraint on the government budget may mean that there are no available counterpart local funds to carry out projects for which foreign assistance has been provided; "unmatched" external funds can stay in the pipeline for a long time. In general, the socio-economic systems of most Latin American countries are not geared for a rapid increase in productive capacity and efficient capital use.

To improve the absorptive capacity of Latin America, government efficiency needs to be improved through structural, political, and administrative reform; educational reform is needed to increase the number of trained management personnel; and economic and social reform is needed to open opportunities for national entrepreneurs and technicians as well as to generate enthusiasm for national development. But such reforms are slow in coming in Latin America. While some progress has been achieved by the Alliance in speeding project preparation, the more fundamental reforms, essential if absorptive capacity is to be substantially and quickly increased, remain to be undertaken in most of the countries.

What the above suggests is that foreign financial assistance provided within a given period is not simply a matter of donor generosity — although this feature is not to be overlooked — but also a matter involving the complexities of recipient capacity for effective use of outside funds. Clearly, a very generous flow of funds to an underdeveloped region can be used up without producing much permanent improvement. This is particularly true when a large portion of the foreign exchange provided by external financial assistance is used to cover balance-of-payments deficits resulting from the import of non-developmental goods and services. Thus, the fact that in recent years Latin America has had to import annually more than $800 million worth of food, due to the extremely rapid rate of population increase and the painfully slow improvements in agriculture, means that, even with fairly generous external financial assistance, developmental results inevitably have been small in countries with food deficits.

Generally, the problem of effective external assistance is relating it to situations which are far less than ideal. The various donor agencies have developed different kinds of policies to cope with the problem. Mostly they have looked for relatively sound, individual development projects in which the borrower, whether government or private industry, stands ready to do its share and is willing and able to cover the costs of the loan, in other words, projects deemed to be technically, economically, and financially "feasible." The assumption underlying this approach is that application for a loan from a private firm or a government indicates that the borrower deems the loan important enough to be willing to bear the costs involved. If the project meets certain technical and financial standards, generally it can be expected to be of use to the nation's productive capacity or needed infrastructure. Projects dominate international developmental financing. Of development loans authorized in the 1961–66 period, about 83 per cent were earmarked for specific projects, while only 17 per cent were in a more general developmental category.

Development projects by themselves do not necessarily add much to a nation's "absorptive capacity." The donor agencies have therefore sought to build up key national institutions needed for development, particularly educational and administrative institutions, and have brought pressures to bear on governments to follow fiscal and monetary policies suitable for rapid development. The latter pressures have been concerned largely with efforts to reduce inflation, to maintain an economically sound balance between import and export prices (e.g., urging devaluation of the nation's currency) and to raise taxes, particularly progressive taxes.

The results have been mixed. While progress in some sectors, particularly in industry, has been fairly good, the overall rate of developmental progress in Latin America has been disappointing. It has been disappointing enough certainly to suggest the desirability of a change in the scope of external assistance and in the lending procedures of the donor agencies. These questions are discussed at length later in this book.

Some Questions about U.S. Assistance

The United States government has been the mainstay of developmental assistance to Latin America under the Alliance for Progress. Its grants and loans to Latin American countries far exceed the assistance provided by the Inter-American Development Bank and the World Bank, by European nations, or by the net investment in Latin America of U.S. private enterprise.[8] Through the end of 1968, U.S. government aid commitments have totaled over $8 billion. This includes AID loans and grants, "Food for Peace" loans and grants, Export-Import Bank loans, loans and grants from the Social Progress Trust Fund administered by the IDB, and contributions to the IDB's Fund for Special Operations (for "soft" loans), the Peace Corps, and the Inter-American Highway.

To a large extent, AID loans have paralleled those granted by the two international banks and other national donors. They have been typical project loans for agricultural development, health, housing, highways, airports, school buildings, and the like. They have been made in response to real needs, and at the request of Latin American governments, private institutions, or cooperatives. Most of them have resulted in useful physical structures (roads, schools, hospitals, factories) or in better processes or improved agricultural practices. Yet, it is hard to grasp the logic of the particular loans made within the broad developmental objectives set for the Alliance.

---

[8] In addition, the U.S. government has provided the largest portion of the capital of the two banks.

Absence of broad-gauge criteria for AID project loans, based on carefully developed strategy decisions and priorities, means that aid is granted for specific investment projects with major attention focused on questions of engineering and financial specifications, provisions about national participation in the financing of the project, importation of the required capital equipment from the United States, and the like. Sometimes loans have been made for specific projects largely because they were "ready to go," while other necessary programs in more productive sectors were given lower priority because they were not "ready." Under project-lending arrangements it is difficult, if not impossible, to maintain any kind of priority system since there is little relationship between need and the nation's capacity to develop "bankable" projects in the high priority areas, education for example. (Toward the end of the U.S. fiscal year, AID officials sometimes desperately look around for "feasible" projects in order to commit money appropriated by Congress.)

Because of the difficulties involved in project lending, AID early began to experiment with "program lending" and in 1967 with "sector lending."

The sector loan approach was introduced as a possible way to encourage needed structural changes in the key sectors of a nation's economy. The AID intention is to use sector loans to assist Alliance countries that are willing to mobilize increasing shares of their internal resources in order to achieve major progress in agriculture, education, or health services. Chile was the first country to take advantage of this new loan technique, borrowing $10 million for educational development and $23 million for agricultural development.

Program loans are of much longer standing. These are relatively large loans tied to broad national development programs. Such loans have been based on two requirements: a demonstrated need, because of the balance-of-payments situation, to increase the nation's ability to import U.S. goods and services; and the adoption of public policies and programs to insure against capital flight or the misuse of domestic resources through inefficient budgeting, reduced local savings, or inflation.

The first experiment in program lending was in Chile in 1962 following a special mission by Teodoro Moscoso and Richard Goodwin, made in part to overcome the slow start of the Alliance. A program loan was feasible because Chile was one of the very few countries with a national plan ready when the Alliance started, thanks to the efforts of some farsighted Chilean *tecnicos*. AID continued to make program loans to Chile, added Colombia, and then Brazil (following the overthrow of the Goulart Administration in 1964) to the select list of program-loan recipients.

Program lending has a number of advantages: (1) it provides greater flexibility for the borrower because the loan can be used to support important activities that are difficult to package into project loan applications and because foreign exchange receipts can be used for a broad range of import requirements instead of just the import components of particular aid projects; (2) it more directly links aid with the nation's current net balance-of-payments situation; and (3) it can tie aid more directly to self-help and reform efforts.

AID has been extremely cautious in its use of program loans; by 1968 only the three countries mentioned earlier had received such loans. William D. Rogers suggests that they were the only countries that had both a balance-of-payments need and a development program comprehensive enough to justify development program lending. A serious problem is that the performance criteria which are most easily used in program lending are those that are more or less measurable in simple arithmetic. Rogers wrote:

> It is easier to determine whether a borrowing nation has met its commitment to reduce its surplus on current account to a numerically defined level than it is to decide whether it has lived up to promises to expand its educational system, to reform rural life or strengthen democracy.

> The American people, and particularly the Congress and the press, have focused on nonessentials, and tended to underestimate the importance of a large U.S. aid effort and to overestimate the extent to which the one rich partner of the Alliance can trade its help for essential reforms. The Executive has learned only slowly that the United States must devote all the resources and style of its presidential leadership and diplomacy to the single-minded task of supporting development in the hemisphere.[9]

Lack of devotion by the donor side of the partnership to the "single-minded task of supporting development" makes it hard to avoid the conclusion that the United States shares some of the blame for the shortcomings of the Alliance. The generous and far-reaching U.S. contribution to Latin America envisaged by President Kennedy in 1961 has shrunk in the last few years not only in scope but, more importantly, in the objectives sought.

Policy makers in the United States, both legislative and executive,

---

[9] Rogers, *The Twilight Struggle*, p. 210.

at times seem to lose sight of the most pragmatic reason for an "Alliance for Progress" between the United States and the Latin American countries — the promotion of rapid, far-reaching changes in the social, political, and economic structures in order to raise living standards and avoid violent, costly revolutions.

If financial assistance is to make much of a difference in tipping the scales the right way, clearly it must be substantial. In actual fact, U.S. aid commitments have not increased over the life of the Alliance; they have flattened out at a level that makes it possible for the United States to help only two or three countries in a substantial way, or many countries in a piddling way. U.S. policy seems to be a kind of middle way with a mixture of large and small grants of money, and little consistent developmental thrust.

Chapter 5

HOW MUCH PROGRESS
IN LATIN AMERICA?

In judging the performance of the Alliance it must be remembered that it was launched during a difficult period. The years immediately before the signing of the Charter were economically unfavorable ones for most Latin American countries. Political and social unrest was widespread through the region. And there was the emotional impact of the Cuban Revolution followed by varying reactions to the subversive activities promoted from Havana.

It had been hoped that the launching of the Alliance would be a significant turning point — that a substantial amount of external aid coupled with a major developmental effort by the individual Latin American nations would propel them into self-sustaining economic growth. But the bright promises of Punta del Este were not to be realized. For most of Latin America, the 1960's, under the Alliance, have seen a continuation of the painfully slow growth of the later 1950's, a growth rate so slow that it would take many generations to bring all Latin American people up to a decent level of living.[1]

Economic Progress

From 1961 to 1967 the economic performance of Latin America as a whole not only fell short of the Alliance goal of an annual rate of growth of 2.5 per cent per capita, but failed to match performance during the fifties. (See Table 9 which summarizes the annual rates of increase in per capita gross domestic product for the individual countries and for the region.) There has, of course, been great variation in the performance of individual countries. As can be seen from the listing below, only seven out of the nineteen countries achieved a 1961–67

---

[1] For a highly critical view of performance under the Alliance, see Simon G. Hanson, *Five Years of the Alliance for Progress: An Appraisal* (Washington: The Inter-American Affairs Press, 1967).

Table 9.   Annual Rates of Increase in Gross Domestic Product per Capita at Constant Market Prices, 1950–67[a]

Country	Average annual rates			1961	1962	1963	1964	1965	1966	1967[b]	Average 1961–67
	1950–55	1955–60	1960–65								
Argentina	1.4	0.9	1.7	5.3	-3.4	-5.0	6.3	6.1	-1.9	0.5	0.4
Bolivia	-1.8	-2.6	2.6	-0.2	3.2	4.0	3.1	3.1	3.9	3.1	3.4
Brazil	2.5	2.9	1.5	4.3	2.4	-1.3	0.2	1.7	1.3	1.7	1.0
Chile	0.9	1.0	1.8	1.3	3.8	-0.8	1.4	3.5	3.4	1.0	1.8
Colombia	2.3	1.1	1.0	2.0	2.1	-2.8	3.1	0.4	2.3	0.5	1.0
Costa Rica	3.2	1.5	1.9	-1.0	3.8	2.9	1.0	3.0	4.2	4.3	3.2
Dominican Republic	4.2	1.8	-2.0	-7.5	10.2	1.5	2.7	-15.0	n.a.	n.a.	n.a.
Ecuador	2.2	1.2	1.2	-1.5	-1.5	0.9	4.8	0.4	2.1	2.5	1.5
El Salvador	2.1	0.9	3.3	1.1	9.7	0.7	4.5	0.9	3.0	-0.1	3.1
Guatemala	-0.7	2.3	3.6	0.9	-0.3	9.3	3.7	4.4	1.8	0.2	3.1
Haiti	-0.4	0.1	1.3	2.3	2.3	-3.5	-3.5	-3.5	-1.2	-3.3	-2.2
Honduras	-0.8	1.5	1.1	0.4	2.4	-1.4	-0.1	4.1	1.3	0.0	1.0
Mexico	2.9	2.7	2.6	0.2	1.5	2.9	6.6	1.9	3.9	3.8	3.4
Nicaragua	5.0	-1.3	4.6	2.9	6.8	3.8	4.1	6.0	0.7	1.4	3.8
Panama	0.3	2.7	4.7	6.5	5.2	5.4	1.8	4.8	7.5	6.7	5.2
Paraguay	0.3	-0.1	1.2	3.0	-1.0	-0.3	0.7	3.3	-0.2	0.2	0.4
Peru	2.6	2.0	2.7	2.8	2.6	2.1	3.0	3.3	2.3	0.4	2.3
Uruguay	2.8	-1.1	-0.1	1.8	-3.4	-2.2	2.8	-0.2	1.4	-3.3	-1.1
Venezuela	4.6	2.4	1.2	-3.2	2.6	0.6	4.3	1.5	-1.2	0.1	1.3
Latin America	2.4	1.8	1.7	2.0	1.2	-0.5	3.3	2.3	1.6	1.6	1.6

[a] These figures are rough estimates at best and revisions are continually being made by national statistical organizations and international agencies.

[b] Preliminary.

Sources: For 1950–60: Pan American Union, *The Future of Latin America's Development and the Alliance for Progress.* Doc. CIES/847, mimeographed (Washington, D.C., 1966). For 1960–65: Pan American Union, *Evolución Reciente de la Economía de América Latina,* Doc. CIES/1138, mimeographed (Washington, D.C., 1967). For 1966–67: Pan American Union, preliminary estimates (unpublished) based upon 1967 CIAP country reviews.

annual average growth of over 2.5 per cent; seven others had moderate growth; and five had little or no growth.

	Average annual increase in GDP per capita, 1961–67
High growth:	*per cent*
Panama	5.2
Nicaragua	3.8
Mexico	3.4
Bolivia	3.4
Costa Rica	3.2
El Salvador	3.1
Guatemala	3.1
Moderate growth:	
Peru	2.3
Chile	1.8
Ecuador	1.5
Venezuela	1.3
Brazil	1.0
Colombia	1.0
Honduras	1.0
Low growth:	
Argentina	0.4
Paraguay	0.4
Uruguay	−1.1
Haiti	−2.2
Dominican Republic	n.a.

The high-growth group includes five of the six Central American countries. These countries started from a very low base, and they are still extremely poor and underdeveloped in most cases, but their economic achievement is impressive nevertheless. They have enjoyed relatively good prices for their export products and their common market has clearly given them a significant economic boost. Mexico is the only large country that has moved ahead rapidly, and it has done very well indeed. For the 1960's, overall, it has one of the world's best growth records. Only one country in South America has achieved the hoped-for Alliance growth goal, Bolivia, the poorest of the continent's countries. Bolivia's performance in the 1960's has been an impressive recovery from the economic deterioration following the revolution of 1952. It has benefited from relatively good tin prices, but it has also moved ahead on a broad economic front, supported by fairly substantial external assistance. Of the high-growth group, Bolivia, Mexico, and Panama have enjoyed the steadiest growth from year to year.

Seven other countries fall into the moderate growth group — arbitrarily taken to be an average annual growth in GDP of 1 per cent–2.4 per cent. These countries contain a much larger proportion of the total population of Latin America than the rapid-growth group (some 140 million, compared to 61 million).[2] Of the moderate-growth group, Peru with a 2.3 per cent rate of growth, has come closest to achieving the Alliance growth goal. Peru's growth in the 1960's essentially has been a continuation of the growth pattern of the 1950's. The "moderate" group includes the three nations — Brazil, Chile, and Colombia — that have received far-above-average Alliance financial assistance. Brazil's mediocre performance of the 1960's follows good, sturdy growth throughout the 1950's. Chile's 1960's performance, by contrast, surpasses its growth of the 1950's by a substantial margin. Colombia has had lackluster economic performance since the early 1950's when it was getting peak prices for its coffee. Venezuela, whose average income is by far the highest in Latin America — largely because of its fabulous oil resources — has had only moderate (and erratic) growth in the 1960's following a period of very rapid growth during most of the 1950's. Nevertheless, Venezuela has moved ahead in a number of important developmental areas.

The five countries that have had little or no economic growth include Argentina and Uruguay, which are among the best endowed nations in Latin America. Their per capita income is topped only by Venezuela. They have the highest literacy rate in Latin America (91 per cent in both cases). They have the highest per capita caloric intake in the region. They have by far the largest amount of agricultural land per capita. But Uruguay has had no economic growth since the early 1950's, while Argentina has had sharp ups and downs, ranging from a drop in per capita GDP of 5 per cent in 1963 to a rise of 6.3 per cent in 1964, with a per capita income in 1967 only slightly higher than it was a decade earlier. Haiti has been badly mismanaged under a harsh dictatorship. (Its connection with the Alliance for Progress is peripheral.) The Dominican Republic, throughout the existence of the Alliance, has suffered from the disruption of civil strife following decades of exploitive dictatorship. The objective of the Alliance agencies in this country has been to lay a foundation for reconstruction and future economic expansion.

[2] Employing 1966 population data.

Rates of overall economic growth are clearly only part of the picture. Generally, and certainly in the economically more advanced countries of the world, it can be assumed that rapid growth will bring at least some gains to all groups in the society, whether it be somewhat better prices for the farmers' products, or more jobs for the marginal population in the slums. But it is hard to avoid the conclusion that in Latin America little of the gain seems to filter down.

The performance of the Latin American countries, with only a small number of exceptions, is even less satisfactory on the income-distribution (equity) scale than in terms of overall economic growth.

In addition to establishing an overall growth target, the Alliance Charter outlined a series of measures and conditions regarded as essential in achieving satisfactory economic and social progress: strengthening agriculture and bringing about land reform; increasing industrial production and productivity; expanding exports; encouraging savings and productive investment; maintaining price stability; reforming taxes and improving fiscal administration, and, in other ways, providing for the mobilization of internal resources for developmental purposes. As there has been only mediocre overall growth performance, it is not surprising to find that performance in these major developmental categories is at best spotty.

AGRICULTURE

Net farm production[3] during the 1960's increased only just enough to keep up with population growth, roughly 3 per cent a year. While total farm production during the past few years has increased some 28 per cent compared with the average for 1957–59 (the base years used by the U.S. Department of Agriculture in reporting on Latin American agriculture), *per capita* output has been at roughly the same level as it was in 1957–59. Per capita output in 1965–67 was substantially higher than at the end of the 1950's only in Central America, Mexico, and Venezuela.[4]

Total farm output has been greatly influenced by the sharp ups and downs of coffee production in Latin America, particularly in Brazil. For example, only 600,000 tons of coffee were produced in Brazil in 1964 when coffee output reached a low point; production in 1965 rose

[3] Total production excluding items needed for further production, such as animal feeds.
[4] As reported in U.S. Agency for International Development, Office of Program and Policy Coordination, Statistics and Reports Division, *Latin America: Economic Growth Trends*, October 1967, p. 18, and reports of CIAP.

to 2,262,000; in 1966 the figure was 1,260,000, and in 1967, about 1,500,000. These variations resulted partly from weather conditions, but also from the requirements for reducing production imposed by the International Coffee Agreement. The virtual ceiling on Brazilian coffee exports, necessitated by the desire of the world's coffee producers to maintain fairly high and stable coffee prices, typified the problems of Latin American agriculture and indicated the necessity for substantial change if farm performance is to be greatly improved.

The problems posed by the limits on expansion of the traditional export commodities were already clear by the time the Alliance for Progress was launched. Farming would have to be greatly diversified and modernized, productivity increased, and new export possibilities developed if the tempo of economic growth was to be substantially accelerated. Although both the U.S. AID agency and the Inter-American Development Bank have given high priority to loans and technical assistance to Latin American farming, the results have been disappointing. The traditional crops are still the mainstays of agriculture in almost every one of the Latin American countries. Thus far only in Mexico have new export crops been developed on a large and economically significant scale, and only there has a genuine, widespread agricultural revolution been under way. Research shows that major increases in Latin American food production are attributable largely to new acreage brought under cultivation. Increases in productivity have been small. In fact, only in the production of traditional export crops, particularly sugar and bananas, has modern technology been introduced to an important degree. Clearly, the tempo of farming improvement has been far below that needed to achieve the Alliance growth target.

In the region as a whole, progress in agrarian reform continued to be painfully slow or virtually non-existent. A knowledgeable official source has summed up the situation as follows:

> The implementation of legislation affecting the agrarian structure is still slow; the distribution of land and other productive resources among the rural population remains very unequal, and potentially productive land, water and human resources are seriously underutilized in the rural area.... The *campesino* class as a whole is still far from achieving satisfactory income levels and complete integration into the mainstream of social and political life in most of the countries.[5]

The slowest progress has been in the critically important area of land redistribution. The most significant land redistribution effort of

[5] Inter-American Development Bank, *Socio-Economic Progress in Latin America*, Social Progress Trust Fund Sixth Annual Report, 1966, p. 46.

recent years has been in Chile (although Colombia has also begun to move in this area at an impressive rate). The Frei government pushed through, against strong opposition, a far-reaching land reform law in 1967. Some 280,000 hectares of formerly private land were distributed to 3,800 families during that year, virtually all in the form of directed settlements. This was more than twice the achievement of any preceding year. Other than Chile and Colombia — and those countries with reform programs that antedate the Alliance (Mexico, Bolivia, and Venezuela) — only a few countries have even proposed land redistribution schemes, much less implemented them. What land has been given away often was in the public domain, much of it of doubtful quality. Resettlement schemes have also proceeded very slowly, and because of their high cost it is likely that future progress in this area will be quite limited.

Not surprisingly, the countries that have made the most progress during the Alliance period are those whose agrarian reform efforts were launched before 1961. Mexico, Bolivia, and Venezuela had earlier undertaken substantial land redistribution schemes; in recent years, these countries have entered a "consolidation" phase where the issue of land redistribution has given way to efforts to provide the beneficiaries with an adequate supply of needed inputs and social services and to create new institutions for production, marketing, storage, credit, and machinery service. These countries still face severe difficulties in fully modernizing their agricultural structures but their efforts are substantial and continuous.[6]

Some aspects of agrarian reform have been carried through. Thus, for example, several Latin American countries have confirmed the property rights of small tenants who held the land as squatters.[7] Also some change has been achieved in guaranteeing wage payments to *hacienda* workers thus eliminating feudal-type obligations prevalent in Peru, Ecuador, and Colombia. Agricultural credit programs have been set up in a number of countries providing loans to small and medium-size farms.

MANUFACTURING

The picture has been brighter for manufacturing than for agriculture. Increases in gross value added by manufacturing activity in Latin

[6] Inter-American Development Bank, *Social Progress Trust Fund, Fifth Annual Report*, 1965, p. 65.
[7] Some observers fear that this may intensify the minifundia problem, however.

America as a whole during the 1960's have averaged about 6 per cent a year, compared with agriculture's 3 per cent.[8] In Mexico and Venezuela manufacturing output rose by 65 per cent and 58 per cent, respectively, between 1960 and 1966. In almost all of the industrially more advanced countries in Latin America, manufacturing progress has been paced by a few new industries, particularly automobile manufacturing and assembly. Although manufacturing production has risen at a faster rate than the overall gross regional product during the period of the Alliance, the rate of increase in some important sectors has actually fallen off since the 1950's, due primarily to the relative decline of import substitution.[9] A comparison of growth rates in specific kinds of manufacturing during 1955–60 and 1960–65 for the region as a whole shows a slowdown in growth for foodstuffs, beverages, and tobacco, from 4.4 to 4 per cent a year; textiles, from 3.2 to 2.8 per cent; petrochemicals, from 10 to 8.8 per cent; basic metal industries, from 9 to 8 per cent; and for metal products, machinery, and transportation equipment, a marked drop from 15 to 7.3 per cent. Substantial increases in production during 1960–65 were recorded by the paper and automobile industries. By 1965, manufacturing was accounting for 23.4 per cent of the total gross domestic product of the region, compared with 20.9 per cent for agriculture.[10]

Two major problems of Latin American manufacturing were recognized by the Alliance from the beginning. The postwar Latin American drive for industrialization had created "an industrial structure virtually isolated from the outside world."[11] Latin America's industries were sustained, in the main, by their ability to get high prices for their products. The base rested not on technical and managerial proficiency, but on protective tariffs that were among the highest in the world. Latin American industry clearly had to be made more competitive, and internal markets had to be broadened by lowering prices. At the same time, the major manufacturing countries in Latin America were finding that the more obvious import-substitution possibilities, mainly in consumer and simpler capital goods, were being exhausted

---

[8] The data are based on reports of eight countries which accounted for 87 per cent of the total gross national product and 82 per cent of the population of Latin America in 1958. AID, *Latin America: Economic Growth Trends*, p. 20.

[9] Inter-American Development Bank, *Socio-Economic Progress in Latin America*, Social Progress Trust Fund Seventh Annual Report, 1967, p. 4. The following sections draw heavily on this report.

[10] AID, *Latin America: Economic Growth Trends*, p. 17.

[11] Economic Commission for Latin America, *Toward a Dynamic Development Policy for Latin America*, U.N. Doc. E/CN.12/680 (April 14, 1963), p. 107.

because of limited internal markets. The next stage of industrialization, the manufacture of intermediate and capital goods, including precision and heavy-duty machinery, would require larger markets than the individual countries offered. It was hoped that the Latin American Free Trade Association, as well as the much smaller Central American Common Market, would provide the framework for greatly expanded interregional trade and the encouragement of capital goods manufacture. The same developmental thrust, it was hoped, would also permit Latin American countries to enter established markets for capital goods in Europe and the United States.

Only modest progress has been made under the Alliance in overcoming these problems. Latin American industry retains its high cost structure, protected by tariffs, quotas, and other barriers to trade. The Latin American Free Trade Association has made little progress since its inception in 1960, plodding along in painful product-by-product negotiations for the reduction of national tariffs. Developments within the small Central American Common Market have been the brightest part of the picture. Between 1962 and 1966, trade among the common market countries increased at a rate of 36 per cent a year. In 1966 locally manufactured commodities comprised about 68 per cent of all goods exported within the Central American Common Market area. Of the remainder of Latin America, only Mexico has succeeded in significantly increasing its export of manufactured goods. Overall, industrialization in Latin America continues along the pathways laid out before the Alliance for Progress. The brightest possibility seems to be the creation of a Latin American common market, which was the focal point of the President's Summit Meeting in 1967 and which has been moved up on the Alliance agenda since the difficulties in achieving rapid growth through "inward-looking" industrialization have become more apparent.

EXTERNAL TRADE

Developments in the external sector, generally the critical element in the relative economic growth of the Latin American countries, have been mixed during the years of the Alliance: broadly favorable in quantitative terms; much less favorable in terms of the rate of change of the basic export structure.

Following virtual stagnation between 1954 and 1961, Latin American exports increased sharply in 1962 and continued to expand thereafter. The value of regional exports grew at an average annual rate of 6.4 per cent between 1962 and 1966, rising from $8.7 billion to $11 billion. A significant portion of export expansion since 1962 was attributable to improved world prices. According to the IBRD price index, commodity prices for the region rose 10 per cent between 1962 and 1966 and the prices of only two of the 13 most important commodities, bananas and cotton, fell during the period. This was accompanied by an increase in the physical volume of exports. The U.N. index of export volume showed a rise for the region between 1962 and 1966 from 123 to 145 (1958 = 100), or nearly 18 per cent. There was a slight decline in the value of Latin American exports between 1966 and 1967, but the 1968 preliminary estimates suggest that this may have been a temporary downturn.

Despite continued expansion of the value of exports between 1962 and 1966, the overall balance-of-payments deficit affecting the majority of countries in the region since the early 1950's kept imports from rising at a rate similar to export growth. During the period, imports rose at an average annual rate of 3.8 per cent and reached $9.6 billion in 1966, with an additional $500 million increase in 1967.

Table 10 shows the growth of exports and imports for the region as a whole between 1950 and 1967. The cyclical nature of the performance of the external sector over the period is apparent. Also it is clear that the services associated with the external trade (payments for shipping, insurance, etc.) and the interest payments on loans and investment income and other capital transactions (shown in column 2) involve a substantial drain on the foreign exchange earned by the region's exports. The extent to which funds leave the region because of inflation or other reaction to economic events or governmental policy, and the extent to which private foreign capital is attracted into the region greatly influences the total import capacity — and, therefore, the capacity to undertake substantial developmental investment. Thus, for example, during 1967, the substantial net private capital inflow (some $821 million compared to $440 million in 1966), including the repatriation of domestically owned funds in the wake of stabilization efforts, permitted an increase in imports (together with a small accumulation of reserves) sufficient to more than compensate for the slight decline in exports.[12] As always, of course, the regional averages represent a wide range of performance among the individual countries. The marked increase in net private investment recorded in 1967 was the result largely of gains in the major countries. In Argentina and Brazil, stabilization and other economic policies appeared to be attracting

[12] According to CIAP estimates. See Table 11.

Table 10.   Latin America: Summary of International Transactions, 1950–67

(million dollars)

Year	(1) Exports f.o.b.	(2) Net services and capital transactions[a]	(3) Total import capacity (1) + (2) = (4) + (5)	(4) Imports[c]	(5) Changes in international monetary reserves
1950	5,996	− 721	5,275	4,840	435
1951	6,966	11	6,977	7,142	−165
1952	6,350	643	6,993	6,958	35
1953	6,939	− 659	6,280	5,960	320
1954	7,335	− 732	6,603	6,798	−195
1955	7,349	− 389	6,960	6,890	70
1956	7,918	− 168	7,750	7,260	490
1957	7,829	821	8,650	8,500	150
1958	7,452	− 457	6,995	7,690	−695
1959	7,650	− 645	7,005	7,220	−215
1960	7,978	− 373	7,605	7,690	− 85
1961	8,104	− 404	7,700	7,950	−250
1962	8,661	−1,001	7,660	8,040	−380
1963	9,200	− 840	8,360	7,860	500
1964	9,756	−1,501	8,255	8,106	149
1965	10,172	−1,518	8,654	8,316	338
1966	11,133	−1,447	9,686	9,624	62
1967	11,060	− 605[b]	10,455	10,134	321

[a] Includes errors and omissions. Up to 1963, it does not include merchandise services included in imports c.i.f. See note (c).

[b] This unusually low figure reflects mainly the inflow of short-term private capital to Argentina after the devaluation of its currency which caused an increase of foreign reserves of that country of about $350 million.

[c] On c.i.f. basis up to 1963, and on f.o.b. basis for 1964–67; as a counterpart of this change of definition in the series, a corresponding adjustment has also been made in column (2). See note (a).

Sources: Pan American Union, *The Future of Latin America's Development and the Alliance for Progress,* Doc. CIES/847, mimeographed (Washington, D.C., 1966); *Evolución Reciente de la Economía de América Latina,* Doc. CIES/1138, mimeographed (Washington, D.C., 1967); and *Principal Trends in the Latin American Economy for 1967 and Prospects for 1968 that Affect Fulfillment of the Aims of the Alliance for Progress,* Doc. CIAP/215, Rev. 2, mimeographed (Washington, D.C., May 1968).

considerable portfolio as well as direct investment. In Mexico, the continuation of domestic growth and stability was reflected in an acceleration of external investments in a broad range of activities. In Venezuela, a slowing down in petroleum disinvestments was accompanied by new investments in other sectors. At the same time, thanks seemingly to stabilization policies, repatriation of national capital seemed to have occurred in Argentina, Brazil, and Colombia.[13]

[13] Preliminary CIAP estimates for 1968, shown in Table 11, indicate some improvement in exports, but diminution in private and official capital flows in comparison with 1967.

The close relationship among the various key factors involved in international transactions, and particularly the close relationship of trade and aid, can readily be seen in the recording of financial inflows and outflows in Table 11 for 1966, 1967, and 1968.

The export performance of the Latin American countries during the Alliance years has not improved enough to suggest that most of the countries are on the way to self-sustaining growth. The region's export increase has been less than that of the rest of the world, excluding centrally planned economies, and its share of all world trade declined from 6.9 per cent to 6.1 per cent between 1962 and 1966.

The relative share of Latin American products imported into the four major world markets continued a downward trend which began in the 1950's (Table 12). By 1966, the Latin American share had fallen to 7.7 per cent, compared with 9.6 per cent in 1962. The displacement of imports from Latin America was particularly pronounced in the cases of the United States and the United Kingdom.

Table 11.   Latin America: External Financial Availabilities and Requirements for 1966, 1967, and Estimates for 1968

(million dollars)

	1966	1967	Preliminary estimate 1968
Requirements:			
Merchandise imports (f.o.b.)	9,624	10,134	10,924
Factor payments[a]	1,920	1,860	2,044
Other services	653	712	699
Exchange reserves	62	321	245
Errors and omissions	134	[b]	[c]
Total	12,393	13,027	13,912
Availabilities:			
Merchandise exports (f.o.b.)	11,133	11,060	11,689
Private capital flows, net	440	821	452
Official capital flows, net	820	973	779
Errors and omissions	[c]	173	992
Total	12,393	13,027	13,912

[a] Payments for external production factors (interest, dividends, royalties, etc.).
[b] As the entry here would be a negative sign, the errors and omissions figure has been entered under availabilities.
[c] Not applicable.
Source: Pan American Union, *Principal Trends*, 1968.

Table 12.   Latin America's Share in Major World Markets, 1962–66

(*per cent*)

Market	1962	1963	1964	1965	1966
European Economic Community	5.9	5.4	5.3	5.2	4.9
United States	20.8	20.3	19.0	17.3	15.6
United Kingdom	6.5	5.9	5.1	4.8	4.7
Japan	7.7	7.9	7.6	8.1	7.7
	9.6	9.0	8.4	8.1	7.7

Source: Inter-American Development Bank, *Socio-Economic Progress in Latin America*, 1967, p. 6.

Mobilization of Domestic Resources

Central to any national development thrust is mobilization of domestic resources. Consequently, the record with regard to savings and investment is broadly indicative of the intensity of national efforts to achieve self-sustaining growth. Table 13 provides rough estimates of the proportion of the gross national product devoted to savings and investment during the period 1957–65 for seventeen countries for which data are available.[14] These estimates suggest that domestic savings in Latin America have generally increased over the years, and in the most recent period at a somewhat faster rate than the rate of income expansion. Investment has also increased, but at a slower rate than GNP. The proportion of the national product devoted to investment has been slightly lower during the Alliance years than in the preceding period. The differences, though not particularly significant (especially in view of the imperfection of the data), are another indication that there was little change in the patterns of economic development during the Alliance years.

A more favorable element in the picture is the seemingly widespread acceptance in Latin America of the need to increase tax revenue by higher tax rates and better administration, and to devote a larger part of these revenues to economic and social development. This movement in the direction of tax reform, in both the legislative and administrative realms, is one of the most favorable aspects of Latin American

[14] These estimates, originated in AID, are presently being revised. They are extremely rough (with savings calculated as a residual after estimating other income and expenditure items), and are therefore subject to significant error. Other estimates of savings and investment, including some partial ones, made by ECLA, IDB, and OAS differ somewhat in the magnitudes shown, but all of them point in the same direction as that spotlighted in the text.

Table 13. Gross Investment and Savings: Seventeen Latin American Republics, 1957–65[a]

Year	Total investment (billion $, 1962 prices)	Domestic savings (billion $, 1962 prices)	Domestic savings as per cent of total investment	Total investment as per cent of GNP[b]	Domestic savings as per cent of GNP[b]
	(1)	(2)	(3)	(4)	(5)
1957	9.4	7.6	80.9	18.9	15.3
1958	9.1	7.9	86.8	17.4	15.1
1959	9.6	8.8	91.5	17.9	16.4
1960	10.1	9.0	89.1	17.8	15.8
1961	10.4	9.2	88.5	17.4	15.4
1962	10.6	9.5	89.6	17.2	15.4
1963	10.3	10.1	98.1	16.2	15.9
1964	11.5	11.0	95.7	17.2	16.5
1965[c]	12.2	11.9	97.5	17.2	16.8

[a] Excludes Dominican Republic, Haiti, and Cuba.
[b] Because they were taken from diverse sources, and converted from national currencies to U.S. dollars, the GNP estimates on which these estimates are based differ slightly from those used in other tables of this book.
[c] Preliminary.
Source: U.S. Agency for International Development, Statistics and Reports Division, *Trends in Production and Trade* (Washington, D.C., 1965).

performance in recent years. There have been both quantitative and qualitative (largely, equity) improvements. As a result of these measures, central government revenues have increased fairly rapidly. As shown in Table 14, presenting data prepared by IDB, central government revenues in constant prices rose from $5.5 billion in 1961 to $7.9 billion in 1966, an increase of 7.3 per cent a year, substantially higher than the annual increase in GDP in the same period. However, variations among the Latin American countries were large. Between 1961 and 1966 the increase in tax revenues exceeded the rise in GDP by more than 40 per cent in Colombia and Peru, by 32 per cent in Brazil and 25 per cent in Chile.[15] At the other end of the scale, in Argentina and Haiti, the tax burden was lighter in 1966 than in 1961.

On the qualitative side, there has been a shift to somewhat greater reliance on the income tax, a simplification and more progressive orientation of sales taxes, and some improvements in property taxation (e.g., in assessments). At the same time, there has been some overhauling of

[15] In Peru, unfortunately, the form of the increase was unfavorable from both the equity and economic standpoints. The major part was an increase in the rate of the national turnover tax.

Table 14. Central Government Tax Receipts in Relation to Gross Domestic Product, 1965 and 1966[a]

(1961 = 100)

Country	Index of tax receipts		Index of ratio of tax receipts to GDP	
	1965	1966	1965	1966
Argentina	76.1	91.3	68.8	83.1
Bolivia	134.7	156.7	108.1	118.9
Brazil	139.1	158.9	121.0	132.1
Chile	132.2	169.9	107.4	124.7
Colombia	136.2	181.7	114.3	144.6
Costa Rica	144.4	155.2	114.6	115.7
Dominican Republic	86.9	122.6	78.9	100.0
Ecuador	142.0	143.4	117.6	115.4
El Salvador	140.0	137.8	108.2	100.0
Guatemala	134.6	130.4	109.1	102.6
Haiti	72.5	70.2	77.0[b]	79.7[b]
Honduras	139.0	152.3	113.1	117.9
Mexico	153.2	153.6	119.0	111.1
Nicaragua	153.1	156.4	110.8	108.6
Panama	140.6	161.9	103.8	109.6
Paraguay	132.6	135.5	113.1	113.1
Peru	176.8	191.3	137.9	141.4
Trinidad-Tobago	133.1	128.0	124.1	116.4
Uruguay	89.0	128.7	86.8	122.8
Venezuela	126.6	137.4	100.0	106.8
Average Index for Latin America[c]	126.2	142.4	106.0	114.3

[a] Tax receipts in Latin America (million 1963 dollars):

1961	5,531.8
1964	6,472.6
1965	6,980.6
1966	7,877.0

[b] Base 1962 = 100.
[c] Includes the 20 Latin American member countries of the IDB.
Source: Calculated by IDB on the basis of official statistics. Inter-American Development Bank, *Socio-Economic Progress in Latin America*, 1967, p. 14.

the tax administration machinery in almost all of the countries, with substantial assistance from the U.S. government (Internal Revenue Service personnel have been particularly helpful), the OAS, and the IDB. Tax officials are being trained in better techniques, delinquent taxes are being collected more frequently, and tax evasion laws are better enforced.

These improvements, though hardly revolutionary, have been made slowly and painfully against the opposition of powerful groups. And basic problems persist. The tax structures in most of the countries are still highly regressive, foster social injustice, and are utterly at odds with any modern economic development strategy. The need for thoroughgoing tax reform remains.

The substantial increase in tax revenues led to a large increase in resources potentially available for investment, but, not unexpectedly, only part of them were actually used for that purpose. Current expenditures generally increased with the rise in tax revenues; in a few countries — Argentina and Uruguay, for example — expenditures substantially exceeded revenues and contributed to inflationary pressures. The rise in central government expenditures was due in most cases mainly to salary increases, increases in public debt service and in transfers to autonomous agencies and government enterprises, and expansion of social services. While most expenditures were largely non-developmental, some were directed to high-priority developmental categories, with marked increases in spending on education and agriculture.

In spite of increases in current expenditures, the volume of resources saved by central governments has increased in most countries. IDB data show that twelve central governments saved a greater proportion of GDP in 1966 than in 1961, seven saved less, and one showed no change. However, movements were erratic from year to year, and there has been no clear indication of steady improvement in most cases.

As the IDB report of 1967 points out: Larger public savings enable governments to finance a larger volume of investment without resorting to internal or external credit, but do not necessarily mean greater financial stability. When governments raise their savings, but expand their investments by even larger amounts, they must increase their borrowings. If they cannot obtain additional loans from abroad or from domestic sources other than banks, they must resort to the banking system and thereby contribute to monetary expansion.[16] If the process exceeds the modest amounts by which individuals and enterprises wish to increase their money holdings at existing prices, the excess tends to generate pressure on the price level and balance of payments. For this reason, the relative amount of government borrowing from the banking system, the rate of increase in the money supply, and the movements in the cost-of-living index are intercorrelated, and are good indicators of a country's domestic financial management.

Summary data for these indicators (presented in Table 15) reveal

---

[16] Mexico, in contrast to most of the other Latin American countries, appears to have been fairly successful in financing its deficits by selling government securities to the private sector and in foreign capital markets, as opposed to financing by expanding central bank credit.

Table 15. Average Annual Percentage Changes in Cost-of-Living Indexes and in Money Supply, 1950-67

Country	Percentage change in cost of living											Percentage change in money supply 1961–66 average
	1950–58 average	1959	1960	1961	1962	1963	1964	1965	1966	1961–66 average	1967ᵃ	
Argentina	22	102	12	19	32	28	18	38	30	27	33	24
Bolivia	76	10	11	7	3	–1	11	5	14	6	n.a.	19
Brazil	17	43	32	43	61	81	85	41	46	60	27	60
Chile	38	33	6	9	27	45	39	26	17	27	22	38
Colombia	9	5	7	5	5	46	2	15	14	15	8	18
Costa Rica	3	0	3	0	6	2	2	–1	2	2	2	6
Ecuador	2	0	4	3	4	5	3	6	3	4	n.a.	9
El Salvador	5	–1	0	–4	2	2	2	0	–2	0	2	4
Guatemala	2	0	–3	3	–1	1	–1	–1	3	1	1	6
Honduras	3	–1	1	0	5	2	4	4	4	3	7	9
Mexico	8	0	8	–3	3	0	3	5	4	2	2	12
Nicaragua	8	–3	3	–2	0	3	2	4	5	2	n.a.	14
Panama	0	0	0	0	0	2	3	0	0	1	n.a.	n.a.
Peru	8	16	3	7	5	10	12	16	8	10	13	13
Uruguay	10	48	36	10	11	44	35	88	50	40	64	39
Venezuela	1	4	2	1	–2	1	–2	5	0	1	2	6

ᵃ The 1967 figures are preliminary; some cover periods other than the calendar year.

Source: Based on International Monetary Fund statistics. Raymond F. Mikesell, Survey of the Alliance for Progress: Inflation in Latin America, prepared for the Subcommittee on American Republics Affairs, Committee on Foreign Relations, U.S. Senate (Washington: Government Printing Office, Sept. 25, 1967), Table 1, p. 3, and Table 3, p. 4.

that changes in the cost-of-living index and money supply varied greatly from country to country. Several countries have experienced some of the highest rates of inflation in the world, while a number have had a record of price stability that compares favorably with that of the United States and Western Europe.

The Charter of Punta del Este had stressed efforts to maintain relative price stability as a key to the realization of the fundamental goals of the Alliance. U.S. AID, World Bank, and IMF loans to the inflation-prone countries have been accompanied from the beginning by pressures for national price stabilization measures. The data show that success in these endeavors has been limited. The reason is evident. As Raymond F. Mikesell has pointed out in his excellent little study of inflation in Latin America:

> Long run viability and satisfactory economic and social progress are not likely to be realized in the absence of reasonable price stability. But when we review the principal self-help measures for development progress outlined by the Charter of Punta del Este of August 1961 — tax reform, improved fiscal administration, the encouragement of savings, strengthening agriculture, increasing industrial productivity, making markets more competitive, expanding exports, and encouraging foreign private investment — we find that most of them are included among the measures and conditions regarded as essential for price stability as well.[17]

In a real sense, the continuing difficulty with regard to inflation in some of the major Latin American countries, including those in which substantial Alliance aid has been concentrated, is a measure of the limited success thus far achieved in realizing the developmental goals of the Alliance for Progress.

Social Development and Education

Concern for social development, as we have seen, antedated the organization of the Alliance for Progress. As interpreted by the Act of Bogotá, social development encompassed a number of services about which people particularly cared — education, health, housing, and water and sewerage, as well as social reforms. The Alliance Charter had set down specific targets for these services and strongly stressed the need to carry out extensive land and tax reforms.

None of these targets has been achieved — not in education, not in health, not in housing, not in water and sewerage, not in land

---

[17] *Survey of the Alliance for Progress: Inflation in Latin America*, prepared for the Subcommittee on American Republics Affairs, Committee on Foreign Relations, United States Senate (Washington: Government Printing Office, September 25, 1967), p. 39.

reform. Only in tax reform, as we have seen, is the picture fairly bright. In each case the gap that remains is tremendous, even in countries where there has been meaningful progress. A sense of the difficulties and of the relatively limited nature of the improvements can be obtained by looking at the field of education.

The major targets set for education were an end of illiteracy by 1971 and provision of six years of free compulsory education for the entire population of school age. Literacy for the region as a whole is now estimated as in the vicinity of 67 per cent; it can be expected to be only slightly higher by 1971. In none of the Alliance countries has the effort to wipe out illiteracy been comparable in scope to that reported under way in Cuba. This is troublesome, no matter how interpreted, particularly since literacy campaigns are generally so closely aligned to the intensity of the national will for rapid economic and social progress.

During the period of the Alliance, the percentage of the school-age population enrolled in primary schools for all the Latin American republics together has been increasing at a fairly steady, but not impressive rate, rising from 49 per cent in 1960 to 56 per cent in 1967.[18] The rate of population growth makes the problem of providing education a difficult and expensive one. Thus, while about 12 million more Latin American children were enrolled in primary schools in 1967 than in 1960, the number of school age who were *not* enrolled also grew — by about 2.5 million. Thus, primary school expansion, carried out through greatly expanded public expenditures for education, proved insufficient to close the enrollment gap. While some gains have been recorded in each of the countries, general standing among the nations has not changed substantially. Currently, for example, four of every five children of primary school age are enrolled in school in Argentina, but only one in every three is enrolled in Guatemala.

The relative gains in secondary education have been more impressive. Secondary school enrollment and secondary school graduates more than doubled between 1960 and 1967; in ten of eighteen countries enrollment increased from two to three times. The number of teachers almost doubled (more than tripled in Mexico). Many of the countries have expanded their vocational training programs to the point where there were over twice as many graduates in 1967 as there had been in 1960.

Growth of enrollment in higher education has been equally impres-

[18] Office of Public Affairs, Bureau of Inter-American Affairs, Department of State, *Latin American Growth Trends*, April 1968, pp. 3–15.

sive — from 510,000 students in 1960 to 880,000 in 1966. As the Inter-American Development Bank points out in a detailed study of higher education,[19] this accelerated growth can be attributed to several circumstances that include the urbanization process, improvement in urban middle-class real wages, a growing awareness by young people of the close relationship between education and social and economic opportunity, and the positive reaction of youth to policies adopted in nearly all the countries to ease admission to the universities. These factors combined with the accelerated population growth rate of Latin America to establish a cumulative growth rate in university enrollment for the region as a whole of 9.5 per cent a year during 1960–66, higher than in the United States.

The drawing power of various specialties is interesting. Three fields are dominant: humanities and training for secondary-level teachers; administration and economics; and medical and health sciences. Next in line are law and engineering. Other groups of specialties, such as agriculture and the natural sciences, are far below. The relative importance of specialties varies from country to country, however; medical and health sciences are pre-eminent in Argentina, law in Brazil, and administration and economics in Mexico. There seems to have been a substantial increase in interest in fields closely associated with the needs of developing economies, but the hold of the traditional fields of medicine, law, and the humanities is still very great, although law is beginning to lose ground to newer fields of interest.

While most of the data on developments in education during the years of the Alliance are essentially encouraging, the fact that almost one-third of the population is still illiterate, that the majority of children leave school before the end of the third year and relatively few reach secondary school, and that university education in most of the countries is tradition-bound and of poor quality suggests that substantial improvements in education remain a basic key to social and economic betterment in Latin America.

The Population Problem

Influencing all economic and social development issues has been the fantastically rapid rate of population growth in Latin America, the highest growth rate of any region in the world today. Progress in Latin America would have had to have been rapid indeed for per capita gains to have been achieved, as is apparent from the data on education.

[19] *Socio-Economic Progress in Latin America*, 1966, pp. 313 ff.

In 1960 the total population of Latin America was 212 million. (It had been 90 million only four decades earlier.) In 1967 the population was estimated at 243 million. Estimates for 1970 suggest a total population of 265 million at present rates of growth.[20] The population is currently growing at a rate of 30 per thousand, the result of very high birth rates and declining mortality rates. There are substantial variations in birth rates among the individual countries, of course, between the extremes of 21 per thousand for Argentina and Uruguay and 49 per thousand for Honduras. A group of countries comprising approximately 70 per cent of the population of Latin America has birth rates between 40 and 45 per thousand. This group includes Brazil, Mexico, Colombia, Peru, and Venezuela. Six Central American and Caribbean countries have rates between 46 and 49 per thousand. At the same time, in recent years there has been a marked drop in mortality rates. In six countries — Argentina, Mexico, Uruguay, Venezuela, Panama, and Costa Rica — the rates are less than 10 per thousand. In other nations, which comprise a large proportion of the population of Latin America, the mortality rate is between 10 and 22 per thousand. It is anticipated that these rates will experience sharp declines. The implications for the future growth of Latin America are obvious if the present birth rate is maintained.

The population growth has reinforced the move to the cities. While the rate of growth of the total population is estimated at 30 per thousand, urban areas are increasing at the rate of 42 per thousand, and rural areas at the rate of 16 per thousand. Thus, the urban population is increasing by 5.3 million persons per year, in comparison with an annual increase of 1.8 million persons in rural areas. At least 2 million persons emigrate from rural areas each year. Unemployment and underemployment in urban areas seem to have been rising at a rapid rate (although data here are scanty). The growth of urban population has greatly increased the pressure for social services, particularly for education, housing, health, and urban sanitation. These services are absorbing an increasing proportion of national budgetary resources, but in most cases overall improvement in the social situation is painfully slow.

The population growth obviously has greatly compounded the difficulties faced by the Alliance in promoting rapid social and economic progress. Only recently has any recognition been afforded this fact by either national leaders or international agencies. The first major region-

[20] Pan American Union, *Principal Trends in the Latin American Economy for 1967 and Prospects for 1968*, OAS/Ser. H/XIV, CIAP/215, Rev. 2 (May 16, 1968), pp. 120 ff. (Preliminary, subject to revision.)

wide conference on population control in Latin America was held in Caracas in September 1967. That was the first meeting at which high-ranking officials lent the prestige of their offices to a discussion of so politically "delicate" an issue.[21] In only a few countries — particularly Chile, Colombia, Costa Rica, El Salvador, and Honduras — have any birth control efforts been undertaken by national health services. In most of Latin America there is still too little awareness of the implications of the demographic developments, and few meaningful efforts have been made to overcome traditional resistance to policies and programs designed to find solutions to the population problem.

Political Progress

The evaluation of Latin American performance in the economic and social realms is complex enough; reviewing political progress is even more difficult.

The Charter of Punta del Este restated a key feature of many inter-American agreements, including the OAS Charter signed in 1948, namely, that the nations of the hemisphere are to be governed by the principles of representative democracy. In practice this has been disregarded by a large proportion of the Latin American republics. The Charter did not establish criteria for judging "democratic" governments, nor did it establish any relation between external assistance and the character of the government requesting it. The United States government could, of course, have made its assistance contingent on the general principle set down in the two Charters, at least in those cases where the perversion of constitutional government was clear-cut. In practice, this has been deemed impossible, among other reasons, because of overriding "security" considerations, particularly the concern that a Communist-led government might come to power. This attitude was behind the enthusiastic United States support of the military "revolution" which ousted the left-leaning Goulart government in Brazil.

Against this background, it is not surprising to find that the Alliance seems to have made very little, if any, difference in the frequency of military coups ousting elected governments, a long-standing Latin American tradition. Shortly after the Alliance came into being, the

---

[21] For a valuable discussion of this conference, see Luis Escobar Cerda, "After Caracas: Problems and Prospects," *Population Bulletin*, vol. 24 (February 1968). See also "Punta del Este, 1961–1967: Early Dawn of a Demographic Awakening," *Population Bulletin*, vol. 23 (June 1967).

military took over from elected governments in Argentina and Peru. Elected if ineffective regimes in Guatemala and Ecuador were ousted in 1963, with the latter experiencing its second political upheaval in two years, the military deposing a man they had put into office two years earlier. The constitutional governments of the Dominican Republic, Honduras, Brazil, Bolivia, and Argentina, and Peru again, as well as Panama, were subsequently overthrown for a variety of reasons, or no reason other than thirst for power.

In judging the role of the Alliance in political events, it is well to note that when President Kennedy reacted to the Peruvian military takeover early in the life of the Alliance by withholding both recognition and financial assistance, he was not only opposed by American business interests in Peru and at home, but received practically no support from the Latin Americans. Obviously, the Latin Americans still were extremely touchy about the possibility of external "interference," and did not accept implementation of the principle of representative democracy as a legitimate feature of the Alliance. Thus, if the United States government wanted to relate financial assistance to the character of the government requesting such assistance, it would have to do so in the face of Latin American resistance.

An alternative approach is to apply the Alliance mechanism to a longer-run goal, that of political development. This notion was given legislative support in Title IX of the Foreign Assistance Act of 1966. It reads as follows:

> In carrying out programs authorized in this chapter, emphasis shall be placed on assuring maximum participation in the task of economic development on the part of the people of the developing countries, through the encouragement of democratic private and local governmental institutions.

As Pat Holt has pointed out, there is nothing new here that was not already in the act, either implicitly or explicitly, but Title IX, together with its legislative history, served to give a new emphasis to programs and problems of political development.[22] Title IX has generated interest among State Department personnel and scholars in the possibility of launching programs that might directly influence the development of Latin American political institutions in democratic

[22] Pat M. Holt, *Survey of the Alliance for Progress: The Political Aspects*, prepared for the Subcommittee on American Republics Affairs of the Committee on Foreign Relations (Washington: U.S. Government Printing Office, 1967), p. 22. This is an excellent brief statement of the problems of political development in Latin America.

directions, for example, through civic education. But such programs are still to be developed.

There is yet another broad political issue that deserves attention. From the very beginning, it seemed evident that progress toward Alliance goals would require widespread political commitment to development and reform.

At an early point, Lincoln Gordon pointed out that "a political mystique is indispensable to the success of the Alliance for Progress."

> Unless the pursuit of economic and social progress, in the terms of the Charter of Punta del Este, becomes a major part of the national political life of participating countries, and unless the great majority of people and organized groups and leaders of influence feel themselves involved and committed to these goals, the Alliance for Progress will not succeed regardless of the technical soundness of individual projects and the amounts of foreign financial support made available to Latin America. The Alliance then will become simply another American aid program but not a cooperative process for bringing about a real change in the actual standards of living, in the prospects for their further rapid improvement, in the sense of participation in progress by all classes and regions of the national communities, and in the security of civil liberties and the institutions of representative democracy.[23]

The importance of developing a "political mystique" also was underlined by a number of Latin American leaders, including Alberto Lleras Camargo, Rómulo Betancourt, and Roberto Campos.

Writing in 1965, Tad Szulc suggested that the Alliance for Progress had been a failure on that score:

> The concept of the Alliance somehow failed to electrify Latin America, contrary to what optimists in Washington had hoped and notwithstanding the early Latin American enthusiasm for the new administration. Despite the noble and inspiring words of President Kennedy, the Alliance quickly proved to be virtually empty of the desperately needed political and psychological content. It was unable to project a mystique that would captivate the attention and imagination of Latin Americans....
>
> What can be concluded, then, is that the Alliance's principal failing is that it has not become an Alliance in a real sense nor the catalyst of a democratic social revolution. Operating in a virtual political vacuum, it is battered by the cross winds of the opposition from the extreme left, which fears its democratic "social reformism," and from the right and business interests in the center, which, for their own reasons, fear these reforms.[24]

[23] Lincoln Gordon, *A New Deal for Latin America* (Cambridge: Harvard University Press, 1963), p. 111.
[24] *The Winds of Revolution*, pp. 239, 252.

The Alliance may have failed to "electrify" a whole continent simultaneously, but the picture is not so bleak as that drawn by Szulc. A not insignificant number of countries have committed themselves to economic and social progress and are struggling to achieve development. As of 1968, this was true of Mexico, most of the Central American countries, Colombia, Venezuela, and Chile. Admittedly, no one country is committed to all the goals and reforms outlined in the Charter. Even a "revolutionary" country like Mexico that is openly committed to rapid growth is doing less than might be hoped in distribution of income and ending the bitter poverty of the small farmers in the depressed regions. But, after all, these are underdeveloped countries carrying the burden of traditions that are essentially antidevelopmental. Political commitment can be expected to be less than total.

Where the Alliance has fallen down is in not finding a way to make the pursuit of economic and social progress "a major part of the national political life" in countries where no developmental sparks had already been set off. Yet even in these countries, there is no doubt that interest in development has been strengthened. If the countries that have not yet made a political commitment to development and reform are to do so within a reasonable period of time, it may well be through the economic and psychological pressures exerted by a regional economic integration movement. One of the major problems for the future is to find effective means to speed this movement.

Chapter 6

THE NEED FOR THE LONG VIEW

THE problem of evaluating an international effort as large and as complex as the Alliance for Progress is formidable, but a review is essential if for no other reason than to provide a basis for discussion that might lead to better approaches in the future.

It could hardly have been expected that fully effective operating concepts or ideal mechanisms for driving the complex undertaking of the Alliance would spring into being at the start. Indeed, concepts and mechanisms will require constant testing, adjustment, and evolution as the Alliance continues, new experience is gained, and circumstances change.

A New Charter for the Alliance?

Should the Alliance, perhaps, have a new charter, and, if so, what changes in Alliance concepts and structure do the first years' experience suggest are needed? If the case for charter revision is persuasive, it probably will be symbolically auspicious to plan for its adoption on the tenth anniversary of the framing of the Charter of Punta del Este. A review at this time of Alliance experience would highlight the progress made towards some of the goals of the original and, at the same time, demonstrate that many matters critical to achieving its goals had not yet been seriously addressed. With the hindsight of nearly a decade's experience, a rethinking of the original charter would also demonstrate that certain goals were unrealistic (as for education and health) while others were unnecessarily vague and haphazard (as for social and political progress). The review would make clear that many of the central elements of the Alliance had not been stated specifically enough. The core concepts and their operational implications for the implementation of Alliance programs, such as "external assistance," national "self-help," and "regional integration" were expressed in only the vaguest terms. While this perhaps was necessary in 1961, the experience since provides considerable guidance for more precise definitions, and a more refined structuring of strategies and policies and the instrumentalities for their execution. Most of all, a review would highlight the fact that thus far the Latin Americans have not accepted the Alliance concept as their own and have not become deeply involved in the enterprise. Strategies will have to be evolved which can generate a true Partnership for Progress.

If the suggestion to frame a new charter for the Alliance were accepted as a useful, indeed indispensable, way of adapting Alliance mechanisms, concepts, and goals to the experience of the past decade and to the circumstances which can predictably be seen to lie ahead, then a careful review of the past and a preparation for the future are now in order. Within this framework, charter revision would be based upon a comprehensive review and study of not only the strengths and weaknesses of existing institutions and concepts, but also of new Alliance concepts, goals, and institutional departures which are better adapted to the task yet ahead.

The very process of review and preparation of the ground for charter revision, if carried out properly, could help to involve the Latin American countries, the international banks, and the advanced countries now in the Alliance, and they might be induced to take an active part in sponsoring and carrying out such a study.

While our understanding of development processes is still far from adequate, we have learned a great deal from experience in Latin America and from cases of successful development elsewhere. The latter are particularly interesting for present purposes, especially when added to the extensive studies that have been carried out on the bases of development of the presently rich countries of the world.[1] The developmental successes of Taiwan, South Korea, Israel, and Puerto Rico in the 1950's and 1960's are particularly informative. In each case one finds a people with a considerable base of education and skill, either of long standing or acquired through an intensive effort on the part of the government to promote education and skill training. These people have come to value national progress and individual achievement, in some cases, directly from government efforts to promote and instill such an outlook. Each has enjoyed basic political stability during the major development-

---

[1] Among the many valuable books in which development experience is analyzed are: Albert O. Hirschman, *The Strategy of Economic Development* (Yale University Press, 1958); W. W. Rostow, *The Stages of Economic Growth* (Cambridge University Press, 1960); Alexander Gerschenkron, *Economic Backwardness in Historical Perspective* (Harvard University Press, 1962); E. E. Hagen, *On the Theory of Social Change* (Free Press, 1962); D. C. McClelland, *The Achieving Society* (Princeton University Press, 1961).

push period, even when there have been important changes in government. Each has sought to bring people at the base of the pyramid into the mainstream of economic, social, and political life — even where democracy as we understand it in the United States is weak and where politics are dominated by a one-party system. Community development efforts in some have been among the best in the world, and all sorts of instrumentalities (including the armed services) have been employed to broaden participation.

It is interesting to note that in each case, governments have put a great deal of effort into evolving sound middle-range and long-range programs for key functions and sectors, such as education, agriculture, and industry, even where national planning is not especially strong. (Of course, national planning has been publicly emphasized because of the requirements for macro-economic information in connection with the receipt of foreign aid.) The emphasis on, and the accomplishments in agriculture have been impressive, and some of the more successful land reforms of modern times are to be found in these countries.[2] Some of them have gone through a veritable agricultural revolution. The other productive sectors also have been the conscious concern of governmental policy and development programs. Each of these places has not merely received substantial amounts of external financial and technical assistance but has made effective use of it. This poses a basic question for the Alliance: What are the circumstances under which a country will make good use of external funds? Put another way, under what circumstances of national behavior can the injection of external assistance make possible a great developmental push to bring a poor nation to an economically self-sustaining basis?

This broadbrush summary of some characteristics of development achievement suggests some of the great complexity inherent in these questions as well as many of the great dilemmas confronting external assistance donors and assistance agencies. Thus, sustained economic development and the capacity to make effective use of external resources to accelerate the process seem to occur most dramatically under national circumstances where the countries have somehow managed, often against great cultural, historical, and political odds, to achieve certain of the political and economic habits characteristic of economically advanced nations. That is, the promise of sustained economic

---

[2] Puerto Rico is somewhat of an exception in this regard; here, industrial development has been by far the most important ingredient, because of the attraction of free entry to the rich U.S. market.

growth, widely shared by the population, seems to have been obtained in countries in which there is a government which is not only seized with a long-term development vision, but which operates competently on the basis of this vision within a broad political consensus permitting long-range continuity of programs and policy. At the same time, broad-based participation of the population, both in the benefits of growth and in the productivity upon which it is based, has somehow been made possible through the dissemination of education and skills and, equally essential in many societies, through very dramatic shifts away from traditional attitudes towards work, achievement, and inherited social structure, in the direction of attitudes and aspirations more consistent with modern economic organization. Concurrently, in each of these countries, there have been profound changes in key productive sectors generally reflecting shrewdly made policy choices and carefully planned governmental investment decisions and programs. Thus, in each of these countries, there appears to have been comprehensive and concerted attacks on the problem of agricultural productivity and on defusing potential political turmoil through reforms altering traditional and inequitable landholding and income patterns. These countries also made notable strides in resolving the great questions of integrating the rural population into the national market economy, both as producers of needed foodstuffs for export and sustenance of city populations and as consumers of the products of the growing urban centers.

In Latin America, the cases of sustained growth and development in Mexico and Venezuela appear closest to the pattern just discussed. Although neither country has relied substantially on concessional foreign financing or technical assistance, each has absorbed, and employed with great skill, enormous quantities of foreign resources and technology. In both countries, one finds patterns of policy choice and governmental behavior that may be instructive and germane to the rest of the hemisphere. Development in both countries has been carefully nurtured by governments operating within a stable policy consensus about the goal itself and the means of achieving it. Also the governments have had reasonable short-term and long-term objectives, and policy making, investment decisions, and programs have followed technically appropriate, successive stages within realistic timetables. Neither of these countries can be said to have reached the stage of self-sustaining growth, and either may yet run into serious difficulties which could undo much of the progress that has been made. Yet, their situation is essentially hopeful, seemingly for the same reasons that give events in Puerto

Rico, Taiwan, Korea, and Israel so hopeful a development cast. That is, development success seems to have made Mexico and Venezuela much more like developed countries in various central respects.[3] Indeed, a distinction should probably be made, and applied to these countries. They should no longer be referred to as underdeveloped countries, but rather, as "poor nations"; i.e., they have already set into place what may be the necessary conditions for development.

The precise question for most countries, and for those giving assistance, is how to fashion development strategies that bring the countries to the stage where the conditions needed for sustained growth and development are well established in the national fabric. Finding the answer to this question is the challenge of the Alliance. In more concrete terms, for example, how can a country educate a mushrooming population when economic instability works havoc with financial and administrative plans for school construction, teacher training, and so on? How can archaic educational systems be transformed into systems that can serve the needs of an economically modernizing society? Must there not be substantial political stability and, under today's conditions of urban concentration, considerable economic growth to sustain massive educational efforts? Yet can there be long-run political stability without mass education? How can needed political stability, coupled with political support for development efforts, be achieved in the midst of protracted and generally unpopular stabilization programs? Through what processes can key government policy-making organs be infused with dynamism and competence in countries where recruitment into high political position or the upper echelons of public service has seldom been based on notions of technical merit or achievement, or where, as in many Latin American countries, the educational structure throws up few men with the technical training needed to man the complex and far-ranging functions and services which government must now assume in modernizing the economy?

Even so cursory a view strongly suggests that in large part the great complexity of the task of the Alliance stems from the fact that the failure of many countries to attain satisfactory patterns of growth and development is rooted in intractable and tangled congeries of economic, political, cultural, and geographic circumstances. Also, it raises ques-

---

[3] Venezuela's developmental progress, which we refer to here, cannot easily be measured by the existing development indices. For instance, GDP and investment growth were far more spectacular in the 1950's than in the 1960's. However, the achievements of that nation in this decade in weaving the basic fabric of development, including aspects like education, community development, and government efficiency, have had a highly significant "modernizing" impact.

tions for the Alliance donors and agencies. Can they devise sophisticated strategies predicated not only on a perceptive understanding of resource needs and technological possibilities, but also upon the political and sociological dimensions of change required in light of these developmentally inhospitable circumstances? Even if they can, should external assistance agencies or donor nations attempt to participate in development programs that touch so fundamentally upon the nerve structure and personality of the aid-recipient countries? Also, there is yet another key question. Does it make sense for external assistance agencies or donors seriously to attempt basic development-inducing assistance in countries that do not demonstrate the development "ingredients" that appear to have jelled in Mexico and Venezuela?

It is a major thesis of this book that it is possible to design assistance strategies and instrumentalities that are sensitive to unique country circumstances and needs, that assistance is most essential for countries still groping towards a viable institutional, political, and sociological base for development, and that this assistance need not offend nor run counter to national sentiments, sense of purpose, or feelings of dignity. It is also a major thesis of this book that, to the extent assistance can be funneled through multilateral agencies, the dangers of incurring untoward or destructive nationalistic resistance to modernizing will be greatly reduced.

There are useful lessons in Latin America, not only in the sustained development of Mexico and Venezuela without much concessionary financial assistance, but also in the advance of some of the other Latin American countries. The not inconsiderable progress of Chile and Colombia in the face of great difficulties, as well as of the Central American countries, surely says a great deal about the value of substantial external assistance, coupled with internal motivation for following sound developmental policies.

It will be no simple matter to bring about a change in the *terms of reference* for major decision making so as to improve the conditions for economic, social, and political progress in the countries of Latin America. But the effort must be made, and, if it is at all successful, the achievement of a decent level of living by the great bulk of Latin Americans may be speeded by at least a generation. Efforts to fill balance-of-payments gaps and finance "bankable" projects within the various countries are not enough. External efforts must be broadened, and priorities shifted to enhance the development ambiance of Latin America as a whole.

The inter-American system has already made some basic moves in this direction with the establishment of economic and social development as pre-eminent in hemispheric priorities. The first decade of the Alliance has created much to build upon, but the scale has been too small and the pace too slow. Unfortunately, the Alliance faces a situation where slow gains and mild improvements are easily dissipated in the excitement and absorption of traditional national politics and parochial interests. Development and progress must become the dominant interest, the path to victory at the polls, and the path to personal and economic gain. The national developmental thrust must be powerful indeed to achieve this. For much of the hemisphere, multilateral efforts are the most promising route to this achievement; they may in fact be the only route.

The broad outlines of such a renewed, larger, more effective multilateral effort can be perceived in initiatives that have already been undertaken. The specific content of the hemispheric organizational and procedural response now awaits elaboration. The crucial next step, it appears, is to find ways of strengthening the three parallel levers of development — national, regional, and international — and a new Alliance charter might give major attention to the following:

National. Encourage a shift in emphasis in national planning and policy toward development of human resources and socio-political structure. Top priority should be given to investment in human beings, and to reforms that make possible greater equalization and greater popular participation in the economic, social, and political elements of national life. There will be need for the mobilization of substantial human and institutional resources to encourage political development, including the strengthening of "participant" institutions, such as political parties, labor unions, mass media.

Regional. Attempt to strengthen region-wide development activities involving all or several of the Latin American countries. Specific measures would have to be agreed upon for speeding the creation of a Latin American common market and the launching of continent-wide and more limited multi-nation development projects. Such a far-reaching regional effort is needed to create a developmental momentum powerful enough to transcend the continual fluctuations in national politics. Discontinuity is a key feature of underdevelopment. Useful starts can readily be lost. Thus, means to enhance the possibilities of continual forward movement are of the greatest importance. This is one of the major promises of a region-wide framework for development.

A suggestion of the possibilities inherent in strong regional arrangements was provided in the middle 1960's by the uninterrupted progress of the Central American common market even after take-overs by military juntas in two of the countries for no reason other than the naked desire for power.

International. Reconstitute the international-assistance aspects of the Alliance for Progress through the coordination of aid and trade activities and multilateralization of all phases of the Alliance. External assistance, experience suggests, can provide its most powerful effect when it brings the recipient nations into the development "business." It is hoped that genuine regional progress will develop from this working together of nation with nation, and nation with donor agency, in the same way that the European Common Market developed from the cooperation of the recipients of Marshall Plan aid.

The three priority areas of attention for charter revision involve complexities that must not be overlooked or underestimated, as they were at Punta del Este. First, creation of the massive educational and specialized training activities suggested by a shift in emphasis in national planning towards human resource development will present staggering organizational and financial demands, given the immense gaps and needs in Latin America, the nature of the existing educational base, and the prevalence of fossilized educational traditions that militate against rational human resource planning. The introduction of serviceable educational concepts and the establishment of an adequate institutional base will require not only a carefully developed strategy and planning approach in every country but painstaking attention to costly and complex program implementation.

Secondly, although greater popular participation in the economic, social, and political elements of national life is clearly desirable as both an end and means of development policy, little is yet known about the political and sociological processes through which participation becomes broader. Few areas of political science and development thinking are more mysterious and less charted than efforts to understand such matters as the types of sustained grass roots community political efforts that can be anticipated as a result of economic changes, crises, foreign assistance efforts, or educational improvements.

Thirdly, regional trade and other development activities cannot be expected to succeed without substantial political and economic accommodation and major changes in national attitude in many countries.

Also, there is little hope for a strong, rapid movement towards South American economic trade integration so long as the major countries are experiencing high rates of inflation and financial instability.

Lastly, making drastic changes in national and international lending agencies will take considerable imagination and political accommodation. The donor countries must be satisfied that their interests are best served by multilateral power of decision over the allocation of resources they make available. And both donor and recipient countries will have to agree among themselves on the role and powers of international agencies, their appropriate size, their functions, and the relationships among these agencies.

Population Growth and Alliance Goals

Projections of certain key indices suggest not only the probable magnitudes involved but the time horizons that are appropriate in considering Alliance plans and policies. Projection is an imperfect art at best and cannot do much more than point to what is likely to occur if certain trends continue along present, or assumed, lines.

Probably the most significant projection for Alliance plans grows out of present population growth trends. Latin America as a region may have the highest growth rate in the world; several of its countries are at the very top of the world list of rates of increase.

At the 1965 estimated rate of average population increase (2.7 per cent), the population of Latin America in the year 2000 would be close to 600 million, compared to a 1965 population of some 235 million. The projected figure for the year 2000 suggests a population for Latin America substantially larger than the total current population of the United States and all of Western Europe, taken together, larger than the present population of India, and not far short of the present population of China.

If economic growth over the next three decades were to continue at roughly the present level, an average for the region of 5.0 per cent a year, the total gross domestic product for the region would rise from the present $80 billion to some $440 billion. A 2.7 per cent rate of population growth throughout the period would provide a per capita income of some $740 for the region as a whole — less than the current level in Venezuela, but higher than that in all other Latin American countries. If the rate of growth of GDP per capita were to be at the level set for the Alliance (an average increase of 2.5 per cent), implying an overall rate of increase of 5.2 per cent per year, the average per capita income in the year 2000 would be about $800, still not a very satisfying amount. Given the 2.7 per cent rate of population growth, it would take an overall growth rate in GDP of 6 per cent per year to provide a respectable average per capita income by 2000; the 6 per cent rate would provide a per capita average level of about $1,030 a year.

Projections of GDP per capita for the year 2000 (with a 2.7 per cent rate of population increase are shown below):

Assumed average growth rate in GDP	GDP (billion $)		Per capita GDP ($)	
	1965	2000	1965	2000
5.0%	80	440	340	740
5.2%	80	470	340	790
6.0%	80	615	340	1,030

What becomes immediately apparent in this type of projection is the critical interplay between the rate of population growth and the rate of increase in the production of goods and services (i.e., in GDP). This is made explicit in Table 16, which shows the significant range of possibilities for Latin America by the year 2000.

The difference between "stagnation," or a dangerously slow increase in levels of living, and "substantial success" could be caused by relatively small differences in the rates of population and income growth. Although the calculations employed in Table 16 are entirely mechanical and do not account for the different implications of a smaller population growth rate as against a much more rapid rate of increase in total GDP, the relationship between population and GDP is a very real one in the sense that even a large increase in the production of goods and services can readily be eaten up by a very rapid population growth rate.

Another way of highlighting the problem for the Alliance posed by the long-term projection of key indices is to bring out the fact that gains in agriculture, industry, and other economic activities would have to be very rapid indeed if there is to be any substantial improvement in levels of living in Latin America should population growth rates continue at present levels. The full scope of the problem can be surmised by comparison with past rates of growth. In recent times, only during the unusually prosperous period of 1950–55 (in the time of the Korean War and before Europe had fully recovered from World War II) did GDP per capita in Latin America approach the 2.5 per cent

Table 16. Possible Economic Futures for Latin America for the Year 2000 with Different Rates and Combinations of Population and Economic Growth

Year and level of GDP per capita	Population		Gross domestic product		GDP per capita	
	Rate of growth, %	Millions	Rate of growth, %[a]	Billion dollars	Rate of growth, %	1965 dollars
	(1)	(2)	(3)	(4)	(5)	(6)
1965	...	235	...	80	...	340
2000:						
Stagnation	3.5	785	4.53	375	1.0	480
Charter-goal level	2.7	595	5.26	480	2.5	805
Substantial success:						
Alternative A	2.7	595	6.80	800	4.0	1,340
Alternative B	2.0	470	6.08	630	4.0	1,340

[a] Combined result of the assumed population growth rate (col. 1) and the target per capita income growth rates (col. 5).

level — actually it was 2.4 per cent. During 1955–60 the per capita increase for Latin America was 1.8 per cent, and during 1960–65 the increase averaged 1.7 per cent. Against this background, one can appreciate what it would take to achieve an average rate of increase of 4.0 per cent per year — the level suggested as appropriate for "genuine success." In countries where the population growth rates are in the vicinity of 3.5 per cent per year, the economic gains would have to verge on the miraculous if a decent life is to be provided for the people at any time even in the middle-range future.

An Appropriate Time Horizon

In looking toward a new stage in the Alliance for Progress, it is essential that a realistic time-frame be established, and that the over-optimism of the earlier phases of the Alliance be avoided. Realism requires that Alliance planning and implementation get away from its year-by-year, crisis-to-crisis scheme of operations and organize itself for a decade-by-decade thrust. Indeed, it is realistic to think in terms of the three decades to the year 2000 as an appropriate time horizon for the Alliance.

One advantage of this lengthened span is that much that now seems impossible is quite feasible when viewed in the perspective of a decade. Another advantage is that truly critical actions can be adequately planned and then executed with care. There is time to do the things that must be done: to survey the natural resources so that new resources can be found and known resources better exploited; to build up the necessary educational institutions so that the many skills needed for development will be available; to create the research organizations that can provide the urgently needed know-how; to create continent-wide networks of transportation and communications that can make regional economic integration possible; to "open up" the continent to help weld the nations together economically, culturally, and politically, and to exploit the potentially rich resources of the now impenetrable interior; to bring about the needed social and political reforms and the broad participation of the people of each of the countries in the developmental task. Simply listing these requirements is to make a case for a long time horizon for the Alliance.

The objection can be made that time is the scarcest of commodities in Latin America. The area faces a crisis now stemming from wide-spread dissatisfaction and bitterness; great things must be done now or it may be too late. There is crisis surely enough, but what is the appropriate way to deal with it? To rely upon flashy "impact" projects here and there, like housing developments that reach a tiny proportion of the people that need housing? To rely upon the installation of a host of infrastructure projects that are relatively easy to plan and build but may or may not induce any discernible direct improvement in the quality of life? To rely largely upon the development efficacy of "program loans" intended to meet estimated balance-of-payments gaps? These do not seem capable of overcoming serious socio-political difficulties. While program lending and infrastructure projects are essential development objectives, they are narrow foundations for progress.

The determining elements in national events can be expected to be the play of national politics and personalities and the ups-and-downs of short-term economic developments. Only in the longer run can there be a change in the terms of reference within which public and private decisions are made and in the atmosphere for socio-economic-political progress. The Alliance *must* bet on the longer run. There really is no choice. But this does not mean that the present should be ignored in the interest of the future. Quite the contrary. Probably the most effective approach for the Alliance *now* is to create a tone of sure and steady improvement. What probably matters most of all is that it be made possible for people to look forward to a real, if gradual, improvement in their situation, and even greater improvements for their children.

If the Alliance for Progress is to achieve its objectives, efforts must be made to: (1) establish a regional framework for development; (2) overcome the major blocks to development; (3) place the Alliance and the national developmental activities on a rational basis; and (4) strengthen foreign assistance. Estimates of the length of time it will take to complete some of the activities on which these objectives depend are shown in Figure 1. Experience in some of the problem areas (national planning and regional economic integration, for example) provides some basis for estimating the time it may take to achieve effective performance levels, but for the tasks that lie mostly in the future one can only make educated guesses. Nevertheless, it is useful to have an overall impression of the time horizons that may be involved.

Establishing a regional framework for development. National efforts at economic development in Latin America need the developmental boost or leverage that a powerful continent-wide thrust can provide. We are dealing with a continent split by physical barriers and national boundaries that make little developmental sense; the continent has to

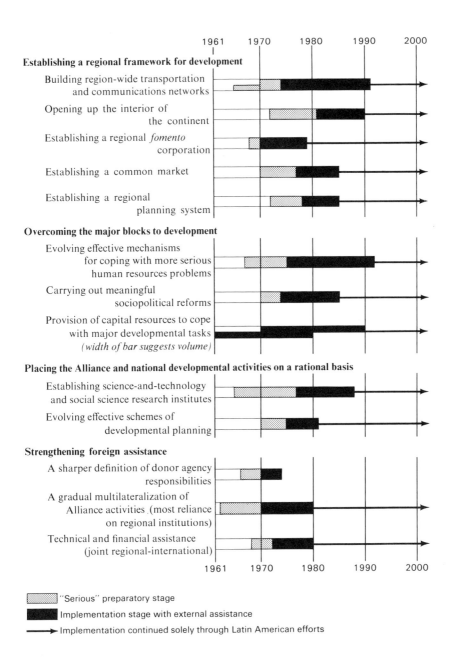

Figure 1. Time horizons for key developmental tasks.

be tied together. The establishment of a regional framework for development will clearly take a long period of preparation. It will probably be
the latter part of the 1970's before a powerful and meaningful regional
push can be launched, and even longer before the full impact of regional
activities will be felt nationally. On the chart, some guesses are recorded
as to the time phasing that might be involved in the laying of such a
regional framework for development.

Overcoming major blocks to development. Despite some variation
from country to country, the most severe problems are: (1) the deficiencies in human resources — the lack of skills, the lack of motivation
for family planning, the lack of entrepreneurship; (2) rigid, hierarchical
social structures and immature political development; and (3) the inadequacies of capital resources for developmental, risk-taking purposes.
As noted earlier, the Alliance has made meaningful progress only with
regard to the last of these, and even here a critically important element,
the improvement in Latin America's capacity to earn needed foreign
exchange through trade, has yet to be tackled seriously. Capital resources will probably be a major problem in the 1970's, as in the 1960's.
In the 1980's, external financial assistance may still be needed but at
a decreasing scale and increasingly for complex and elaborate undertakings, such as "opening up" the interior of the continent. The needed
improvements in education, the establishment of an effective family
planning movement, and the carrying out of needed socio-political
reform are likely to require the longest time horizons.

*Placing the Alliance and national developmental activities on a
rational basis.* This will involve greatly strengthening the base of knowledge in a number of key areas. Some are directly associated with public
developmental activities, as in the case of natural resources surveys.
Others are somewhat less directly associated, as in the case of research
in important areas of science and technology and in social science. It
will probably take another decade to bring these activities to an effective
and mature level.

Strengthening foreign assistance. Here, at least in theory, one can
be relatively optimistic about achieving useful results in a relatively
short period of time, since the changes called for are largely institutional
in nature. There are no major hurdles, for example, of the type involved
in efforts to improve human resources in poor countries.

It is assumed that each activity will require a "serious" preparatory
stage, during which the majority of the Latin American countries will
be establishing the needed institutions, doing the necessary underlying

research, developing the necessary political support for the activity, or in other ways laying a foundation for its successful implementation. This stage is suggested by the grey bar on the chart. Even before the given "preparatory" activity is widespread in the region, however, it can be assumed that one or a few of the Latin American countries will have started the activity somewhat earlier than the period designated on the chart.

The period of *actual implementation* that can be anticipated among *a majority* of Latin American countries, after the preparatory stage, is shown in darker shading on the chart. The length of the shaded bar is meant to suggest the period over which external technical and/or financial assistance will probably be required. An arrow extending beyond this period is meant to suggest that the given activity can be expected to be carried out thereafter largely through Latin American personnel and funds.

Here, too, the "seriousness" of the effort is the main consideration, rather than the fact that something is under way. Thus, it is suggested that the serious stage of regional economic integration is still well in the future, even though the Central American Common Market has been making substantial progress, and a free trade area for the remainder of Latin America already is in existence. Here the consideration is one of *proportion* and *relative effectiveness*. The people of Central America comprise only some five per cent of the total population of Latin America. The Latin American Free Trade Area, as it now functions, is still short of a "serious" preparatory stage and well short of a meaningful execution stage.

In summary, it might be well to note again that there is no meaningful basis for making time projections for the various activities that seem to be needed to achieve the objectives of the Alliance. Only broad guesses can be made. Yet these can serve the purpose at hand, which is to give content to the key point made here: to be successful, the Alliance must change its approach from a year-to-year basis to a multiple-decade outlook.

The remainder of this book examines the various components that have been identified as important in the development of the poorer countries — improvement of human resources, social and political reform, regional economic integration, information and research, and planning — and points to possible improvements that might speed the desired economic, social, and political progress within the various Latin American countries.

Chapter 7

PRIORITY MEASURES FOR DEVELOPMENT

IN the vast panorama of Latin American development, two features stand out in bold relief. The first is that, with only a few exceptions, the Latin American countries today face three formidable threshold barriers to mobilizing themselves for development: (1) deficiencies in human resources, (2) weaknesses in social and political institutions, and (3) lack of export earnings to meet the foreign exchange needs of extensive development programs. Sustained, long-run progress throughout much of Latin America is unlikely until these thresholds are passed.

The second feature is the absence of a strong technical and institutional base for rational development policies. To design means and strategies that are specifically appropriate to the ends sought there must be: relatively refined data and reliable information; the generation of know-how in key developmental fields, including science and technology; sound planning institutions and processes; and effective implementing institutions. These have yet to appear in most countries of Latin America.

The most unfortunate aspect of these barriers to development is that they, in large part, are self-reinforcing. For example, where there is a shortage of trained manpower, as in most of the Caribbean and Andean countries, the skills, attitudes, and capacities required for the needed educational reform programs may not be available. At the same time, traditionally-oriented social and political institutions resist the recruitment and effective use of the few highly skilled technicians and administrators who are available and who, given political support and executive responsibility, might spearhead modernization efforts. Where exports earn far too little foreign exchange to cover the many import items required by a full-fledged developmental program, a country may find itself in the dilemma of having to borrow large sums over a long period of time to pay for its imports but being unable to sustain a heavy interest and repayment schedule. A country can go broke trying to keep from being poor.

The aid agencies must take a hard look at priorities and at the operations and organization of their lending activities. Primary concern must be shifted from project selection and standards and the details of monetary and fiscal policy to the more fundamental elements of the development process. A new approach probably would result in a shift in the central composition of the lending and technical assistance activities of the international agencies. There might also be quite different approaches in activity design (e.g., far greater emphasis on sectoral than on project lending, far greater emphasis on training), in program implementation (e.g., far greater demands on most borrower countries to concentrate on implementation processes), in the conditions upon which these resources are made available (e.g., clear-cut, unequivocal political support for key institutional reforms), in the time frame in which assistance activities were phased, and in the weight given to multi-country trade and investment activities.

Categories of Recipient Countries

The Alliance for Progress action groups and related donor agencies have had some difficulty deciding when they should treat all Latin American countries as exactly equal and when each must be treated specially in the light of its special circumstances. In practice there is a mixture of both.

All the major donor units (IDB, AID, the World Bank, and IMF) have country desks manned by people who follow in detail the developments within each country, and AID maintains country missions as well as desks. Financial and technical assistance is largely negotiated through such desks, or missions. Under this system, there is a strong tendency for agency personnel to get too deeply involved with the economic minutiae of the country of their responsibility. Short-term issues and matters related to isolated projects and programs tend to dominate, while broad objectives and long-term strategy for the aid programs as a whole are subordinated.

But the basic patterns for providing aid to the Latin American countries follow general, across-the-board rules. Each country is supposed to prepare a development plan; fit "bankable" individual projects within the plan; and negotiate the projects with the donor agency. Little Honduras or desperately poor Bolivia supposedly have the same standing as Brazil or Mexico in these matters. While this may soothe national feelings, it is unrealistic.

What seems to be called for is finding a somewhat more workable middle ground. National projects or programs must be carefully built upon detailed analysis, fact collecting, and planning, as well as persistent detailed attention to implementation progress and problems. Also, at least until recipient country personnel can be trained, the assistance agencies must retain responsibility for much of this detailed project or program design and review. Indeed, with the probable increases in project and program complexity in the future, it is likely that the IBRD and IDB will change their present policies and assign resident staff to many countries for detailed review of projects. At the same time, it is essential that assistance activities be better tailored to long-run strategies. The project-by-project approach based largely upon the availability of "bankable" loans must now give way to a long-term approach that will attack the basic impediments to development.

A useful long-term approach might be to shape basic program and activity design in such a way as to give emphasis to the elemental barriers to development identified at the beginning of this chapter. For purposes of analysis, the countries can be grouped into categories according to the extent to which these barriers appear to impede their development progress. While the categories overlap to some degree, they furnish a useful framework for identifying core problems and suggest appropriate priority goals. Adjustments in execution could then be made within the broad strategy to meet the special conditions, particularly the current political conditions, of each aid recipient.

The first of the three broad categories comprises those countries in which the paucity of human and institutional resources is so great as to make meaningful planning and comprehensive program implementation extremely difficult or even impossible. This is the plight of most of the Central American and Caribbean countries, and of Bolivia, Paraguay, and Ecuador. It is useless to expect countries in this category to develop or implement complex plans or programs, or substantially to advance development through investment or major institutional changes without outside assistance coupled with a tremendous increase in their pool of skilled and educated persons.

The second category, which overlaps the first, comprises those countries where the probabilities of rapid development without substantial social-political reform seem slight. At a minimum, these are countries where, if economic growth were to take place, it would be on a highly unstable base with only a small proportion of the total population receiving any gains. While basic social reforms — particularly to achieve broader participation in national life and greater equity in economic rewards — are needed in all Latin American countries, only in some does the existing social-political situation seem an insurmount-able barrier to broad-scale development. These are the countries where the heritage of the Spanish period, with its rigid social hierarchy, is still particularly strong, and where the ruling elite is opposed to modernizing changes in any of the important segments of national life. Peru falls into this category, as do almost all of the countries in the previous category, the latter thereby doubly blocked from rapid, substantial development.

A special case involves countries where one or a few regions fall into this second or "reform" category, while the remainder of the country is in a more favorable — though far from totally satisfactory — situation. This is true of countries that are not fully integrated as nations and where regionalism is a dominant fact of national life. The Northeast of Brazil falls into this category, as do some of the hinterland regions of Colombia which are largely removed from the modernizing influence of the aggressive middle classes of the country's three major metropolitan centers.

In a class all by itself, but properly belonging to this second cate-gory, is Argentina — a country that has puzzled Latin American scholars for decades and is the despair of anyone concerned with the development of Latin America. For one thing, it already has had con-siderable development. For another, it seems to have all the attributes normally associated with a country ripe for rapid economic growth. Yet its fuller development is blocked by internal political chaos and lack of cohesiveness. For that reason it belongs in the second category. It is not likely to move ahead rapidly unless substantial changes are made in the social and political arrangements of the country. Outside funds alone will make little difference.

A third category encompasses countries whose development is seriously blocked by trade inadequacies. This covers a large proportion of Latin America, excluding only Venezuela with its rich oil exports, Mexico with a variety of export industries and a high income from tourists, and to some degree Argentina with its basically rich export base. Development in the other Latin American countries will be limited, except for brief periods of high export prices, by their inability to earn enough foreign exchange from exports to finance the imports needed for major investment programs. For them, trade expansion is clearly an essential requirement for the development of self-sustaining economic growth. But this normally takes time; meanwhile, external financial assistance is needed to fill the gap left by insufficient foreign exchange earnings. Not only must import needs be considered in such aid, but the capacity of the country to carry different levels of interest and repayment burdens as well.

Given the complexity and pervasiveness of these problems, categorization inevitably becomes complicated. If the first category (serious human resources deficiencies) were referred to as the "A" category, the second (deficiencies in socio-political structures) as the "B" category, the third (inadequate capacity for earning needed foreign exchange) as the "C" category, only a few countries would fall into one category alone. Most would more appropriately be categorized in multiple groupings. Most of the Caribbean countries would be of the ABC grouping, Peru and Panama might be thought of as being an AB type, while Chile might be said to fall into a BC grouping. Such awkward designations may not add very much to the aid picture — it would not exactly contribute to good relations between donors and recipients to have the former referring to "ABC types," for example — but the basic concept is essential in designing appropriate strategies for external assistance.

If the logic of the situation prevails, and aid agencies modify their approaches, substantial changes will inevitably be required in the aid apparatus. At least two kinds of change seem particularly urgent. One is to put the great problems of human resources inadequacies, socio-political reforms, and trade arrangements on a comparable footing with the financial aspects of aid giving. The other is to achieve more coherence in the whole assistance apparatus.

I

Improvement of Human Resources

The process of development is carried forward by people who are willing to work for a better future, who can vote in their own interest, who can produce farm surpluses, start businesses, manage factories and run factory machinery, administer government agencies, draw plans and carry them out and buy the products made by others. Modernization is impossible without such "human material."

The need in Latin America goes very deep. The developmental requirements are large and quite subtle. They call for changes in outlook and behavior with regard to working, saving, having children, and taking risks and for changes in the relationships between employees and employers and between subordinates and superiors. They call for a large variety of skills. Education is obviously important, but clearly not just any kind of education. It must be education that produces attitudes and skills conducive to greater productive efficiency, greater regard for civic responsibilities, and an infinitely greater capacity to accept and adapt to technological and social change.

EDUCATIONAL NEEDS

With few exceptions, education in Latin America is inadequate for a serious developmental push. In the countries where thoroughgoing educational reform is most glaringly needed, the priority given to education in governmental budgets is small. To make matters worse, in most countries the limited resources that are allocated to education are poorly spent. It is common, particularly outside the capital or large cities, to find schools in which there are no books available to teachers or students, and the teachers are not only untrained, but barely literate. There are few facilities for teacher training or supervision, and teachers are usually among the lowest paid members of their very poor communities. In short, the educational systems of most countries strongly reflect the values of the past, when education was seen as a prerogative of the elite, and the essentially rural, highly stratified social structure placed no premium on the development of a skilled and enlightened mass citizenry.

As Galo Plaza, former President of Ecuador, and present Secretary General of the Organization of American States, has pointed out:

> In Latin America, the political and social environment produced a system of selective aristocratic education dominated by the Church, for the purpose of preparing for service to the Crown or the Church. In the North, education was greatly influenced by the scientific achievements in Germany and England and acquired a sense of social responsibility, while in Latin America, French culture, which was the highest expression of Latin culture, became the dominant influence with its emphasis on culture for culture's sake.[1]

Although new ideas and values are challenging the existing educational systems, and popular demands for education are becoming a potent political force, traditional ideas still dominate educational structures in most countries.

Reform of the school systems faces immense difficulties. The popu-

[1] Galo Plaza, "Education for Change," *Americas*, vol. 16 (September 1964), pp. 11–15.

lation explosion has swamped the systems of many countries, so that even keeping abreast of the population needing education has seriously strained resources. Traditional values, and a still pervasive indifference to the direct link between economic progress and education, slow efforts to increase financial support and to bring about reforms required if the education systems are to meet national needs. There is a vicious circle. The needed reforms require sophisticated and hardheaded planning and administration, considerable research and experimentation, and flexible legal and administrative procedures and practices. All of this requires a large cadre of well-trained, adequately paid teachers and administrators who are modern in outlook. Existing educational patterns and the traditional attitudes toward mass education have prevented the development of these preconditions. Consequently, even where larger budgetary allocations are made for education, it is less than likely that meaningful programs can be mounted without major efforts in changing many cultural, legal and institutional patterns. For most countries, also, it is doubtful that significant progress can occur within the next decade without substantial foreign technical assistance.

Thus far, the donor agencies have responded to the severe educational problems in Latin America in various ways. In 1966, the United States government declared that in the future, in its international development program, highest priorities should go to education, health, and food. AID funds already have helped to build thousands of Latin American classrooms and have provided for a variety of educational programs including assistance in technical and vocational education. AID has financed the cost of assistance by U.S. universities to Latin American universities. Some of the former have established branch campuses to foster the exchange of faculties, students, and ideas. Peace Corps volunteers have helped a number of communities to build schools, and some of them serve as teachers, often in remote villages, while others work to advance community development. The Inter-American Development Bank has concentrated on higher education. The World Bank has only recently turned its attention to education.

While the value of assistance in a given field cannot be measured solely by the volume of loans made available, it is not insignificant that the total loans and grants provided to education during the first eight years of the Alliance are but a small percentage of these loans. There are a number of reasons for this. Educational projects tend to have a far smaller foreign exchange component than physical infrastructure projects such as electric power plants. Also most of the Latin American educational ministries have failed to produce "feasible" projects. Comprehensive education programs need many years to develop, large technical staffs, and, generally, great initiative. Without such initiative, the international agencies are not attracted to investing in these complicated undertakings. Probably the most important reason, however, is that education has not been singled out as an especially high priority area for lending. Had the international agencies taken greater interest in education in Latin America and used their considerable influence to stimulate greater interest in this sector, the level of activity — and of progress to date — would no doubt be far greater.

Since education is of such critical importance, particularly in the Category A countries, the Alliance should undertake a far more vigorous role in this field. It could, for example, be particularly helpful if substantial funds and technical resources were allocated for long-term *education-manpower development programs.*

The best way to mobilize this effort might be to establish a new agency, a Human Resources Commission (discussed more fully in Chapter 11) to stimulate priority attention to education, as part of or in close association with the Inter-American Cultural Council, one of the three constituent agencies of the OAS.

It is particularly important that there be a clear understanding on the part of the Latin American countries and the donor agencies that the development of education-manpower programs is to receive a very high priority and that the foundations for human resources development must be laid no matter how expensive and time-consuming such an effort may be. Parallel to the preparation of such programs should be a forced draft effort to train educational planners and administrators who could man the future educational planning programs in their countries. Basic to the success of these programs is, of course, high level political commitment in each country to their implementation.

A key element in education-manpower programs (now being tested in the AID secondary education sector loan in Brazil) should be the application of the basic ideas in "systems analysis." This would involve making broad-based studies of the human resources problems and potentialities within each country.[2] Such studies would normally include

[2] See Frederick H. Harbison, "Human Resources Development Planning in Modernizing Economies," *International Labour Review*, vol. 85 (May 1962), pp. 2–24. "Manpower analysis cannot always be based on an elaborate or exhaustive survey. It is seldom possible to calculate precisely the numbers of people needed in every occupation at some future time. But, whether statistics are available or not, the purpose of manpower analysis is to give a reasonably objective picture of a country's

detailed analysis of curriculum weaknesses at each level, salary structures, arrangements for financing, and projections of increased requirements in light of new strategies, analysis of whom the system now
reaches and fails to reach and why, an inventory of existing physical
plant and teacher training institutions, and analysis of administrative
practices and shortcomings. Studies of this kind, though inherently
complex and time-consuming, are essential for rational strategy formulation.

The development of long-term educational-manpower strategies
and programs should have several useful consequences, particularly
for Category A countries. First, it would put into focus the critical
importance of assigning high priority to human resource improvements
in national development plans and in external assistance. Second, it
would furnish an estimate of the needs, define the scale of the required
national effort in terms of specified objectives, and delineate the role
of external assistance and how much is needed. Third, planning studies
and strategy formulation are likely to make planners, politicians, and
educators more fully aware of the systematic elements of the education
process. This should help to avoid the kind of difficulties encountered
in the past, when programs proved to be ineffective and wasteful because
key components, such as training teachers, were left out or lagged.[3]

However, planning and strategy formulation do not get translated
into needed budget responses, new legislation, or vigorous and imaginative administrative solutions and policies without political will and
determined administrative support of change.[4]

---

major human resources problems, the interrelationships between these problems,
and their causes, together with an informed guess as to probable future trends. Manpower analysis is both qualitative and quantitative, and it must be based upon wise
judgment was well as upon available statistics. In countries where statistics are either
unavailable or clearly unreliable, moreover, the manpower analysis must be frankly
impressionistic." Harbison sets out the logical objectives for such manpower analyses:
(1) identification of the critical shortages of skilled manpower in each major sector of
the economy and an analysis of the reasons for such shortages, (2) identification of
surpluses, both of trained manpower as well as unskilled labor, and analysis of the
reasons for such surpluses, and (3) the setting of targets for human resources development based upon reasonable expectations of growth. Such targets are best determined
by a careful examination and comparison, sector by sector, of the utilization of
manpower in a number of countries which are somewhat more advanced economically and socially.

    [3] A useful treatment of education planning in Latin America is: UNESCO, Inter-
national Institute for Planning, *Problems and Strategies of Education Planning,
Lessons from Latin America*, ed. Raymond Lyons (1965).

    [4] Of course, the very effort of undertaking the planning and strategy formulation
exercise can be of great value if consciously undertaken as being, in part, an effort
to mobilize the necessary consensus. The sense of urgency which has sometimes
impelled national governments (as well as international agencies) to move quickly

Planning and strategy formulation mean little until they are put into practice. Detailed studies must be made of all the costs involved in setting up the comprehensive education system, and other studies and plans are needed to define overall educational needs and establish broad policy priorities. But the translation of plan analysis and policy priorities into effective investment programs is by far the most difficult task. If complex programs are to succeed, their various elements must be meshed, and bottlenecks must be anticipated and eliminated. This is why the importance of a systems approach to education was stressed earlier. In Latin America, lack of systematic coordination and of persistent attention to detail is the shoal upon which many well-intended programs have foundered.

Next, the techniques and strategy of assistance given by international agencies must be very carefully thought through. If the international agencies are to aid in this effort, they must agree among themselves that human resources development is a primary priority concern, and they must establish mechanisms for effectively coordinating their activities. The Human Resources Commission mentioned earlier would be one such mechanism.

In working towards agreement on priorities and mechanisms, the international agencies must be prepared to accept long-term responsibilities because the job is both large and complex. Everything cannot be done at once, nor can it be done in a short period of time. Priority goals and tactical or strategic first steps will have to be decided upon and carefully tailored to the circumstances in each country. Indeed, for many countries, the frailty of indigenous institutions requires that programs be begun on a modest scale, perhaps restricted in the first instance to basic pilot and institution testing and building operations in limited geographic areas.

Finally, international agencies must recognize from the outset that their task is that of providing supplementary financial and technical resources, and that the success of the programs will depend upon the support, enthusiasm, and participation of domestic institutions and leaders. In some countries it will take years to build up from pilot or small programs to the stage where an effective, nationwide response can be expected. International agencies must be prepared to identify

---

has led them to skip over the necessarily protracted, and often frustrating consensus-building job, with the result that their otherwise satisfactory plans have often yielded no implementation response by the agencies or ministries for whom they were prepared.

not only the overall needs and program possibilities, but the specific state, federal, and municipal institutions that are prepared to assume greater responsibilities.

ENTREPRENEURSHIP

Even when illiteracy and semiliteracy are overcome, individual entrepreneurial activity and the formation of entrepreneurial attitudes are inhibited by a host of factors. It would seem particularly valuable for both international agencies and national policy makers and planners to give far more attention to this aspect of the development process than they have in the past. Many countries might profitably study the processes through which the vibrant and energetic entrepreneurship found in their slums has grown and flourished. Unofficial credit mechanisms, unusual forms of business holdings, internal enforcement of fair competition, group insurance arrangements, and instances in which slum productivity has penetrated into larger urban or rural markets might yield very important suggestions. Institutions providing small-business credit and technical assistance supporting slum entrepreneurship might yield far higher social and economic returns than the very costly housing, resettlement and welfare programs which are now being developed in most countries for slum dwellers.

Similarly, as has been the case in Mexico, development bank support of promising, selected entrepreneurs who demonstrate a capacity for larger undertakings could become an important source of bringing to light entrepreneurial talent.

There are many other steps that might be taken in tax and commercial law, capital market regulations, export and import regulations, and credit terms and rates which could reveal other latent entrepreneurial energies and talent. International agencies and national planners and policy makers have not really begun to systematically explore these possibilities.

If economic development is to be pressed forward, the inducement (or "hothousing") of entrepreneurship and the training of management skills must be high on the order of business. Alliance funds and personnel should be allocated to these purposes.

Some of the following might be done:

1. Maximize *management training by Latin American and foreign businesses*. Special tax or financial inducements could be given to these businesses for the costs of conducting "qualified programs," with part of the financing of such costs covered by Alliance funds.

2. Strengthen management training *in the Latin American universities* in business, engineering, law schools, and schools of public administration. (A great deal is already being done in this direction, but it is far short of the need.)

3. Provide *credit* for risk-taking enterprises of every kind and size through government development banks and *fomento* organizations, through the commercial banking system (possibly employing the technique of a "private enterprise fund" evolved by the World Bank in Colombia), and directly through the international banks in the case of the larger businesses. The credit facilities should include "storefront" banks and other facilities to bring credit and technical assistance to the poorer communities.

4. Establish institutions to provide every kind of assistance a risk-taking entrepreneur or business manager or government-enterprise manager may need, including adequate credit, technical assistance (in production, marketing and administration), applied research in the solution of production and marketing problems, and physical facilities conducive to profitable operations.

5. Undertake detailed economic, social, and cultural *studies* of entrepreneurial behavior and attitudes in different population cross-sections in the same country. Such studies should be practically oriented toward devising policy and institutional responses for encouraging incipient entrepreneurship.

POPULATION AND FAMILY PLANNING

If the quality of human resources is to be improved in Latin America, the existing situation in which so many families breed children whether they want them or not will somehow have to be changed.

Latin America has the highest rate of sustained net population growth of any major region of the world. In 1920 Latin America had 90 million inhabitants. By 1965 the population had increased to 235 million. At the present rate of increase, the population will have grown to almost 400 million by 1980 and possibly more than 600 million by the year 2000.

The rate of population increase is far from uniform throughout Latin America, however. It ranges from a rate comparable to that of the industrialized countries in Argentina and Uruguay (1.8 and 1.2 per cent annual increase) to the remarkably high rates of more than 3 per cent a year in Mexico and Brazil, and 4 per cent a year in Costa Rica.

Rapid population growth poses particularly serious problems for development in countries where the rate of economic growth is low or modest either for a country as a whole or for certain sectors (particularly farming, fishing, forestry and sometimes mining). Mexico and Venezuela, for example, enjoy relatively high overall rates of growth, but conditions in many of their rural areas are as miserable as those found in the very poorest countries. Moreover, in all of the countries with rapid rates of population increase there has been a flood of migrants to the cities far beyond the cities' capacity to provide jobs or even the most rudimentary public services.

But even the sector picture hides too much, deals too much with averages. The population problem is at its core a human resources problem. When parents produce so many children that cannot be cared for, a significant part of a generation is condemned to brutal poverty and misery. The children get very little education; they also get very little food and health care. They get locked into the vicious poverty circle.

The explosive population growth has become a matter of some concern to the various organizations associated with the Alliance for Progress, with U.S. agencies taking a lead role. Moving cautiously in an area of so much delicacy and emotionalism, the Alliance agencies, at times in concert with private groups, have launched only small programs so far. But a greater awareness of the problem has been produced. Some governments have responded by establishing research and information units; for example, Peru has set up a Center for Studies of Population and Development within the Ministry of Health and Public Welfare, and Venezuela has set up a Population Department in the Ministry of Public Health.

Nevertheless, a great deal more can and should be done in respect to research, education, and information. We know so little as yet about how to shortcut the usual "automatic" forces that are conducive to smaller families. (The widespread use of birth control practices tends to follow rather than precede improved living conditions and to be characteristic of areas in which a high degree of mobility and competition for status tend to encourage the small-family system.) In every aspect of the problem additional knowledge is urgently needed.[5]

Governments that want to initiate birth control programs should know that they can count on substantial help from the Alliance agencies.

[5] In this regard, the Ford and Rockefeller Foundations have been making a magnificent contribution.

In general, the Alliance agencies should put discussions of the population problem and family planning on the same plane as discussions of
education and health and treat them as critical aspects of the problem
of improving human resources in general.

II

Social and Political Reform

Outside influence on national activities touches a most sensitive
point when the issue is basic social or political reform. Such reform is a
matter of political and economic power, and many groups, particularly
those who may have most to lose in the short run, are not likely to
welcome outside interference, no matter what the Charter of Punta del
Este may say about reforms. Strong nationalistic sentiments at all levels
of society also limit the extent to which external agencies can become
involved in these fundamental domestic issues. But rapid economic
growth and widespread social progress cannot take place in Latin
America in countries run by, and for, a small ruling clique, or suffering
from political malaise or a social and political structure that blocks
effective developmental programs.

For various reasons, external funds have been and are being provided to such countries in spite of the infertile soil for development.
Organizations such as the World Bank and the Inter-American Development Bank have to respond to requests for individual project loans.
The standards of evaluation applied — the intrinsic value of the projects and the capacity of the country to repay the loan — do not necessarily involve issues of basic socio-political reforms. Sometimes the
banks may press for some tax improvements, but normally such pressures are for marginal administrative changes rather than substantive
changes with regard to equity of burdens.

Also the international and U.S. government agencies have had
programs in these countries for many years. It would take a substantial
wrench in patterns of institutional thinking to cut or eliminate programs
for reasons which did not prevent substantial investments and activity
in the past, particularly since much of this activity, when judged on a
project basis, has been useful.

In many instances where the politics of recipient nations are more
resistant to reforms than seems desirable, aid strategy has been based
on the assumption that the preconditions for broader social reform and

political change are higher and sustained economic growth and social and political gains will evolve only as the economy develops and economic opportunity becomes correspondingly broader. In many of these countries, the U.S. and international agency strategies seem to assume that their leverage lies on the economic side, and that this leverage will create conditions in which better political processes can flourish.

Another important reason, particularly from the United States point of view, is that economic assistance is considered to be a key mechanism for preventing economic deterioration and political chaos. According to this view, economic assistance will lead to economic growth, and agricultural, educational, and other reforms, which in turn will lead to more open politics. The strategy assumes that a major reduction in external assistance levels would jeopardize this objective and increase the possibility of authoritarian political reaction. The great dilemma in this position is, of course, that there can be no certainty that these assumptions are correct, or that present aid is doing much more than supporting a status quo, which makes meaningful development (which cannot simply be equated with economic growth) extremely difficult, if not impossible, within this century.

Finally, there has been the anti-Communist consideration, which has played a significant role in U.S. aid decisions, principally in the Dominican Republic and Panama, and for a brief period, in Brazil. While the significance of this consideration tends to be exaggerated by many observers of U.S. assistance programs, these motives, at least in the countries mentioned, have been important. There has been a tendency to play up the Communist threat even where disturbances represented resentments and frustrations on the part of an oppressed peasantry or city workers and these resentments had no clearly demonstrable Communist dominance or overtone.

The incongruity of supporting rightist or "status-quo" regimes that are not likely to advance the objectives of the Alliance for Progress is obvious to all. Liberals in Latin America have become increasingly cynical about U.S. intentions, and U.S. officials are often uncomfortable with an apparently inconsistent U.S. policy. The failure of most Latin American governments to produce the promised reforms and the failure of the U.S. government and the international agencies to find more effective means of encouraging needed reforms or to identify themselves with reform objectives add up to the greatest failure for the Alliance to date.

The dimensions of this issue can be understood most clearly in the context of the heavily political bent of the Alliance as it was conceived. At the start the Alliance was considered by its principal architects as an ideological and political program for change in the Americas, a call to liberalism and political and social decency. Financing mechanisms and assistance levels were, in an important sense, really secondary considerations. What captured the imagination and stimulated enthusiasm were the political goals of social and economic reform, insistence on democratic processes, and the sense that, with effort and cooperation, a new social and political order could be constructed. The ideological and political enthusiasm of the early Alliance days could not be expected to remain undiminished, particularly as the difficulties of achievement became better understood, but little of the enthusiasm seems to have survived at all. For men of good will, Alliance rhetoric has come to have an empty ring.

No one who has been a close observer of the Alliance can mistake the seriousness of this failure. One stark conclusion seems evident, and must preface discussion of political and social reform issues: the United States must either openly and clearly accept responsibility for a major role with regard to socio-political reforms in Latin America, despite the political difficulty of this position, or abandon the Alliance for Progress and limit itself to the financial support of the international agencies and to the practice of making loans for transitory political purposes through diplomatic channels. And let it be said bluntly: An Alliance whose dominant theme is anything but bringing about basic social and political reforms is nothing but a political expedient.

U.S. attitudes and actions can have a great deal to do with what happens. During the Kennedy Administration a strong U.S. position against the military taking and holding power in Peru and Argentina in 1962 dampened the ambitions of the military in several other countries. Also, the strong U.S. pressures had a great deal to do with the rapidity with which the military returned the government to civilians.

A clear-cut United States position on these matters is essential in terms of its own self-interest. The world will be a far safer place if Latin America is prosperous and stable. Also, since change is inevitable, the United States will be far better off if it is identified with the forces of progress and decency.

It is often argued that basic reform must be left to the Latin American countries themselves, and that the U.S. government and international agencies should only provide support after these reforms are undertaken. This argument, in essence, represents an abdication of responsibility with respect to many countries, and is inconsistent with the long-term interests of the United States and the development agencies in the modernization of the hemisphere. It is evident that many Latin American governments have not taken Alliance social and political goals seriously and that, at best, most countries have made only token efforts. It is also clear that without strong, sustained international pressure for reform the future will probably be no different. Outside influence cannot be expected to make national elites preside over their own demise; reform and change must come through internal political processes. Yet over time sustained external pressure for reform cannot help but be felt. From this point of view, the great shortcoming of the United States and international agencies has been their failure to evolve a coherent political strategy, tied to the sensitive application of resources for stimulating or encouraging political forces within the Latin American countries that would support reform policies.

To draw up such a strategy will not be an easy matter, given the hard actualities of indifference, opposition, or incompetence at the top. How can programs be conceived, introduced, and implemented that make the political leadership realize that, for its own survival, it must become more responsive to the needs of its constituents? The prevailing view, that by promoting growth and stability the people on the bottom will benefit and political evolution will occur, is hardly good enough. Hardheaded insistence on reform seems to be a better starting point.

The implication here is not that there are simple solutions or black and white answers, nor readily available techniques. At the minimum, the United States and Alliance agencies must regain their political credibility as being supporters of major reform. Devices to this end are available to the United States, such as carefully planned Presidential policy statements and indications of interest in hemisphere reform activities, a thoroughgoing revision of its assistance legislation relating aid to the scope and speed of reform, and the provision of generous funding and high-level technical assistance for reform programs.

Possibly the greatest barrier to the possibilities of social and political progress in most countries of Latin America is the alliance against social change between conservative civilian ruling groups and the military, or at least a coincidence of basic interests between them. It is in these countries that outside forces — and most of all, the United States government — can play an important role for or against progress.

Can anything be done from outside that will discourage the Latin

American military from playing an active role in their nations' politics and encourage them to revert to their more legitimate role as ultimate defenders of the constitution?

Again, the issues are several and complex. The military come to power most frequently because they are a long-established elite group with clear loyalties to themselves as an institution, a strong identification of their institution with the national interest and destiny, and a sense that they are the last resort of national integrity. There are few other institutions, and seldom any of national scope, that can make or enforce similar claims. Often the military come to power because the civilian political groups or parties are unable to govern effectively or to resolve their disputes peacefully. Political parties frequently are little more than a transient grouping held together by a strong leader or short-term interests.

Given the vacuum in political organization, intermittent military governments may be inevitable, particularly in times of economic crisis or rapid social and economic change. The United States and external assistance agencies must find appropriate responses to this reality. At the very least, they could show less than enthusiastic support or approval of those governments, and express their disfavor when such governments impose authoritarian measures (just the opposite of the United States reaction in Brazil in 1964).

The aid agencies must attempt to promote institutional and economic changes that will help remedy the political pathology out of which recurrent military dictatorships emerge. At the same time, of course, insistence on political decencies and attentiveness to basic reforms must be the hallmark of the assistance relationship.

U.S. and international-agency policy making should have a strong, almost overriding bias against military or status-quo-preserving tendencies and towards genuine and articulate support for reform. It is precisely because situations are seldom clear-cut that a strong bias must be firmly built in to guide choice and shape policy. Without such strong guidelines, short-run policy and immediate political expediencies inevitably win out. For example, we can either rely on the military in many countries to serve as a barrier to Communist take-overs or civil strife and anarchy and accept this as the best practical solution to their problems, or rely strongly on pressure for social, political, and economic reforms. We can't have it both ways.

If we opt to rely on progress on several fronts, then we must do everything that an outsider can decently do to prevent the military from interfering in civilian affairs, particularly when reform-minded governments are in power. Here the risks are great and it will take strong nerves.

BROADENING PARTICIPATION

Probably the critical feature in all the many elements that tend to be included under the heading "social reform" is a major broadening of the base of political, economic, and social participation within a nation. It is most important that people have reason to believe that justice and fairness prevail.

Participation can mean many things, and its form may vary from one culture and nation to another. But its consequences are everywhere similar: a feeling of having a stake in the society. This can make all the difference between people who feel that they have little to lose in a violent revolution and those who, no matter how little they may actually have, feel they have a great deal to lose. Perhaps more importantly it can mean a difference between a people who are economically unmotivated and unproductive and politically apathetic, and a productive and alert citizenry. The first condition is where the present danger lies — so many people in Latin America are without a meaningful stake in their societies. The many people at the bottom must be given a stake as quickly as possible.

The Alliance Charter provides little specific guidance concerning this problem. It refers generally to many elements which are necessary for providing the poorer people of a nation with a sense of sharing and belonging, but the major objective itself does not come through. This lack of precision and clarity of concept has had unfortunate consequences. The most significant response to a sense of the need for "social progress" was the establishment of the Social Progress Trust Fund in the Inter-American Development Bank (described in earlier chapters) to help finance so-called "social projects." While the Fund operated, most of its resources were allocated to housing, water, and sewerage projects. After four years the Fund was largely used up, and the little remaining was combined with the other Bank operations on the reasonable premise that such projects did not really differ in any special way from other kinds of projects.

The establishment of a fund for limited "social" projects was a meager and inadequate response to the need for social and political progress. But one false start is not a reason for neglecting these critical problems. It is evident that steps must be taken to advance social progress in Latin America, and that social progress cannot be achieved through a number of scattered projects. For purposes of discussion, the areas of future emphasis may conveniently be grouped into two categories of major consideration: social reforms and political development.

SOCIAL REFORMS

One useful device might be the re-establishment of the Social Progress Trust Fund — but this time to assist in the financing and implementation of land reform and basic infrastructure for the urban poor.

Even more desirable, perhaps, would be the establishment of a fund to help Latin American governments to design and implement *any* major reform program that clearly serves to broaden participation in national life and to increase distributional equity. At the outset, at least, concentrating on one or two key areas would seem to offer the best prospects for success. Land reform should be one of these areas. Establishing a strong Alliance institution specializing in aiding land reform would be an effective tactical first step in re-establishing a belief in the Alliance as a force for political and social reform.

Another area of possible concern for the fund would be the condition of the urban poor. As conceived here, the fund operations would differ substantially from the earlier Social Progress Trust Fund. The fund would continue to support activities yielding basic urban infrastructure, such as water supply, sewerage, and drainage (all of which can be characterized as health programs), but its operations would be designed to stimulate broadened participation in the planning and execution of projects at the municipal level, to strengthen local government institutions by requiring that all projects be largely self-financing, and to promote financially viable mechanisms in the borrowing countries capable of continuing the programs after the fund has furnished "seed capital."

Thus, as contemplated, fund lending to national or state governments must *require* the establishment within the recipient nation of an urban-infrastructure loan fund that in turn would lend to municipalities for "qualified" projects. This approach would have several advantages. First, relatively modest international inputs could serve as a magnet for attracting considerable domestic resources. Fund lending might require a substantial contribution from national or state resources and additional contributions from any municipality which, as sub-borrower, received financing for its projects through this mechanism.[6] Second, the fund could put an end to the practice of providing resources for municipal facilities through the federal budget. The allocations are usually made on a "pork barrel" basis, and inevitably fall very short of needs. The municipalities would become responsible for the construction and maintenance of their facilities and would have to arrange for loans from the fund and marshal their own resources to pay off the loans. This would eliminate a substantial drain on national budgets and place the costs and responsibilities where they belong — on the municipal user. Third, this type of operation would greatly strengthen local governments.

To reduce funding problems, the fund could take the lead in developing consortium arrangements with other donors, such as AID and the World Bank. The fund could then serve as a "broker" institution. It would make the studies and analyses and do the technical spadework, but other agencies would make most of the loans.

POLITICAL DEVELOPMENT

Developed nations are characterized as much by the breadth of the base of political participation and the largely general-interest purpose of governmental action as they are by their industrialization or degree of affluence. As Hugh L. Keenleyside has pointed out:

> The distinction between a developed and underdeveloped society does not consist alone of a contrast in material circumstances. It involves the quality as well as the degree of the integration of social and political institutions with modern means of industrial production. . . . The highly developed countries . . . have demonstrated a steadily growing sense of responsibility to their own peoples — and, to a lesser extent, to others.
>
> On the other hand nothing is more disheartening in visiting the less developed countries than to observe the almost total lack of interest in the welfare of their poverty-stricken compatriots that is displayed by a varying but usually considerable proportion of the customarily small group who possess wealth and exercise authority.[7]

National political development may seem at first blush to be outside the scope of legitimate external influence. A closer look suggests

---

[6] Subloans made to municipalities could be backed by city bonds. While today there is almost no market for them in Latin America, this device could become an important mechanism for developing this potentially significant mechanism for municipal financing.

[7] Hugh L. Keenleyside, *International Aid: A Summary* (Toronto: McClelland and Stewart, 1966), pp. 38–39.

that where political development is viewed as the evolution of an ever-widening participatory role for the citizen in the economic and political processes of his country, and the development of institutions through which political interests and change find responsive and adaptable means of mediation, external influence is no more sinister than the conventional provision of technical and financial resources for promoting growth. Indeed, the distinction between these is blurred since the infusion of resources and skills aimed at promoting growth cannot help altering political balances and processes.

The thesis advanced here is not that international agencies should enter into partisan political affairs or take sides in any specific controversy or issue, but that donor countries and agencies can, and must, find out how their assistance can be more sharply directed towards opening up participation in the recipient countries.

The argument has already been made that a firm stand by the external donors on the question of basic reform cannot help but strengthen forces for change and democratization. In more specific terms, technical and financial support of projects or programs with a heavy reform content can also serve political purposes. For example, a major lending program that extends secondary or primary education facilities to large groups of people for whom education has hitherto not been available cannot help but leave a large, indelible imprint on future political balances and political structure in the region or country affected. Political development is too close to the heart of the development process to be treated as a marginal or secondary consideration in the strategy of assistance agencies and donors.[8]

The notion that broader participation is a valued development objective is based on the assumption that processes of meaningful change are, by and large, more likely to occur where those affected have the opportunity to give political expression to ideas about the direction that change should take.

Political development cannot be defined with precision, but it can be said that it looks towards modification in national life in the direction of (1) a broader base of participation of individuals and groups, (2) a greater sense of (national) community, (3) the creation or strengthening of institutions for introducing and mediating change effectively, and as non-divisively as possible through the political process, and (4) greater

---

[8] The U.S. Congress has recognized the importance of the subject. Title IX of the Foreign Assistance Act of 1961, as amended in 1967, has directed the U.S. AID to seek ways of promoting political development through "community development" and related means.

responsiveness of the government through more effective performance (relatively rational decision making and honest administration). Opportunities for international agencies to furnish technical assistance and resources which strengthen these processes are substantial, even if there is no well-established formula for designing and implementing activities which further these goals, or for measuring success or progress. For example, strengthening communications media and providing for the rapid, accurate, and widespread dissemination of information would do much to increase the opportunity for many citizens now cut off from events outside their small communities to act rationally in their own and their community's interests. Where the legal profession plays a key role in shaping institutions and procedures through which change comes and clashes between economic interests are resolved, political development strategy should focus on the strengthening of the legal profession and legal institutions. Similarly, broader citizen participation in labor unions and civic or municipal associations or professional groups may be essential in many countries if people are to understand their own society and their opportunities and responsibilities.[9]

THE ROLE OF REGIONAL ACTIVITIES: THE POLITICS OF REGIONALISM

Given the sensitive nature of the whole field of political development, the United States government would probably be well advised to rely as much as possible on multilateral organizations. Multilateralism here has a significance far beyond offering an alternative to bilateral or unilateral actions. Multilateral organizations, whether they strengthen labor unions or mass media, provide loans or technical assistance for land reform or tax reform, set up research organizations concerned with political development, or conduct similar activities, offer one of the best training grounds for national political leadership now available. It is no accident that men such as Eduardo Frei and Carlos Lleras Restrepo, who have taken active part in inter-American organizational efforts, are currently among the most knowledgeable and progressive national leaders in Latin America.

The international agencies — whatever their shortcomings, and they are many — establish a rational, developmentally-minded tone

[9] A set of activities to advance political development is provided by H. Field Haviland, Jr., in "An Operational Strategy for Political Development," A paper prepared for a Brookings Institution Symposium on The Theory and Practice of Political Development, September 12–16, 1966. See also Bruce H. Miller, *The Political Role of Labor in Developing Countries* (Washington: The Brookings Institution, 1963).

which has a strong spillover into national activities. A major extension of political development and social reform activities through the international agencies, if the past experience is any guide, will help significantly in generating reform-mindedness in the Alliance for Progress. Clearly, the Alliance and its constituent agencies cannot afford to move into their second decade without reviewing their strategies and purposes in terms of the need for political development.

III

External Capital Resources

A country may have a socio-political framework conducive to rapid economic development and the human resources to carry out the necessary developmental tasks and still not be able to make adequate progress. If it is to create a modern productive system, it must also have the necessary capital, including foreign exchange for essential imports.

A nation's need for external funds is directly tied to its rate of economic growth. As noted earlier, production in Latin America as a whole will have to increase at an annual rate of some 5.2–5.5 per cent to achieve the Alliance's ten-year goal of a per capita increase of 2.5 per cent. For most countries of Latin America this is probably too low a rate to achieve self-sustaining development within a reasonable period of time; an increase rate of GNP closer to 6 per cent would provide a more comfortable margin.

Using such goals for annual increases in GNP (specifically, 5.2 per cent and 6.1 per cent) and comparing them with "historical performance" of 4.5 per cent annual GNP increase, Chenery and Strout have estimated the amount of foreign assistance that would be needed in 1975 with different assumptions as to the annual rate of increase in exports, and also different assumptions as to savings and investment. (See Table 17.) Basing their estimates on the relationships among these key aggregate factors over a fairly long period in the past, Chenery and Strout indicate that (excluding Venezuela) $5 billion a year would be needed in 1975 to achieve the Alliance goal if low exports were to prevail (i.e., with exports increasing at the "historical" rate of 3.6 per cent), as compared with $3.8 billion under "high exports" conditions (i.e., exports increasing at the rate of 4.8 per cent a year). The external needs would be less ($3.23 billion) and GNP higher (6.1 per cent) under more favorable savings and investment conditions — what they call "upper-limit performance."

Table 17.   Latin America:[a] Alternative Projections of Net Foreign Resources Needed in 1975

	Assumptions			
	Historical perform-ance (A)	Planned development		Upper limit perform-ance (D)
		With low exports (B)	With high exports (C)	
	(. . . . . *per cent* . . . .)			
Annual rate of increase of GNP	4.5	5.2	5.2	6.1
Annual rate of increase of investment	4.2	5.8	5.8	7.5
Annual rate of increase of exports	3.6	3.6	4.8	4.8
Marginal savings rate	12.1	14.1	16.9	21.8
Marginal import rate	16.4	16.6	18.2	14.5
Annual rate of increase of foreign resources	4.9	9.4	7.1	5.6
	(. . . . . *billion U.S. dollars* . . . . .)			
Net foreign resources needed in 1975:				
Excluding Venezuela	2.87	5.00	3.80	3.23
Including Venezuela[b]	2.73	4.60	2.91	2.57

[a] Excludes Cuba, Uruguay, Dominican Republic, and Haiti. Includes all other Latin American members of the Alliance for Progress, plus Guyana, Jamaica, and Trinidad-Tobago.

[b] Assumes that Venezuela will continue to be a capital-exporter country, and that it will have a surplus in the balance-of-payments current account, which would enable it to provide financial assistance.

Source: Based on Hollis B. Chenery and Alan M. Strout, "Foreign Assistance and Economic Development," *American Economic Review*, vol. 56 (September 1966), pp. 679–733.

The estimates of foreign resources needed in 1975 compare with $1.55 billion for 1962 in the Chenery-Strout compilations if Venezuela is excluded, and with $800 million if the Venezuelan external current-account surplus is subtracted from the net resources deficit of the other Latin American countries.[10] As can be seen, even in the most favorable of the alternatives — assuming a maximum internal effort and the "high" rate of growth for exports (Alternative "D" in the table) — the total external resources needed by Latin America in 1975 will be more than twice the 1962 amount. And the figure will be very much higher if there is no substantial increase in export earnings.

If a satisfactory rate of growth of GNP is to be maintained, the regional need for external resources will continue to increase for several decades, unless exports grow at a faster rate than the Chenery-Strout

[10] These are not the actual 1962 figures, but the result of averages derived from a time trend.

"high" of 4.8 per cent per year. The amount needed in 1985, for instance, would be several times the present level, and the needs could conceivably continue to grow even beyond that date.

The exact figures in this type of exercise are not of great importance — too many assumptions have to be made, and substantial changes in the coefficients have to be expected, but the general orders of magnitude are suggestive and the basic relationships *are* important. The key point to note here is that substantial economic growth and industrialization in an underdeveloped country cause a rapid and substantial rise in imports. At some stage, a nation can dampen import growth by producing some of the consumer goods and even some of the capital goods formerly imported. But, except for the larger countries, the process must soon play itself out. Recent studies of Latin American economic development, as a matter of fact, suggest that most Latin American countries have reached the stage where import substitution can no longer be expected to be a prime mover of economic growth. Given the present stage of technological advancement, the size of the national markets, and the structure of imports that could be substituted, the possibilities for further substitution are too limited to diminish total import requirements in significant amounts. If that is so, then some feasible combination of foreign aid, foreign borrowing, foreign private investment, and increasing exports must be relied upon. Of these, increases in exports offer significant advantages as the core feature of an economic expansion program.

It should be noted that the long-term impact on national economies of a given amount of foreign aid is substantially different from that of a similar increase in exports. Reviewing Latin American economic development during the period 1950–1965, Chenery and Eckstein arrived at the conclusion that most countries in the region showed a greater propensity to save from export income than that from domestically originating income. They found no such relationship between foreign aid and internal savings.[11]

[11] Chenery and Eckstein show, *in fact*, that, in many countries of the region, an increase in the foreign resources inflow seems to coincide with a reduction in the total amount of internal savings. Hollis B. Chenery and Peter Eckstein, "Development Alternatives for Latin America," paper presented at the Conference on Key Problems of Economic Policy in Latin America, The University of Chicago, November 1966.

In a recent study, Harry G. Johnson similarly concludes that "foreign aid can close a prospective balance-of-payments gap without any extra saving effort by the country concerned, whereas to close the same gap by trade requires not only that the country supply the goods, but that it increase its domestic saving to the extent of the additional export proceeds."

Harry G. Johnson, *U.S. Economic Policies Toward the Less Developed Countries* (Washington: The Brookings Institution, 1967), p. 53.

But the trade versus aid argument is not at all one-sided. Foreign financial assistance makes possible an immediate net increase in the total resources of a developing nation and therefore permits a substantial increase in investment levels without a reduction in consumption; the latter is usually socially and politically unacceptable.

EXPORTS AND SERVICES

A Latin American export promotion effort would have to try to cover all the existing possibilities, for the goal to be achieved demands the maximum realization of the foreign exchange earning potentialities of the region. Four main categories can be distinguished: "traditional" commodity exports; exports of goods to other Latin American countries; new exports of goods to the rest of the world; and tourist and other service industries.

Traditional Exports. This group covers the products composing the bulk of Latin American exports of goods: coffee, sugar, bananas, cocoa, wheat, meat, cotton, wool, oil, copper, iron ore, and tin. Most countries of the region depend on one or two of these products for more than 50 per cent of their foreign exchange earnings — in some countries, the proportion is as high as 80 or 90 per cent.[12]

For this group of products, the aim clearly should be to avoid severe market fluctuations and to assure a continuous, even if modest, growth. With a few exceptions — copper, meat, and petroleum, for example — the exports in this category cannot be expected to provide a large part of the needed growth. World demand for coffee and sugar, in particular, is basically inelastic.

In this field of traditional export products, important contributions could be made at the international level. The fluctuations in the world prices of the basic Latin American exports often impose severe difficulties on the Latin American economies. An indication of the range of such fluctuation is provided by IMF estimates which show that the average unit value of all Latin American exports was 11 per cent lower for 1958–66 than for 1950–57. The difference between the years of highest prices (1951–54) and the lowest level of the period (1962) was more than 22 per cent (see Table 18).

The data reproduced in Table 18 suggest why Latin American leaders have been urging the adoption of international price-stabilization

[12] For a valuable analysis of Latin American exports, see Donald W. Baerresen, Martin Carnoy, and Joseph Grunwald, *Latin American Trade Patterns* (Washington: The Brookings Institution, 1965).

Table 18.   Latin America: Unit Value of Exports, 1950–67

(1958 = 100)

Year	Index	Year	Index
1950	103	1959	93
1951	117	1960	94
1952	112	1961	93
1953	108	1962	91
1954	117	1963	93
1955	108	1964	100
1956	107	1965	102
1957	108	1966	104
1958	100	1967	104

Source: Index compiled from International Monetary Fund, *International Financial Statistics*, various issues.

schemes that would assure the Latin American countries of a relatively steady flow of foreign exchange earnings from their basic exports.

Certainly, in view of the difficulties faced by the countries that are so dependent on a few basic commodities, a strong case can be made for establishing a network of international stabilization schemes on the model of the International Coffee Agreement, as well as a system of compensatory financing that could be operated through the International Monetary Fund. But of even larger potential importance would be a change in the policies followed by the industrialized countries of North America and Western Europe in relation to some of the basic export products of Latin American and other developing nations. The United States could make a magnificent contribution to the welfare of the developing countries if, in the spirit of progressively freeing international trade, it would change its policies in such fields as the import quota restrictions imposed on oil and sugar, the subsidies given to domestic cotton producers, and farm supports and tariffs. The industrialized countries could benefit if they ceased to subsidize some of their less efficient producers and took advantage at the same time of the increased export possibilities that would result from the enlarged import capacity of the underdeveloped countries accompanying the freer access for their traditional exports.[13] We should have learned long ago that we benefit more from expansionism than from restrictionism.

Exports within Latin America. The possibility of the Latin American countries achieving higher export earnings rests in large part, possibly the major part, on enlarging markets for new, as well as some traditional, exports by an effective integration of the Latin American economies.

[13] For a thoughtful treatment of these issues, see Johnson, *U.S. Economic Policies.*

The probabilities are high that the establishment of a genuine common market in Latin America would eventually provide substantial export opportunities not only for existing manufacturing industries, but for the introduction of new processed products. At the same time, export opportunities for raw materials and semi-processed goods would be particularly bright because of the relatively short distances involved.

Effective economic integration would provide the means for import substitution at the regional level, and thereby reduce the foreign exchange needs of the region as a whole.

New Exports to the Rest of the World. The possibilities of increasing non-traditional exports on a really substantial scale depend on the development of a worldwide, rather than purely regional, trade. But the producers of products for worldwide trade must be efficient. As pointed out earlier, the tariff and exchange policies followed in many Latin American countries have caused the emergence of high-cost industries currently not in a position to compete in world markets, and in some cases not even in regional markets. With the exception of Mexico, Latin American countries have not followed policies designed to promote new export activities or to increase the efficiency of existing plants to permit them to compete with the manufacturers in more advanced countries.

There is need for an overall reappraisal of many economic attitudes in most Latin American countries. Monetary, exchange, and tariff policies will have to be reshaped in an export-oriented direction. Development credit institutions and assistance to private entrepreneurs in both technical problems and market research also should give high priority to export possibilities. All this, and more, should be reflected in the content of national development plans.

It should be recognized that some steps in this direction are already being taken. Mexico's development bank, *Nacional Financiera*, is actively encouraging export-oriented investment in several industries, complemented by market research and promotion in Europe and the United States. Colombia is exporting textiles to South Africa. Brazil and several other countries of the region are exporting manufactured articles. Also, in several of the more recently prepared development plans, especially in the case of Uruguay, attention is given to the problems of potential outside markets for the more important industrial projects proposed in the plan, together with a technical analysis of the optimum size of the new plants in order to assure a cost structure that would permit competition with foreign producers.

However, even if the most rational internal plans and policies were adopted, success in this field for the Latin American countries will require the assistance of the industrialized countries and donor agencies. Each of the following forms of assistance would be helpful: (1) increased financing for national development (*fomento*) institutions and development banks; (2) an increase in loans to private Latin American industrial firms, and particularly an improvement in the terms of the loans; (3) provision of production, marketing, and managerial knowledge; and (4) trade preferences that would improve the competitive position of Latin American firms in the markets of the industrialized countries.

The first three points suggest a much greater emphasis than in the past on the directly productive sectors. As emphasized at a number of points, development financing should be directed to the high priority items, no matter how much effort is required to develop "bankable" projects, rather than to projects that happen to be easy to prepare. Industries, whether agricultural, mining, manufacturing, or service, that have good export potentials should be the targets of the greatest effort and support by the donor nations and agencies.

Trade preferences are probably equally important. The Latin American countries, as well as the other underdeveloped nations, are at a tremendous disadvantage in competing with the industrialized countries in world markets. There are many reasons — both humanitarian and involving enlightened self-interest — why the industrialized countries should accept the basic principles underlying the position taken by Latin America and other developing countries at the meetings of the United Nations Conference on Trade and Development in Geneva. This would mean that the United States, Canada, Western Europe, Japan, and possibly the Soviet Union, would unilaterally and substantially lower tariffs and other trade restrictions that apply to manufactured goods exported by the underdeveloped countries. While some industries in the advanced nations will be hurt from such a lowering of tariffs — generally the least productive industries in these countries — the cost of easing adjustment of such industries and their workers would, in all probability, be quite limited and yet would represent a major contribution to the welfare of the underdeveloped world. Besides, the industrialized countries, in the long run, would benefit from the substantial increase in trade that would accompany such a policy.

Tourist and Other Services. Another way of achieving substantial additional foreign exchange earnings would be for Latin American countries to increase their exports of services. A major element here is tourism. It is a striking fact that Mexico is the only Latin American country that takes advantage of the possibilities in this field.

In this jet age, it should be possible to promote Latin American tourist circuits that could benefit most countries of the region in two different ways: by attracting U.S. and European tourists to tours of Latin America, and by diverting to the countries of the region some of the money Latin Americans spend on visits to other parts of the world. It would be useful to provide external financing for a hemispheric network of hotels, plus entertainment and transportation facilities, that could enhance tourist trade. Mexico, in the multilateral framework of the Alliance, could provide technical assistance in this field to her sister countries.

Other useful measures to increase foreign exchange earnings could be taken in the air and sea transportation fields. Mergers or a variety of cooperative arrangements among Latin American marine and airline services would permit a reduction in the present large foreign exchange outflow for services now mostly provided by foreign carriers.

PRIVATE INVESTMENT AND LOANS

The possibilities inherent in foreign private investment and loans have been underplayed in recent years. In fact, some ill-will has been directed at foreign private investment — for understandable reasons.

In only a few years since 1950 has the inflow of private capital not been offset by the much larger outflows in profits, royalties, and interest remittances. United States investors received $5.7 billion *more* than they invested in Latin America (excluding Cuba) during the period 1950–1963. Total earnings by U.S. firms during that period were about $11.5 billion; total investment was about $5.8 billion, of which $3.2 billion was new investment and $2.6 billion came from reinvested earnings.[14] While the contribution to the development of the economies of the Latin American countries made by private foreign investment is there for any fairminded person to see, it still must be recognized that the result is a net drain on Latin America's limited foreign exchange.

Of no small significance is the fact that even the relatively small amount of new foreign investment in Latin America in recent years has largely gone into industries aimed at national markets (automobiles, drugs, etc.) rather than into new export (foreign exchange earning)

[14] Estimates based on data published by the U.S. Department of Commerce.

industries. In most of the Latin American countries, the foreign firms have been attracted by their ability to sell in national markets protected by high tariffs. Usually, they have no interest in promoting manufactured exports from Latin America; international corporations have other subsidiaries that supply markets in other countries. This is no "plot," but is a result of the conditions set up by high tariffs in Latin America and of the relative costs of producing in different regions of the world. The results, however, cause a good bit of resentment in Latin America.

Particular resentment is also directed against foreign businesses that have built up some specific export industries — those based on the exploitation of natural resources, the national "patrimony." In addition, there is resentment against foreign investors who do not seem interested in the formation of joint companies with nationals owning a large part of the enterprise. Finally, local firms resent having to compete for the limited amount of local credit with foreign firms that often are the preferred risks because of the home-office strength behind them.

Of course, the question of foreign investment involves very much more than the issue of the availability of foreign exchange, but the latter is not an unimportant part of the picture. Foreign investment is particularly useful in export trade because of the well-established market connections the outsiders often have. If it could be attracted into the "newer" export areas which the Latin Americans are particularly interested in developing, foreign investment could make a significant contribution.

Probably the greatest opportunities for attracting the kind of foreign investment in which Latin Americans are most interested would come through the development of a regional common market. Here, as in so many other fields, the major possibilities lie in the establishment of effective combinations of public and private activities. A good bit is already being done. The United States government has a substantial "guarantee program" to insure U.S. investors against the risk of expropriation, inconvertibility, and the like. AID and the Export-Import Bank have provided help in a variety of ways to private businesses trying to establish themselves in Latin America. European governments have also set up various instrumentalities to assist their businessmen in making investments overseas. Generalized programs of this kind, however, are only partially effective because they are geared to businesses that have already decided to invest in Latin America. The Latin American countries must carry the main burden of attracting outside private investment. Intensive industrial promotion, as well as special concessions, subsidies, tax relief, and other means should be employed to increase the flow of foreign investments to Latin America.

A great deal also might be done to ease Latin America's foreign exchange problems in the realm of *private borrowing*. The rates for private borrowing, and particularly for "suppliers' credits," tend to be quite stiff — reflecting both the general shortage of capital and the high risk attached to such credits. Loans on such terms aggravate the foreign exchange problems of the Latin American countries since they serve to load them down with a too-heavy debt. U.S. officials and officials from various Latin American organizations have at different times tried to interest European countries, whose banks make most of these loans, in the possibilities of "softening" the terms of the suppliers'-credit-type loans, but with relatively little success.

The time may now be ripe for a carefully prepared conference, jointly sponsored by the Organization for Economic Co-operation and Development (OECD), the General Agreement on Tariffs and Trade (GATT), and the inter-American organs, specifically on the subject of suppliers' credits and private-public lending arrangements. With limited objectives and limited scope, such a conference might have a chance to bring about improvements in the terms of private lending. One of the more attractive of the possible arrangements that might be discussed is that developed by the British government in its aid to India. It involves government underwriting of private credits to finance sales of British products to India so as to achieve much improved lending terms. The theory in proposing such a conference is that any significant help to Latin America by the Europeans would probably center on easing credit terms in the sale of their goods and services. This could make an important contribution to the solution of Latin America's foreign exchange problems.

EXTERNAL FINANCIAL AID

In the area of foreign loans and grants a number of subjects deserve attention. A great deal depends on the ratio of grants to loans and on the terms of the loans. The theory that loans are preferable to grants is simple enough. It is assumed that, when the cost of borrowing is relatively high, a country will borrow only what it has to; and that a country will tend to waste resources it receives without any cost to itself. But the answer to waste is not to be found in the mere requirement of debt repayment. The government doing the borrowing is not likely to worry about future debt repayment beyond its four- to six-year term of office. The best way to control waste is to provide substantial help to national planning and execution of plans and careful evaluation of both.

A strong case can be made for the establishment of different interest rates, adjusted to a system of priorities, as well as for the establishment of a cooperative system among the donor agencies that would involve careful study of the changing debt picture of each country.

The donor agencies have charged different interest rates, but in a seemingly random fashion. On the theory that to speed Latin American development, lending activities should be planned as carefully as developmental activities, it would be extremely helpful if a system of priorities were set up that would encourage certain activities through grants and "soft" loans. This would follow the same principle that underlies the federal grant-in-aid system in the United States — to encourage certain activities essential to the welfare of the whole country, particularly when considered from the long-run point of view. Thus, for example, grants might well predominate in the categories of family planning, certain aspects of land reform, assistance to universities for the establishment of research centers, and for many of the international infrastructure projects essential to successful regional economic integration. A possible feature to prevent abuse might be the requirement of national matching of the grants. Other categories would be established for soft loans (including some with a zero interest rate), limiting the harder loans to activities and projects that are basically self-supporting over the longer run, such as electric power and other major infrastructure, and those of lower priority in developmental terms.

Table 19.   Aid Component in Borrowing $10 Million at Different Terms

Rate of interest	Terms		
	Number of years for amortization (1 payment a year, no grace period)	Actual market value of total amortization and interest payments assuming an 8% commercial rate	Aid component of loan ($10 million minus actual market value)
8%	5	$10,000,000	–
6	20	8,747,000	$1,253,000
5	20	8,121,000	1,879,000
2	35	5,016,000	4,984,000
0	45	2,703,000	7,297,000

Source: Pan American Union.

Table 20. Terms of Loans Authorized by Official Agencies under the Alliance for Progress

Agency	Average grace periods[a] (years)		1st semester		Average amortization periods[a] (years)		1st semester		Average interest rates[a] (per cent)		1st semester	
	1961	1964	1966	1967	1961	1964	1966	1967	1961	1964	1966	1967
Export-Import Bank	3.16	3.71	1.9	2.3	15.24	11.88	7.8	9	5.41	5.5	5.5	6
World Bank Group:												
IBRD	4.18	4.71	4.8	4.7	13.95	22.79	15.9	17.3	5.75	5.5	6	6
IDA	10	10	10	10	40	40	20	40	0.75	0.75	0.75	0.75
Inter-American Development Bank:	2.98	3.38	3.4	3.6	14.60	19.60	17.54	15.55	3.9	4.34	4.08	5.09
Ordinary capital fund	3.99	4.02	3	3.8	10.32	19.45	11	11.6	5.75	5.9	6	6.5
Special operating fund	3.81	4.45	3.8	3.4	10.63	16.10	18.5	19.5	4.37	3.88	3.8	3.8
Social Progress Trust Fund	1.59	1.76	[b]		20.69	21.48	[b]		1.78	1.72	[b]	
Agency for International Development	7.72	9.70	10	10	22.75	28.71	30	30	1.60	1.97	2.5	2.5

[a] All values shown in table represent annual averages arrived at by weighting all loans in respective subgroup, in accordance with their amount.

[b] No loans granted as resources were fully committed by the end of 1964.

Source: Pan American Union.

Costs of borrowing, depending on the interest charges and the length of the repayment period, can vary substantially. Borrowing at commercial rates imposes a heavy interest-payment and amortization burden on a poor country. Loans by the international lending agencies are generally at terms more favorable than the prevailing commercial rates for individual loans. But the aid, or subsidy, involved can vary over a broad range. It is worth noting the true aid component of $10 million in different kinds of loans, as shown in Table 19, ranges from zero to $7.3 million.

Against this background, we can examine the outstanding loans authorized by the different lending agencies (Table 20). It will be seen that the regular loans of the three banks — which make up the great bulk of the loans made by these institutions — carried interest rates in 1967 of 6–6.5 per cent and quite short amortization periods, suggesting a relatively limited component of true aid or subsidy. Only U.S. AID was providing a substantial subsidy in its lending.

It would be generally helpful if, in the Alliance reporting, the concept of "aid" was carefully defined and carefully used. This would be helpful in giving everyone concerned a more accurate view than is available at present as to how much "aid" is given to various countries and for various purposes. While a certain element of arbitrariness is inevitable, the logic is clear; namely, that there should be included under the "aid" category, in addition to the total grants, the difference between the gross amount of lending and the discounted value — at "normal" market prices — of the debt service so acquired by the recipient country. In certain instances, such as loans with an annual interest rate of close to commercial prime rates and a relatively short repayment period, the "true aid" component of the external financing is almost negligible. This is not to say that a straightforward international banking function is not exceedingly useful. But the function should be distinguished from aid.

Chapter 8

RATIONALIZING THE ALLIANCE

MORE information and sustained research are urgently needed. There also is a need for much better planning, both by the recipient countries and by the lending agencies, and a continuing evaluation process to see how the Alliance is progressing. In short, *there is a great need to rationalize the whole process of helping Latin American countries to help themselves.* There should be less groping in the dark.

Information and Research

Where great resources are involved and problems are both severe and complex, the desirability of taking as much guesswork as possible out of developmental activities is obvious. Moreover, governments throughout the hemisphere are assuming a larger role in the control of their economies, and international coordination is requiring ever-finer policy tuning, but the supply of information is not growing. In fact, the "information gap" may be getting larger.

This gap is symptomatic of the general backwardness of governmental operations in the hemisphere and reflects a basic lack of "effective demand." In an earlier period, when public sector bureaucracies operated within a traditional framework where policy or program accomplishment was neither expected nor attempted, they needed only the scantiest information base. Most of the first major forward moves in modern economic information techniques were taken by the central banks, partly in response to the pressures from the international institutions. Improvements in information on national government revenues came later, again under similar pressure. An increase in demand for national accounts and other economic data has come more recently from national planning agencies and the Alliance for Progress. Here, progress has been halting and mixed; national planning is resisted in some of the Latin American countries and the pressure for sound national planning on the part of the international agencies has been less than persistent, particularly since the demise of the Committee of Nine.

The information gap is even more severe in the case of data other than the traditional economic indices. For example, given the fact that the population increases could defeat all efforts at economic and social improvement, key demographic series are urgently needed, including those that throw light on the relative effectiveness of various approaches to slowing down the fantastically high birth rates. There is also great need for indices or measures on a number of key social, economic, and political questions that can tell us whether any meaningful progress is being made or not. For example, year-by-year indices of income received by the poorer half of a nation would inform officials on both the recipient and lending sides if there are improvements in equity. It is hard to develop effective national development programs if it is not even clear whether major objectives are being achieved or not. Clearly, these types of statistics must be strongly encouraged.

In the case of basic and applied research, as with information, again there is the question of effective demand. In countries that have only recently begun to evolve serious programs to increase agricultural productivity and to encourage more rapid industrialization, it is difficult for policy makers to realize that a lag in agricultural and technological research can condemn even an ambitious national development effort to very slow and painful gains. It is even harder for policy makers to appreciate the importance of research on social, economic, and political problems and on policy itself. Thus, demand for such research is slow in coming and, as a consequence, the needed research infrastructure for development is not being built as it should be.

In these circumstances, the international lending agencies should probably focus on creating effective demand for data and research, and not merely assist with the improvement of data-gathering and research techniques. For example, for Brazil and other major countries, it might now make great sense for the major lenders to take the position that after a certain date they will make loans only for activities for which the country itself has prepared and submitted well-designed, factually supported proposals. If the burden were put on the responsible ministries to do this kind of job, there is little question that a respectable product would eventually emerge and that, as a necessary by-product, considerable advances would be made in the country's data and information-generating, research, and evaluating procedures. The sort of international pressure that stimulated "modernization" of the hemisphere's central bank information might serve as a rough model for other sectors. A useful approach, as spelled out later in the chapter, would be the selective international subsidization of foundation and research institutes in the Latin American countries. This approach differs from the currently predominant one of technical assistance collaboration, and it will require international support for a longer period than lending agencies are accustomed to think about. The subsidies would have to be continued until there was enough local appreciation for the product of these institutions to attract the support of domestic resources.

Three of the many approaches that might be taken to close the information gap are discussed below.

1. *General "planning" information and research.* Sound up-to-date statistics are the lifeblood of good planning. Clearly, then, lending agencies have a vested interest in encouraging substantial improvements, quantitatively and qualitatively, in basic statistics.

There are few ways of finding major gaps in data as effective as preparation of a national plan. But today there are no techniques for following up once the gaps are known. Planning agencies and other executive staff offices and top policy makers merely learn to do without. This often means that major decisions are made on inadequate evidence. (Information on price changes, for example, is sometimes so much out of date that the government is not certain when it is making monetary and fiscal decisions whether an inflationary turning point has been reached or not, so that the adopted governmental policy may actually be aggravating the situation.) To compound the data problem for the Latin American countries, each of the various lending agencies requires countries requesting loans to provide information on general economic matters as well as on the specific programs or projects to be financed, but each agency wants the information in a form most convenient to it. Thus, recipient countries find themselves endlessly busy trying to provide data to meet a bewildering variety of specifications.

A much needed reform would be to make external requests for data as uniform as possible. If this were done, it would have the healthy effect of forcing donor agencies to examine the need for the information they were requesting, probably reducing measurably the present burden on borrowing countries. It also would provide an opportunity to work out "model" statistical data essential for all major needs: national planning, decisions by international financing agencies, and harmonizing of national policies with plans for regional economic integration.

It is probable, however, that two or even three levels of sophistication in the data model would have to be evolved to fit the wide range of data capabilities among the Latin American countries. For those at the lower part of the spectrum, for example, the major need now is to concentrate efforts on a few key items, such as short-term *up-to-date* economic indicators which can provide a current picture of developments within a national economy — figures on employment and unemployment and on output of the strategic or representative industries (beyond electric power production which is sometimes the only really up-to-date figure available). In every instance, even in the case of the more sophisticated governments, there is need to strengthen and speed up the flow of information on government expenditures and revenue collection, which generally run a course very different from the budgetary commitments made at the beginning of a fiscal year.

To people not intimately acquainted with the problems of development in the poor countries, reference to specific data series must seem a small detail. But here we have the classic "for-want-of-a-nail" situation. At present the powerful and elaborate aid machinery we have built is like a modern well-digging machine following a man trying to find water with a divining rod.

If the job of gathering information were well and thoroughly done by, say, 1975, CIAP should then be able to provide an annual report on developments in Latin America and on projections and financial assistance requirements for the next year or two. The CIAP report would serve much the same purpose as the Economic Report of the President in the United States. However, the CIAP report must say more. It should devote almost as much attention to social and administrative issues as to the economic ones, because the former are critical in analyzing the process of development in Latin America.

2. *Information and research related to high priority government operations.* There is a real need for natural resources surveys and for research on agricultural improvement, land tenure and agrarian reform, population control, educational improvements, the relation between health and productivity, and urban and regional development. Experience in all parts of the world has shown that such research is essential to sound operation of governmental ministries in these critically important fields.

In most Latin American countries, some start has been made on agricultural research. Experiment stations are common throughout Latin America, and they are beginning to carry out a substantial amount of field research. The same is not true of other important fields. Thus, for example, geological, soil, and water surveys in most countries of Latin America are far below a desirable level.[1]

Reports on results of the more successful resources surveys suggest the economic potentialities involved. For example, in Chile, the results of a study of forest resources attracted $22 million in U.S., Canadian, Japanese, and French capital, plus $20 million in domestic financing, for pulp and paper mills. Chileans anticipate that they will soon be earning $30 million annually in foreign exchange through expanded timber exports. In Mexico, a survey of forests in the state of Durango found 40 million acres of usable timber, leading to a $47 million investment.

Even more neglected than research in the field of natural resources is directly productive research on human resources, urban and regional development, and management problems. In these areas there are no established traditions of research in most of the Latin American countries, and there are very few institutions equipped to do such studies, though in a few instances an excellent beginning is being made.

A good example is urban and regional research. A high proportion of all infrastructure investment tends to go into the urban communities so that even limited improvements in efficiency and effectiveness in the handling of the urban infrastructure could provide substantial savings or greater returns. Learning how to cope with the problems associated with the flood of migrants to already crowded cities could bring very handsome social returns. But very little research is now under way which might point the way to improvement of this critical problem. With government operations organized along functional or service lines, the *regional* impact of governmental outlays and investments can fall far short of what is hoped for. That is, the impact on a given region might well be dissipated if the combination or "mix" of public efforts does not provide any economies of scale or a strong multiplier effect. There is, therefore, need for research on regional development to furnish an informational base for a better organization of governmental functional activities as well as to highlight instances where a specific regional type of activity is called for.

[1] Note should be taken here of the highly important contribution that has been made by the United Nations in this area, formerly by the UN Special Fund and currently by the UN Development Programme. Much of the credit for the progress made in the building up of basic institutions for natural resources survey and research should go to the UN leaders who early recognized the importance of this field to the welfare of the underdeveloped countries. The technical assistance provided to various Latin American countries by the Natural Resources unit of the Pan American Union also deserves recognition.

3. *Research in the social sciences and the natural sciences and technology that is not directly related to current governmental planning or operations but important to understanding and ultimately guiding development.* It is important to the design of truly effective development programs that much more be known about the workings of the national economies — about the forces making for inflation, about savings and investment patterns of different population groups, and about the relative advantages of different industrial location patterns. Gaps in knowledge about social change are particularly glaring. There is much to be learned about the forces and agents of change in various cultures and subcultures, and how these forces can be strengthened and guided towards modernization. There are great gaps in our knowledge of political development as well, but at least some of them could certainly be filled through comparative and other kinds of political science studies.

Research in science and technology also has a key role to play in the promotion of development. In the twentieth century, basic scientific research and applied scientific and technological research have become widely recognized as important factors in economic growth. In fact, organized research and development, intimately linked on the one hand with science and on the other with the engineering and management arts, is one of the great social inventions of our time.[2] While there is a huge reservoir of accumulated science and technology that can be drawn upon, research specifically oriented toward characteristic problems and possibilities of each nation is necessary. This is obviously true in the case of the tropical countries — a substantial part of Latin America — since much of the available technology is essentially oriented toward the temperate zones. Tropical medicine, tropical agriculture, and tropical housing are among the subjects that need specialized research attention. In addition, scientific and technological research on industrial products and processes can do a great deal to advance industrialization and industrial modernization. This has been amply demonstrated in the work of the technology centers of Mexico and Brazil.

SPONSORING RESEARCH

Here, as with the collection of basic data, the main task of the donor agencies is to help strengthen key activities. In fields such as agriculture

---

[2] Stanford Research Institute, *Scientific Research and Progress in Newly Developing Countries* (Menlo Park, Calif., 1961).

and health the governments are themselves aware of the value of improved information and knowledge. In other critically important areas the traditions for research are lacking or the subject is politically sensitive; in these instances, international funds, substantial technical assistance, and other forms of encouragement may be needed.

Research on human resources (including educational improvement and fertility control) and on social reforms might well be encouraged through the coordinating agencies proposed in earlier chapters, the Human Resources Commission, and the revived Social Progress Trust Fund. The sponsorship of research in these fields, with appropriate sensitivity to national feelings and politics, should, in fact, be among the most important functions of such "umbrella" organizations.[3]

One of the most needed and attractive possibilities is the establishment of a regional coordinating unit to study the problems of urban and regional development. A small unit, possibly in the form of a foundation, sponsored jointly by several of the donor agencies, and established in Latin America, could help greatly in encouraging needed research related to urbanization and regional development. This might well be combined with an effort to encourage the training of professionals capable of contributing importantly to public programs in the field of urban and regional development.

To encourage natural resources surveys — one of the key areas in the "operational" category — the Alliance agencies might increase the funds available to the United Nations Development Programme so that it can extend its support of natural resources studies in Latin America. The United Nations has done such a sound job in this field that it ought to be encouraged to continue its efforts to build up the basic capabilities for resources surveys in the various countries of the region. Beyond this, the Alliance agencies might well choose to sponsor special studies on resource exploitation possibilities that cross national lines in order to encourage international cooperation and to provide a firmer basis for regional economic integration.[4]

---

[3] A promising development in this general area has been the creation of a Special Fund for education, science, and technology to be administered by the executive committee of the Cultural Council of the OAS. The fund is to finance technical assistance and research undertakings in Latin America in these fields. This effort would be strengthened by the establishment of a strong Human Resources Commission and supplemented by the re-establishment of the Social Progress Trust Fund.

[4] A significant beginning has been made in the organization of a cooperative effort by the OAS, IDB, and the United Nations for the study and future development of the Plate River Basin in cooperation with the five countries concerned (Argentina, Bolivia, Brazil, Paraguay, and Uruguay).

In the case of more general research in the social sciences and in the natural sciences and technology related to development, a logical role for the donor agencies is to help strengthen existing research centers within the various Latin American countries, to encourage the establishment of new centers where needed, to encourage a network of institutional partnerships, and to encourage clearinghouse activities.

Significant progress in the social sciences has already been made in Latin America, and there is a fairly solid foundation to build on. For example, in October 1966, representatives from some thirty social science research institutes in Latin America concerned with problems of development met in Caracas (under the leadership of Victor Urquidi of Mexico) to examine possibilities for useful cooperation, including the establishment of a clearinghouse function. This was followed, in October 1967, by the establishment of a Latin American Social Science Research Council. This council, like the one in the United States, exercises a broad coordinating function over research and statistics. Clearly, it would be sensible to employ these coordinating mechanisms in planning and carrying out assistance to research in Latin America.

The international agencies should see to it that financing does not pose an unnecessary restraint on the development of needed information. More and better information should be recognized as an essential part of the *overhead* of running the Alliance, and funds should be set aside for this purpose. Consideration might be given to the technique employed in road building in the United States, where 1.5 per cent of total highway expenditures is set aside each year for highway information and research. The technique of automatic allocations to information and research in the case of the Alliance (1.5 to 2 per cent of all loans and grants made would be a reasonable amount) would not only help furnish needed funds for data improvement and research on problems of Latin American development, but would have the added value of establishing the importance of a constant search for a better understanding of the issues involved, and for better methods of achieving the goals set.

The trouble in the past has been that the Alliance has functioned as if it were likely to go out of business at any moment, so that the only things that have counted have been more or less immediate impact projects, particularly those with high visibility. The problems of information and research, which are long-term, have been shoved into the background. As a result, the Alliance taken as a whole with, of course, significant exceptions, currently functions like a disorganized ministry in a poor and backward country. It is as if modern management and policy tools had never been discovered. If the Alliance operation is to reach some degree of maturity, and substantial effectiveness, it will have to face the information and research issue squarely, and carefully build up the capabilities of the Latin American countries in this area. The knowledge gap must be closed step by step.

Planning

Criticisms of national plans and planning like those quoted below run through the evaluation reports of the various ad hoc committees set up by the Committee of Nine. Taken together, they paint a rather dark picture of the state of planning in Latin American countries.[5]

> Although appreciable efforts have been made to make . . . [the development plan of the Government of Colombia] more widely known, knowledge and understanding of it continue to be limited. . . . For example, in the contacts Committee members had with labor leaders, it was observed that Colombian workers are genuinely interested in the General Development Program but not sufficiently acquainted with it, nor do they fully understand their own great responsibility in carrying it out. . . . Beyond doubt there is an excessive and disadvantageous inadequacy of statistics, especially with respect to national income and current data for appraising the progress of investments. A more thorough analysis must also be made of relationships between the various economic sectors. . . .[6]

> The present planning system has not yet, despite the progress made, succeeded in organizing the basic ideas to permit a sufficiently well-prepared selection of goals for the Peruvian economy. . . . The existing projections represent at present merely a theoretical model. . . . A plan cannot be limited to the determination of objectives of production, savings, investments, balance of payments, etc. It is indispensable that it should also define — in order to permit the proposing of concrete operational forms — adequate structural reforms, forms to overcome foreseeable obstacles, minimal conditions for a successful accomplishment of required efforts, and the methodology by which the Plan can be adapted in

---

[5] A diagnosis of Latin American planning as of 1965 is provided in Panel of Experts, Alliance for Progress, *The Planning Process in Latin America* (Washington, D.C.: Pan American Union, 1965). See also the analysis of Latin American planning by the United Nations Committee for Development Planning, *Report on the Second Session, 10–20 April 1967*, Economic and Social Council, Official Records, Forty-third Session, Supplement No. 7 (New York, 1967); and United Nations, Department of Economic and Social Affairs, *Planning and Plan Implementation*, Papers submitted to the Committee for Development Planning, Second Session, Santiago, Chile (New York, 1967).

[6] "Evaluation of the General Economic and Social Development Program of Colombia," Report presented to the Government of Colombia by the Ad Hoc Committee, July 1962.

case the actually suggested operation does not achieve the foreseen results.... [7]

As in most Latin American countries, one of the factors that limits
Ecuador's development is the lack of a sufficient number of investment
projects, properly studied as to their technical and socio-economic
justification.... [8]

It is easy enough to spot the shortcomings. The national planners
themselves are well aware of them. It is more difficult to understand
what is behind them, and very much more so to see what might be done
about them in the future.

When the Alliance was formed, the U.S. and international agencies
were well aware that the Latin American countries had very limited
capability in the planning field, but their short-run perspective kept
them from undertaking major programs to overcome this serious shortcoming. Fortunately, the United Nations Economic Commission for
Latin America had established the Latin American Institute for Economic and Social Planning (ILPES) — in cooperation with the OAS
and IDB — before the Alliance came into being, so that some Latin
American planners could be trained.[9] However, while the Institute was
supported by the United Nations, the OAS, and the Inter-American
Development Bank, it did not have enough resources to train anywhere
near the number of planners needed if nineteen countries were to prepare
plans, all but one or two of them for the first time. An additional difficulty was that until the Alliance had made national planning an important feature in acquiring external financial assistance, planning had
been of interest only to the technicians. ILPES-trained planners tended
to be proficient in the macroeconomic tools, but had to learn the
realities of politics, administrative capacity, and project preparation
mainly "on the job."

Because of the long-established ECLA emphasis on long-range
economic programming, and no specification of planning standards
by the Washington-based agencies, it is little wonder that most of the
countries either tried to develop five-year or ten-year comprehensive
plans far beyond their administrative capacities or, at the other extreme,

---

[7] "Evaluation of the 1964–1965 Public Investments Program of Peru," Report
submitted to the Peruvian Government by the Ad Hoc Committee, October 1964.

[8] "Evaluation of Ecuador's General Plan for Economic and Social Development,"
Report submitted to the Ecuadorian Government by the Ad Hoc Committee, August
1964.

[9] Some training in national planning was also being provided at Latin American
universities, particularly in departments of economics, but on a very small scale.

limited themselves to short-term public investment programs. The first years of the Alliance saw the strange phenomenon of Bolivia, the poorest country in South America, presenting a "comprehensive" ten-year plan, while Mexico and Brazil presented what amounted essentially to short-term government investment programs. The Committee of Nine pressed individual countries to establish planning efforts in keeping with their inherent capabilities, but the Committee had neither the staff nor the authorization to help interested countries to set up appropriate planning systems. The Committee of Nine could "preach" — as exemplified by the quotations above — but it could be of little help with major international technical and financial assistance for planning or with the establishment of adequately endowed training and research institutes in each of the countries.

What can and should be done that will provide sound planning, say, three or four years from now and into the future? This is a question the lending agencies must now ask. Some needs are particularly apparent.

NATIONAL INSTITUTES FOR EDUCATION AND RESEARCH IN PLANNING

Each country should be encouraged, through funds and technical assistance, to set up a planning institute that would work closely with the government but be independent of it. While regional institutes (such as ILPES in Santiago) can be helpful in carrying out clearinghouse functions, training teachers, and in preparing materials, they cannot do the major educational and research job themselves. A regional institute may train three or four planners from each country each year, but this is a drop in the bucket, particularly since many of the people trained at such an institute will be lost to the field; they get drawn away into other work or displaced by frequent changes in government. *National* institutes could not only provide a much larger number of trained planners but could enable them to stay in the field even when there are major changes in government — if they are well enough endowed to absorb such people in their research and service activities.[10] In all of the countries, and particularly in the larger ones, emphasis needs to be placed on training and research in urban and regional planning, combined with the more comprehensive issues of national planning.

[10] Probably in the case of the Central American and Caribbean countries, a single regional institute would be more appropriate than separate national ones.

COMMON GUIDELINES FOR PLANNING

The lending agencies should invite the Latin American countries to join them in establishing common guidelines for national planning. The development of such guidelines might well be one of the major "outputs" of the proposed effort to mark the tenth anniversary of the Alliance, and might be closely related to the establishment of common statistical requirements.

By working together on the requirements that they themselves would have to meet in seeking international assistance, the political and technical leaders in the various countries would gain a much deeper appreciation of the potentialities and limitations of national planning. Such guidelines would greatly simplify the task of evaluating national plans and provide a framework for the annual reviews of CIAP as well as for the lending activities of the donor agencies.

The guidelines should be evolved through the joint effort of the recipient countries and all the major donor agencies, and provision should be made for their periodic revision.

This is not the place to consider in detail what such guidelines should appropriately contain. However, it might be useful to examine a few of the major weaknesses in Latin American developmental planning and to suggest what might be done to cope with them. It should be stressed that what follows is highly selective, intended to illustrate some of the requirements rather than to spell them out.

(1) Participation in the planning process

A key problem in Latin America, as in most of the less developed parts of the world, is how to bring planning into the mainstream of political decisions and into the mainstream of national life. Unless a national plan reflects serious commitment on the part of the government and serious intent on the part of the major private groups in the economy — business, labor, agriculture, and the professions — it can never be implemented. This point has been made forcefully in the planning literature.[11]

The planning guidelines should aim at achieving broad involvement by government ministries and major private and cooperative groups in

---

[11] For excellent analyses of the requirements and of what might be done to meet them, see W. Arthur Lewis, *Development Planning: The Essentials of Economic Policy* (New York: Harper & Row, 1966); Albert Waterston, *Development Planning: Lessons of Experience* (Baltimore: The Johns Hopkins Press, 1965), and *Planning Economic Development*, ed. Everett E. Hagen (Homewood, Ill.: Richard D. Irwin, Inc., 1963).

the preparation of national plans. Attaining this objective would be given a powerful boost if it was established that major support by the international agencies was contingent upon: (1) representatives of the more important private groups in the nation being consulted in the preparation of the plan; (2) each of the major sector programs having the backing of the key ministries concerned; and (3) the major policies and programs proposed having legislative and presidential approval.

(2) Advancing regional economic integration

To date not a single plan produced by a Latin American country outside of Central America has included a series of programs and projects to advance regional economic integration, nor has any analyzed the extent to which proposed national developmental policies are consistent with the objective of integration. If a Latin American common market is to be realized between 1970 and 1985, each Latin American country will have to work out plans to gear national production to the limitations and potentialities of a regional market. This involves serious study to determine the production areas in which the nation has particular advantages, the possibilities of complementary specialized production in the more complex areas (as in the iron and steel, chemical, and automobile industries), and a review of national policies to avoid beggar-thy-neighbor effects and to advance international harmonization of policies. In this area, more than in any other, it is essential that the planning guidelines be thoroughly discussed and agreed upon by the Latin American countries in order to create a regional context within which national plans could be prepared and executed.

(3) Developmental strategies

The strongest feature of national planning in Latin America has been the treatment of macroeconomic elements. This normally covers historical data and projections over the plan period of: gross domestic product; national income and to some extent its distribution; private and public savings and investment; capital-output ratios; public expenditures and revenues; and balance of payments, including exports and imports, foreign exchange earnings, and the anticipated foreign exchange gap — the last being often the main point of the exercise. However, while the macroeconomic elements of a national plan look to the future, they are essentially derived from historical data and only slightly modified by the actual programs and projects that have been worked out by the various ministries. Thus, while the macroeconomic elements tend to make up a consistent, integrated planning framework, which provides excellent terms of reference for economic policy, they are not themselves *a plan for development.*

The main planning art is to find a way of bringing together the material resources, the human resources, and the financial resources of the nation to achieve specific developmental goals.

The achievement of any ambitious objective, such as a rapid increase in industry, the modernization of agriculture, or a substantial improvement in education, calls for an orchestration of many elements: the building of infrastructure, the provision of public services, changes in public policy to induce certain private actions, research and development, and many others. The art of planning, like the art of government, involves a search for the appropriate "mix" — the right things, in the right proportions, at the right time, and in the right places. This underlines the importance of evolving effective techniques of "integration" or "coherence" in planning.

The task of bringing elements together harmoniously is extremely difficult, particularly in the face of the continuing infighting among ministries and sections of the country to achieve personal and group advantage. Under present Latin American conditions, the most effective approach to an integrated plan — and one that would also serve to balance off the present overemphasis on "bankable" infrastructure projects — would probably be for central planning offices to focus on: (1) selected sector plans for the directly productive activities, particularly agriculture, mining, and manufacturing; and (2) urban and regional development.

Individual projects would continue to be analyzed in cost-benefit and general feasibility terms and as part of the various sector programs. The additional feature would be the review of individual projects in terms of their contribution to selected urban and regional development programs.

Once the planning methods are worked out satisfactorily, it should be possible for a nation to apply for a loan to help finance a four- or five-year total program for agricultural development or for industrial expansion or a long-range urban or regional development program.

The purpose of the proposed guidelines would be to promote planning that emphasizes the subjects of greatest strategic importance and that treats them with full consideration for all their requirements, including such matters as administrative personnel and financial resources, public policy changes needed, private groups that must be involved, and the external assistance required. A few of the substantive considerations that might well be considered in drawing up planning guidelines are briefly treated in the sections that follow.

(4) Planning the production sectors

Latin American plans, as suggested earlier, tend to be centrally prepared "paper" plans; what is said in them has relatively little resemblance to what the ministries involved actually do or what the government's price, wage, and subsidy policies are with regard to the directly productive sectors.

Centrally prepared plans, with their emphasis on macroeconomic elements and public works, generally have very little useful to say about agriculture, mining, and manufacturing. "Bankable" public projects in these sectors, under current standards, are few. Since these sectors in most countries are largely in private hands, and the relation of governmental planning to the private sector is tenuous at best, plans for the directly productive sectors turn out to be mainly hopeful projections, peppered with largely miscellaneous infrastructure projects.

What is urgently needed are realistic plans for the development of each of the major productive sectors that provide a useful base for public action. Governments will have to treat the problems within each sector and the possibilities for improvement in a broad framework. Here, the macroeconomic aspects of planning can play a valuable role. Not only should they serve to clarify and specify the main objectives of development policy, but they should provide the framework within which sectoral planning can be carried through. They can specify the resource limitations over time and provide needed information for individual entrepreneurs concerning the overall "demand horizon" anticipated for the future — thereby providing a useful guide for individual investment and production plans.

One might well ask if national plans are needed to achieve such ends. In fact, the reader may find it odd that the tremendously important subjects of agriculture, mining, and manufacturing are discussed in a section concerned with planning rather than in their own right. The form of discussion stems from the concern of this book with the leverage on Latin American development that might be exerted by the donor agencies. For the maximum leverage to be exerted by such aid, it is necessary that it be related to broadly conceived overall programs so that it can play an appropriately catalytic role.

While each of the productive sectors has its own special character and its own special needs, the broad requirements for the kind of sector planning that is called for under Latin American conditions can be brought forth by concentrating the discussion on one sector — agriculture.

Agriculture has frequently been neglected by governments in development strategy in Latin America. This has had an unfortunate effect on both farm exports and on food production for internal consumption. Statistics compiled by the United Nations Food and Agriculture Organization show that from 1961 to 1966 Latin America's total food output increased by less than one-tenth of one per cent per capita. Many of the countries find themselves having to divert funds from income-earning developments to pay for food imports. In 1965, for example, Peru spent approximately $90 million on food imports, Chile $60 million, Venezuela more than $100 million, Brazil nearly $200 million.[12] It has been estimated that between now and the end of the century, the region's total food production must increase by nearly 240 per cent just to keep up with the growing population.[13] This estimate makes no allowance for exports.

There is strong resistance in most Latin American countries to effective agricultural planning. Large landowners may welcome specific projects that are directly helpful to them, but they tend to resist the entry of government into broad-scale programs, because these may open the door to major changes they oppose. Many government officials and planners, either consciously or subconsciously, see in agriculture everything they dislike about the existing scheme of things — backwardness, ignorance, stagnation — and they put their faith in modern, often large-scale, industry; for them, agricultural planning seems to be a useless exercise or the way into an operational morass. On the other side, the small farmers and the farm workers, who can gain most directly, are generally not organized to press for agricultural programs.

This situation, plus the fact that agriculture is so important to the successful development of Latin America, provides the rationale for

[12] Joseph Grunwald and Philip A. Musgrove provide a thoroughgoing analysis of Latin American agriculture and its problems in their unpublished study of natural resources in Latin American development. This analysis, as well as the writings of Theodore W. Schultz, Arthur Mosher, and others, together with reports of the Inter-American Committee for Agricultural Development, have provided the statistical and conceptual foundations for this section on agriculture.
[13] Montague Yudelman, *Agricultural Development in Latin America: Current Status and Prospects* (Washington, D.C.: Inter-American Development Bank, October 1966).

both pressure and help from outside to encourage broad planning and specific action programs in the recipient countries. There is much to do. Everything from farm credit and irrigation to disease control and research seems important — and everything is costly. Everything takes so much time; the payoff always seems so far away.

The appropriate role of planning in agriculture is exactly what common sense would suggest that it ought to be. It should search out opportunities for greatly increased output and productivity. It should concern itself with the more crippling problems and suggest the best ways of overcoming them, whether in the realm of land tenure, agricultural credit, or whatever. It should work out the appropriate rates and directions of public and private investments to build up the natural resources, the human, the capital, and institutional resources.

A focus on agriculture provides an extremely useful base for decisions on the conservation, development, and use of land and water resources. In a poor country, it is difficult, if not impossible, to get adequate support for investment in natural resources surveys, research, education, and related elements unless it can be shown that such investment brings positive returns. Land development and conservation measures, resources surveys, and research are all enormously expensive. The scale, the form, and the timing of all such investments must be related directly to productive possibilities.[14]

The problem is particularly great in the case of "new land" development where major capital investment may be needed for forest clearings, flood control, irrigation, drainage or desalination, transportation and other major infrastructure, as well as direct assistance for settlement in some cases. But problems are also involved in using more capital or intensifying labor use on land already considered developed. In both cases, a careful weighing of the anticipated costs and benefits is very much in order.

Agricultural planning must concern itself with physical inputs beyond land and water. Particularly important in this category are chemical fertilizers, high-yielding seeds, and pesticides. In recent studies it has been pointed out that Latin America's farms are among the most underfertilized in the world, using only about 10 per cent as much

[14] For a useful discussion of the application of this principle to natural resources survey, see Orris C. Herfindahl, *Natural Resource Information for Economic Development* (Baltimore: The Johns Hopkins Press for Resources for the Future, 1969). Nathaniel Wollman has outlined the requirements for decisions on water resources development in his study, *The Water Resources of Chile* (Baltimore: The Johns Hopkins Press for Resources for the Future, 1968).

fertilizer per cultivated acre as those in Europe and in North America. Agricultural policy and planning should seek to help farmers get fertilizer at relatively low prices and teach them how to use it. Farmers also will have to be helped with pest control, tools, improved practices, water supply, extension services, and farm credit.

Where land is held in large and mainly unproductive farms, because farm ownership itself provides sought-after status, a change in land tenure can provide the beginning of an improved system of farm production, particularly when combined with a sound program of agricultural extension and credit. But the relation of land tenure to agricultural production is not always so straightforward. There are large productive farms that can only be divided at a loss of productivity, and there are many areas of too small farms, minifundia, where consolidation is essential for increases in farm production. Clearly, there is no formula that can be applied across the board. One thing is clear, however. There is much to be gained by treating land tenure and agricultural production as interrelated components in agricultural planning.

The planning of governmental policy vis-à-vis the farm sector is also of key importance. An example is price policy. Governmental price policy in some of the Latin American countries seems self-defeating; often aimed at keeping costs to the consumer low, it may well hold back the increase in production needed to maintain reasonably priced food. A key requirement is for information on the elasticity of supply of farm products. Such information is needed to determine when it is useful to promote higher farm prices. Techniques for raising prices to the farmers — to induce increased production — can extend from government purchases of farm products at guaranteed prices, to a reduction of middleman costs, to direct subsidy to the farmer for producing specified crops. The prices of inputs that farmers must buy if they are to modernize — fertilizers, pesticides, other chemicals, tools, equipment, machines, fuels, and repairs — are also of major concern. Often prices of such inputs are high because of inefficient production protected by tariffs, monopolies and/or government price policies. In all too many instances in recent years in Latin America, government price policy, far from encouraging expanded output, has served as a drag on agricultural production, and particularly on food production for domestic consumption.[15]

[15] For an excellent analysis of the problems touched on in this section, see Theodore W. Schultz, *Economic Crisis in World Agriculture* (Ann Arbor: University of Michigan Press, 1965).

Good agricultural planning has to be continuously concerned with the relationship between agriculture and industry. Expansion or improvements of certain kinds of manufacturing activities can be among the most important levers for agricultural progress. For example, there is clearly a need for the expansion of modern, competitive fertilizer plants in most Latin American countries. Modern processing plants can greatly enlarge the market for farm products and encourage farmers to improve the quality of their output. In many instances the establishment of a canning or frozen-food plant can stimulate more and better output in nearby farms than can an army of extension agents. It is very impressive, as Schultz points out, to see how rapidly farmers will bestir themselves and begin to use better methods when there is a well-established market for their products, particularly if the market is nearby.

By identifying the elements that will promote progress in the agricultural sector and showing how these can be brought together, agricultural planning achieves its strategically significant role.

There is not much to be gained by extending the discussion to all of the productive sectors. But there is an important general point to be made. A central focus in national planning on the major production sectors is called for by several key facts in the current Latin American situation: food production is just barely staying ahead of population growth and must be greatly increased; all of the Latin American countries need to expand their exports if they are to maintain a rapid rate of growth; and the industrialization drive needs to be intensified and broadened beyond the substitution of consumer durables. Planning can help in the achievement of the high-priority goals.

(5) Urban and regional planning

A second major focus for planning in Latin America should be in an urban and regional context. This is not yet widely appreciated in most of Latin America. There is an uneasiness about the many problems and pressures generated by the explosive rate of urbanization and about the painfully slow progress in the countryside, but this has not yet been related in a meaningful way to decisions made by national governments or in planning to guide such decisions.[16]

The disturbingly rapid rate of the population growth in Latin America has been accompanied by very significant migration from the

---

[16] Chile is the main exception in this regard; it is beginning seriously to concern itself with urban and regional planning. Regional planning has also received some attention recently in Argentina, Brazil, Venezuela, and some other countries.

rural to the urban areas. This is fundamentally altering the traditional social, economic, and political relationships. While the population growth rate of Latin America is generally accepted to be on the order of 2.9 to 3.0 per cent, the rate for the urban population is estimated at roughly 5 per cent, approximately half due to migration. The rates vary greatly, of course, from country to country.[17]

According to estimates of the Economic Commission for Latin America, the urban population grew from about 60 million in 1950 to about 115 million in 1965 — from 40 per cent to 50 per cent of the total population. ECLA estimated that by 1980 about 60 per cent of the population would be urban. Measured in terms of people, the anticipated growth in urban population is even more striking — an increase of more than 100 million between 1965 and 1980 as compared to 54 million in the preceding fifteen-year period. In giant Brazil, which has had the fastest rate of urbanization since 1950 but is still less urbanized than Latin America as a whole, 30 million people are expected to crowd into the cities by 1980, more people than the total population of any but the two largest nations in Latin America.

The problems of Latin American urbanization are immense. Unemployment in the cities is extremely high. The shift from rural to urban status is taking place before there is substantial industrialization in the cities. But, then, the migrants have few skills. The attraction of urban services and facilities plays a large role in bringing migrants to the cities, even though there are limited prospects for immediate employment. The demand for these services and facilities has become a powerful political fact-of-life, and enormous financial commitments have to be made to expand urban infrastructure. Rough estimates suggest that during the first six years of the Alliance, investment in urban infrastructure amounted to one-third of total public investment. In spite of this, basic needs in health, education, housing, urban transportation, and water and sewerage were hardly touched.[18]

If the cities generate problems for a nation, they also generate great opportunities. This is the more important part of the equation. The city is a good place to do business. It is the place that attracts the higher skills, the place to get the necessary business services, and to gain from the economies of scale. The city has — or at least it can have — a tempo and an environment that is conducive to development. Major

---

[17] Pan American Union, *Social Aspects of Urban Development*, CIES/1138 (May 17, 1967).
[18] *Ibid.*

cities are the sources of most modernizing influences in a developing country.

Once the city is properly seen as the factory and the store and the school and the hospital, then it can be seen that the efficiency and the quality of the urban environment, the relation between cities, and the relation between cities and the countryside are truly important subjects for developmental planning.

The spatial aspects of development are significant not only in dealing with the metropolitan regions and a system of cities within a nation, but also in exploiting unusually attractive resource and industrial-location opportunities within given regions of a nation and in tackling the problem of extremely depressed regions. Latin America has made progress here, having undertaken some of the most significant regional development efforts in the world. The development of the Guayana region in Venezuela (directed by an independent corporation) is one of the most ambitious frontier-development efforts ever launched. It involves the creation in a formerly "empty" region of a heavy industry complex based on iron and steel and plentiful power (the latter involving the construction of the huge Guri dam), the creation of a new town (Ciudad Guayana), the establishment of a host of new public services and facilities, and the development of the region's agricultural potential. The development of the Cauca Valley in Colombia, again through the instrumentality of an independent corporation, stands as one of the best examples of multipurpose river basin development in the underdeveloped world. Somewhat less ambitious river basin projects are to be found in several other Latin American countries. The program to further the development of the desperately poor region of northeast Brazil and to raise levels of living is certainly one of the most noteworthy depressed-area efforts in the world today. This program touches almost every aspect of life in northeast Brazil, ranging from great infrastructure works to special incentives to attract industry to agricultural extension work and the teaching of specialized skills.

The full potential of many rich resource areas in Latin America can probably be developed only through an advanced type of regional planning. Extensive development of such areas, some of which cross national boundaries,[19] will call for the creation of extremely expensive

[19] An impressive number of multinational opportunities of this type are described in the report prepared by the Development and Resources Corporation (David E. Lilienthal, *et al.*) for the Inter-American Development Bank, *Multinational Investment Programs and Latin American Integration* (Washington, D.C., September 1966).

infrastructure works. Complex development of this variety often calls for a definite policy with regard to attracting industry, recruiting, settling, and training workers, and providing incentives for the modernization of agriculture, and it can be carried out in a coherent manner only if the nation is prepared to undertake regional planning both in the field and at the national-government center. The planning carried out in the field can serve a particularly valuable purpose if it is designed to bring persons and institutions within the region into the planning process. The central planning is needed here, as in urban planning, to provide a framework for the planning done in the field.

This leads back to the point made earlier: national planning can usefully guide a development program only if it focuses on cities and regions as well as on sectors. As John Friedmann has pointed out, urban and regional planning deals with matters that are especially close to the vital interests of people and, consequently, close to the political pulse beat of the nation. People's concerns are with the points of actual and potential impact of investment decisions, precisely where the bitterest conflicts are engendered.[20]

While urban and regional planning can hardly be expected to provide any magic ingredient to bring Latin America out of the "paper planning" stage into a more meaningful stage, it can help to introduce elements of concreteness and reality which have largely been lacking in the past.[21]

THE LOGIC OF SELECTIVE PLANNING

Whether common guidelines for planning are established or not, if the lending agencies are to stimulate more effective development strategy and better application of policy, they will have to focus their efforts selectively on major sectoral and discrete geographic areas. Planning, beyond the macroeconomic level, must be thought of in specific terms as part of a concerted "input" to bring about major progress in high-priority sectors or areas within a nation. The issue is

[20] John Friedmann, "The Urban-Regional Frame for National Development," *International Development Review* (September 1966), p. 9.

[21] Harvey S. Perloff, "Key Features of Regional Planning," *Journal of the American Institute of Planners*, vol. 34 (May 1968), pp. 153–59. A valuable bibliography of materials in urban and regional planning is provided in John Friedmann and William Alonso (eds.), *Regional Development and Planning: A Reader* (Cambridge: M.I.T. Press, 1964). For a treatment of the major considerations that should go into regional planning, see Joseph L. Fisher, "Concepts in Regional Economic Development," *Papers and Proceedings, Regional Science Association*, vol. 1 (December 1957), pp. W1–W20.

how to determine realistically what the opportunities are and what is a sensible order of priorities in order to apply intensive "planning treatment" to agreed-upon sectors or geographic areas to which some of the limited national resources, supplemented by international loans, are to be applied.

Hope of across-the-board *detailed* planning for every sector and/or geographic area is unrealistic in any of the Latin American countries. But a selective sectoral and area approach is quite feasible, and could be the keystone of effective future national planning and international agency strategy. The "intensity" and timing of planning efforts might vary considerably from one sector or region to the next in any given country.

This kind of planning strategy suggests that in the search for coherence in governmental policy and actions, at least for the next decade or so, it might be more appropriate to develop annual operating plans than to rely entirely on improvements in the four- and five-year plans.

In conclusion, two points are stressed. From the beginning, the Alliance encouraged national planning. Unfortunately, the planning mechanism had to be given overwhelmingly difficult tasks before it could be properly constructed and tested. Under severe pressures to produce immediate results, Latin American planners not unexpectedly fell back on the things that could be found most easily and that mattered most to their political leaders — foreign exchange figures.

The lending agencies were the ones who provided the pressure. If they have been unhappy with the results — and they have been — it does not make their reasons for encouraging planning any less valid. It merely suggests that it is time they did something substantial to improve the situation and to help the Latin American countries evolve a meaningful type of planning. The countries that are seriously interested in development will welcome such assistance and guidance; the others may as well improve their planning mechanisms and try to have them in working order when they *are* ready to move ahead. On the other side, the donor agencies need the guidance of national plans if they are to provide assistance in a form and according to a priority system that is appropriate to each national situation and set of objectives.

Chapter 9

DEVELOPMENT ON A CONTINENT-WIDE SCALE

MOST large-scale developmental activities, to date, have been organized within the framework of national boundaries and carried on through existing national institutions. Unfortunately, most of the nations of Latin America are too small to provide a satisfactory developmental framework. They are too small as markets for modern industry, and therefore tend to lose the great possibilities inherent in the economies of scale of many mass-production types of industries. They are too small to have within them all the skills needed to organize the necessary government programs of development and a broad range of major private businesses. They are too small for substantial diversification to help avoid severe economic ups and downs, or to achieve a broad and sturdy economic base. And they are too small to achieve a good bargaining position in international trade, or in other international economic affairs. Brazil, Mexico, and Argentina do not suffer the same limitations as the smaller countries, but they need larger markets if they are to engage in the profitable production of specialized capital goods. These countries stand to gain substantially from the formation of a Latin American common market.

In Latin America, as in developing regions elsewhere, development has been most uneven, and there are pockets of progress and wealth surrounded by an expanse of underdevelopment and misery. The pockets of development are quite advanced. São Paulo, Rio de Janeiro, Mexico City, Lima, Buenos Aires, Santiago, Caracas, and a number of other cities are vigorous and modern. There also are some rich farming and mining areas where methods used are advanced and incomes are relatively good. But outside these areas lies a vast, poor hinterland barely touched by modern progress, and then only in superficial ways. Clearly, an important problem for Latin America is how to turn its great cities from *pockets* of modernity into *centers* of development.

A major part of the problem is how to overcome the developmental limitations of national boundaries and national institutions. A logical answer is to complement national institutions with regional institutions designed specifically for the large-scale development of both multination regions and intranational regions.

The Latin American nations and the inter-American system have already begun to bring such complementary activities into being. The Inter-American Development Bank has been particularly active in this direction. The problem now is to provide a solid base of understanding and appreciation for the need for such an approach so that the scale and momentum can be greatly increased.

Continent-wide integration and development will require changes in many directions, including the construction of transportation networks, frontier development, and "opening up" the interior. These are discussed in some detail below.

Transportation in a Regional Framework

The major connection between the countries of Latin America from the earliest days has been ocean transport. It still is today, and will for a long time be the chief mode for international trade. However, while ocean transport has certain advantages over land transport, in lower initial capital costs and greater flexibility and mobility, it does not provide the same developmental leverage as does land, or even river, transport. A trunk railroad or highway is likely to produce a ribbon development of towns along its entire route and encourage the construction of feeder routes. A community situated anywhere along such routes can tie into a whole transport network and be able to acquire needed goods and to send out its goods. This is not true for ocean or air transport which leave vast intermediate stretches untouched. Latin America's great dependence on ocean and air transport has been one of the more important factors in the highly uneven development of the continent, the growth of islands of prosperity in a sea of poverty.

The dream of tying together the various nations through a single continental network is an old one.[1] More than three-quarters of a century ago there was a proposal for a Pan American Railway that would stretch from New York to Buenos Aires. The proposal grew out of the desire for greater political and social integration among the Americans and, more concretely, the desire to increase trade and to exploit more fully Latin America's resources. The project was given

[1] This section draws heavily on the highly informative study of Robert Brown, *Transport and Economic Integration of South America* (Washington: The Brookings Institution, 1966).

official approval at the First International Conference of American States in Washington in 1889–90. But despite the support the proposal received, including funds appropriated by the U.S. Congress to survey the route, the project died. As Robert Brown points out, such a north-south railway was far ahead of its time, and it is not surprising that capital could not be found to embark on such a venture.

Construction of national railways began around 1850. These were designed mainly to connect mining centers and agricultural areas with ocean and river ports to facilitate exports. By 1900, there were some 27,000 miles of rail lines (compared with 193,000 in the United States at the same date) in largely disconnected and relatively small systems.

Shortly before World War I, an unusual North American promoter, Percival Farquhar, tried to establish an integrated international railroad system. He acquired a number of existing lines and tried to construct interconnections to fill out the systems in southern South America, using European capital. With the outbreak of war, however, he could no longer obtain new capital and his scheme collapsed. No serious effort has been made since to utilize the transport potential of the many disconnected railways in that part of the world.

The formation of the Latin American Free Trade Association led to new interest in international railway transport, and in March, 1964, representatives of the railroads of Argentina, Bolivia, Brazil, Chile, Ecuador, Paraguay, and Uruguay met in Argentina to establish the Latin American Association of Railroads (ALAF). "Perhaps," suggests Brown, "if this association is successful in carrying out its program, Farquhar's vision will at last become reality."

As the railway age gave way to the highway age, the dream of interconnecting the Americas was transferred to a movement for a Pan American Highway System. In the early 1920's, the idea of a Pan American highway was strongly supported by automobile clubs in South America and backed by North American automobile manufacturers as well as by more visionary Panamericanists. It received official international approval in 1923 at the fifth inter-American conference.

From an early date, it was accepted that the Pan American System should be composed of the highways connecting the capitals of neighboring countries, but the actual choice of routes was broader. The system, which is still under construction, contains a network of around 30,000 miles of paved and "all-weather" gravel roads. It extends from four major points along the U.S.-Mexico border through Central America and, after skipping the "Darien Gap," a difficult jungle area between the Panama Canal and Colombia, links all the capitals of South America with one another, but sometimes very circuitously.

The interest of the Latin American governments in the system is underlined by the fact that the costly investments have been financed almost entirely by Mexico and the South American countries with little foreign assistance. The United States did contribute $170 million of the estimated $285 million cost of the Central American segment, but very little to the remainder.

Some segments of the system are heavily used by trucks and buses, but there is relatively little traffic across national boundaries. What international traffic does exist is concentrated primarily in areas where frontier regions of adjoining countries have developed considerable commerce. This situation will change if South America is successful in bringing about closer economic integration. In the meantime, administrative obstacles plague international highway transport. Frequently trucks from one country are not permitted to enter a neighboring nation and costly transshipment is required at the frontier. Surely nothing can be more irrational than to invest millions of dollars in highways and then build bureaucratic roadblocks that make it impossible to use the system.

International river transport can also provide continent-wide developmental leverage. In several areas of South America, river transport already is of considerable importance and, if properly coordinated with ocean, highway, railroad, and air transport, could contribute greatly to economic integration. The River Plate and Amazon River systems are among the largest in the world, but their true potential has hardly been tapped even though these are areas where sustained investments could probably bring high rates of return.

Brown points out that the River Plate system composed of the Plate itself, and the Paraná, Paraguay, Upper Paraná, and Uruguay rivers, in addition to other navigable tributaries, could well be used for transport between the Argentine part of the Latin American industrial heartland and large parts of the supporting hinterland lying in Argentina, Paraguay, Uruguay, Bolivia, and Brazil.[2] Tributaries of the Amazon could be used to develop the eastern portions of Peru and Bolivia. Given the great contribution that efficient river transport could have on economic development and integration, it is unfortunate that improvements in the waterways have been so long delayed, especially

[2] A study of transport problems and possibilities is under way as part of the joint IDB-OAS-UN-INTAL study of the River Plate Basin.

as the delay is due in no small measure to narrow political considerations.

For most international passenger travel in Latin America, air transport is clearly the most useful. Even though buses and private automobiles will become increasingly important between adjoining countries, only air transport can provide the rapid passenger service between the capitals and larger cities which is indispensable for successful economic integration. Air freight traffic is already considerably more important in Latin America than in the rest of the world. However, despite the relatively well developed cargo service within the borders of many of the South American countries and between these countries and the United States and Europe, there is still little traffic from one Latin American country and another. In many areas, air cargo transport seems to offer a significant opportunity for economical and efficient transport. Air transport also has definite advantages over highway construction where undeveloped areas are cut off by mountain barriers or where the territory between presently populated centers and a new frontier area has little economic potential. In a number of countries, small planes, often run by the air force, are the only links between isolated communities in the interior and the major cities. The extension and strengthening of such small-plane systems can play a useful developmental role in the frontier areas of the continent, as they have in Alaska.

Transport development is a key factor in the economic expansion of Latin America and in regional economic integration. Such development will be costly and difficult, and it must be related to the economic geography of Latin America. Robert Brown, building on the transportation studies of ECLA, the World Bank, and other groups, has provided a valuable analysis of the transport problems of South America in terms of nine regions: a "heartland" (Region I), a supporting hinterland (Region II), and then seven other regions following economic-geographical divisions, each with a special relationship to the industrial heartland and to its own contiguous regions. Brown's suggestions for surface transport priorities both within and among these regions are summarized in Table 21; the diagonal entries represent priorities for internal transport within each of the nine regions, and the other entries refer to interregional transport. The ordering of the transport media in the individual entries indicates the priorities that Brown believes would enable new transport investment and policies to make a maximum contribution to economic integration, especially as regards industrial products. While the specific delineation of regions and indication of

Table 21. Transport Investment Priorities in South America

Regions: Both Origins and Destinations	I	II	III	IV	V	VI	VII	VIII	IX
I. Industrial heartland in Brazil, Argentina, and Uruguay*	Highway/ Railway River Ocean	River Railway Highway	Highway Ocean Railway	Ocean	Highway & River/ Railway	Ocean	Ocean	River & Ocean	Highway Ocean Railway
II. Supporting hinterland**		Railway/ Highway/ River	Highway Railway	Ocean	Highway & River/ Railway	Ocean	Ocean	River & Ocean	Ocean/ Highway
III. Chile			Highway Railway	Ocean Railway	?	Ocean	Ocean	Ocean	Ocean
IV. Highlands of Bolivia and Peru				Highway Railway	Highway	Ocean	Ocean	Highway & River Ocean	Ocean
V. Eastern slope of the Andes					Highway/ River	?	?	River	?
VI. Colombia and Venezuela						Highway/ Railway/ Ocean	Highway Ocean	River & Ocean	Ocean
VII. Ecuador							Highway Railway	River & Ocean	Ocean
VIII. Amazon Basin								River	River & Ocean
IX. Northeast Brazil									Highway Railway

Note: Ordering indicates priority for investment and development. A slash between two media indicates equal priority. An "&" between two media indicates that they are used together. "Ocean" refers both to ports and to the organization of shipping services. ";" indicates that priorities cannot be determined at present. The main diagonal is internal transport within each region. Other squares correspond to interregional transport. Only half the table is shown because the same transport media are used for transport in both directions.

* This region covers the southern coastal part of Brazil from approximately Belo Horizonte in the north to Pôrto Alegre in the South. From this latter city it narrows and includes only a thin strip along the coast of the rest of Brazil and of Uruguay, ending in Montevideo. Then it jumps the Plate River and includes a portion of Argentina to the south of the Paraná River encompassing the important cities of Rosario, Buenos Aires, and Bahía Blanca.

** This region should ideally include the whole of Paraguay, all of Uruguay except for the coastal area in Region I, that part of Argentina not in Region I, and the Brazilian state of Rio Grande do Sul south from Pôrto Alegre, the southern sections of the states of Mato Grosso and Goiás, and Brasília, the new Federal District. It would also encompass the southern part of Bolivia. The region has been modified somewhat for analytical purposes to include the whole of Paraguay and Uruguay, that part of Argentina not included in Region I, the Brazilian Federal District and provinces of Mato Grosso, Goiás, and Rio Grande do Sul, and the Bolivian department of Santa Cruz.

Source: Robert T. Brown, *Transport and Economic Integration of South America* (Washington: The Brookings Institution, 1966), p. 214, Table 9–1.

investment and policy priorities are clearly preliminary, the presentation does serve to highlight the value of a continent-wide approach to the development of transport in South America — and, by extension, to all of Latin America.[3]

With respect to air transportation, which is not covered in the table, the Latin American countries will probably have to work out cooperative arrangements among themselves. The many small national airlines are not making optimum use of the opportunities offered by the jet age, and the formation of joint companies may be very much in order.

The need for continent-wide development and integration is also apparent in ground services. It has taken nearly two generations for the Pan American Highway System to approach completion, and, even now, large trailer trucks cannot carry loads across national boundaries, routings are inflexible, and services are not integrated with those offered by the railroads. The ports are not equipped to handle modern maritime traffic, nor do they have automatic equipment where shipping volume calls for it. A great deal of international integration and improvement of maritime services is needed to prevent ocean transport in Latin America from becoming hopelessly out of date.

The Alliance has a truly important contribution to make with regard to transport. The Alliance instrumentalities must take it upon themselves to work out jointly with the individual nations the strategies that will speed the integration of national transport companies, the modernization of transportation facilities, the harmonization of transport policies, and the joint improvement of services.

Frontier Development as a Factor in Integration

Bordering areas offer especially rich opportunities for extending integration and for overcoming the barrier of national frontiers. The Alliance instrumentalities, and particularly the Inter-American Development Bank, have begun to exploit these opportunities and have sponsored a number of programs for joint development of border areas in Central America and in the north of South America.

The most ambitious efforts to date have involved joint development of the Colombian and Venezuelan border areas and the Colombian-Ecuadorian frontier area. The logic of this development stems

---

[3] Three regions might be added to round out the picture; probably, Central America, Mexico, and the Caribbean islands.

not only from economics and geography, but also from history. These three countries for a brief period were part of a single nation, Gran Colombia, under the leadership of Simon Bolivar. The vision of this great leader nearly a century and a half later still has a certain appeal. Cut off from the industrial heartland in the southern part of the continent by great distances, and by the towering Andes and the Amazon region, these countries might well become a closely interlocked and significant subregion. In fact, the region has a number of features, such as great distance from the core manufacturing zone, its own rich petroleum resources, and extensive plains, that tempt comparison with the Southwest region of the United States.

A multifaceted program for the Colombian-Venezuelan border area is in the process of evolution, based on an Inter-American Development Bank report. The report outlined the problems of the frontier zone, which has more than 45,000 square miles and nearly two million persons, and suggested a specific set of programs to advance its development.

The regions on both sides of the frontier are physically similar and are less developed than the remainder of either country. A number of factors have been "agents of frontier integration." Smugglers, in "correcting certain inequalities in prices," have promoted trade of a kind. The discovery of oil in the Lake Maracaibo area has attracted Venezuelan farm workers, and their jobs have been filled by workers from Colombia. Many families own land which extends across the frontier, and for many cattlemen there is no frontier. Also, many Venezuelan families send their sons to study at Pamplona in the Colombian province of Norte de Santander, which is famous for its schools.

There also are many common problems. In the north they are associated with inadequate water, nomadism, and smuggling. In the central area, they are deforestation, free pasture, and, in some parts, lack of water. In the Llanos, the southern plains, there are severe problems arising from the progressive loss of water in the rivers and from successive droughts and floods.

A program has been evolved that seeks to overcome these specific problems and to promote greater interchange and more rapid economic development. In the north, wells are to be drilled, irrigation extended, and Indians settled on the land. In the central area, the emphasis is on conservation of land, improvement and diversification of agriculture, and improvement of cattle raising methods. In the southern plains a serious effort is to be made to control the course and flow of the rivers, to control floods, and to drain waterlogged areas so as to open up great stretches of the Llanos to cattle raising and farming. Also, efforts are being made to improve cattle breeds and to control cattle diseases.

The IDB mission which studied the frontier zone did not favor a single plan for the whole region on both sides of the frontier, but suggested a series of specific programs including programs for roads, river basin development, irrigation, land settlement, and industrial development. It also proposed the creation of a permanent organism for consultation, coordination and joint action, and the formalization of a series of bilateral agreements.

An equally extensive program has been prepared by the Inter-American Development Bank for the development of the Colombian-Ecuadorian border area at the request of the governments of the two countries. The program proposed includes 71 individual projects and would cost roughly $100 million, with about a third to be financed from outside sources. It is designed to benefit some 600,000 Colombians and 400,000 Ecuadorians living in the 46,300-square-mile border zone.

The implementation of both programs is still in the future, with many political, administrative, and technical problems to be overcome.

Another development has been the formation of an Andean group by Colombia, Ecuador, Venezuela, Peru, Bolivia, and Chile to foster subregional economic integration and development. This group has already established an Andean Development Corporation to help implement these objectives. While this is basically a political venture to help offset the economic and political power of the large Atlantic nations, it could have a significant impact in a number of fields. This grouping has geography against it, but politics favors it. Its durability will provide some insight into which is more important under Latin American conditions.

"Opening Up" the Interior

The vast undeveloped interior of South America (about four-fifths of the land mass) has from the earliest times stood as a great barrier to any kind of development. Walter Lippmann has described the Latin American countries as "a string of islands surrounded on one side by the oceans and the other by an unpenetrated wilderness." He suggests that if there were nothing but wilderness between the Rockies and the Alleghenies there would be no political union in the United States, no great industrial system, no economic base for political stability, and no affluent society. And he goes on to say:

> The central task is to stir up and finance the South American equivalent of the opening of the West in North America. It is in the truest sense of the term an engineering problem — to build roads, to connect the great river systems of the Amazon, the Orinoco, and the La Plata, to build landing fields, to make the jungle lands habitable with modern refrigeration and modern science.[4]

The opening up of the interior is a dream that has inspired South Americans for a long period of time. But the results so far have been largely talk. Pioneering there has been, but most of it has been extremely limited in scope or temporary in nature like the pioneering that accompanied the penetration of the Amazon Valley during the rubber boom of the latter half of the nineteenth century.

Now, however, a serious attempt must be made at opening up the interior and integrating the continent. Population growth alone should demonstrate the immediacy of the problem.

Unfortunately, the kind of pioneering that involves not only national dynamism but a willingness to sacrifice comforts and traditional ways for later satisfaction would seem to be on the decline. What is needed is not the kind of pioneering that went into the construction of Brasília, for this was an "opening of the interior" based on a new seat of government, with centralized administration as the developmental lever, and with all the comforts of the most advanced city living and with an emphasis on aesthetics.[5] Nor does the answer lie in the kind of pioneering where great numbers of individual families and small groups surge into the wilderness, clear the forest and prepare the land, and live without any comforts and without public services. This type of movement can be useful in the case of a very limited extension of the present frontier, as is happening all along the rim of the Amazon Basin, but it is not appropriate for a major attack on the empty interior. A central problem, therefore, is the evolution of an appropriate and effective strategy for opening the interior in a generation or two and not over centuries. This question should occupy Alliance officials in a major way.

---

[4] "A Look at South America," *Washington Post*, December 14, 1965.

[5] What has been significantly developmental has been the spontaneous colonization that has taken place at various points along the highway built to connect Brasília with other major cities.

An effort of the size involved here should have a focus; otherwise it might be dissipated by vagueness as well as vastness. Such a focus would be provided by the organization of an effort to develop the Amazon River drainage basin. The Amazon and its tributaries drain a very large portion of the unexploited South American interior: more than half of Brazil, the southern half of the three "Guianas," a good portion of Venezuela, two-thirds of Colombia, part of Ecuador, more than half of Peru, and two-thirds of Bolivia. This area is *the* great barrier to tying together the countries of South America. And it has a "mystique" that can help generate the necessary political backing. What is needed is a carefully planned and strongly organized effort. To attract substantial financial and human resources from every part of the world, there must be some assurance that the great investments involved are likely to provide commensurate returns.

Herman Kahn and Robert Panero have described the difficulties involved in the development of the Amazon Basin and have outlined some of the requirements of a major attack on the Amazon.[6]

> Strangely enough, the Amazon is one of the few remaining large river basins of the world which has not been comprehensively investigated and analyzed in terms of flood control, irrigation, and power generation, even though it is navigable its full length and even though there are existing trading cities and airports along its full length. The very magnitude of the water volumes and distances involved, as well as the climate of the area, tends to discourage comprehensive investigation and complicates any attempt to analyze flood control or regulatory devices. Amazonian "experts" tend therefore to know only pieces of the area, and an over-all view is difficult to develop.

The main stem of the Amazon and its tributaries extend through all the northern part of the continent so that water routes come within a relatively short distance of many of the major cities. Unfortunately, although the main stem itself is fully navigable, few of the tributaries are. If it were possible to render the major and minor tributaries more navigable than they now are by eliminating natural barriers, or by designing new generations of river craft that would be able to navigate these streams in an efficient and economical manner, or by some combination of both methods, direct traffic would be feasible between the industrial centers of Buenos Aires, Montevideo, and São Paulo and the raw material producing countries of Venezuela, Colombia, Ecuador, Peru, and Bolivia. "If this traffic becomes possible and economical,

[6] "Nuevo Enfoque del Amazonas," *Progreso* 65/66, Revista del Desarrollo Latinoamericano, Una Edición Especial de *Visión*, pp. 134–141.

Brazilian automobiles could be sold in Colombia in return for Colombian coal; Colombian coal deposits in the high Andes, not currently exploitable, would become economical. Brazil imports coal and Colombia has, for all practical purposes, cut off the import of automobiles to preserve hard currency."[7]

At the same time, even though the interior of the continent represents four-fifths of the land mass, very little of this land is suitable for colonization. If the flood stage of the main stem of the Amazon could be significantly reduced, by some economical combination of man-made lakes, river diversion projects, and/or control of the Amazonian sources, hundreds of thousands of square miles of heavily silted, new land would become available. At present, only leached, lateritic soils exist above flood stage. Preliminary examination of some of the tributaries suggests that there are cases where it would require only a relatively small effort to effect control at natural points. It might be possible, therefore, to obtain some direct control of the flood stage of the main stem of the Amazon through a number of small projects. This would result in the drying of currently flooded lands, and in increased navigability of tributaries.[8]

Important possibilities, not mentioned by Kahn and Panero, also lie in land clearance, mostly jungle clearance, in areas not subject to flooding. Some significant beginnings have been made, particularly in Brazil, at the edges of the formidable jungle. Thus, a number of huge ranches have been developed in an area along the Araguaia River, one of the large tributaries of the Amazon, and within reasonable land distance of major markets for beef in southeastern Brazil. The forest here is being cleared by teams of largely unskilled workers using mainly hand tools and fire, and it is reported that each worker can clear an average of ten acres in forty days.[9] The large investments now being made, mostly by entrepreneurs from the rich southern states of São Paulo and Minas Gerais, are stimulated by Brazilian government tax waivers.

[7] *Ibid.*, p. 138.

[8] That these matters are not purely technical ones, but involve significant political considerations (including concern about national security and national status) was underlined by the furor caused by the Kahn-Panero proposal in Brazil. Several groups, and particularly some representatives of the military, bitterly attacked these proposals as an opening wedge for "U.S. imperialism" in Brazil. It was even suggested that the United States was interested in the development of Amazonia because it intended to settle some of its Negro population there. One would hope that over time, and given genuine international sponsorship, a less parochial and narrowly nationalistic view would prevail.

[9] Juan de Onis, "Brazil is Rolling Back the Amazon Jungle," *New York Times*, January 17, 1966.

Half of corporate federal income taxes can be invested in the Amazon region instead of being paid to the tax collector.

A serious international effort, involving the active participation and support of the six nations within the Amazon Basin, is called for, organized and backed by the Alliance for Progress. The tasks would probably include the following:

1. Analysis and evaluation of current technological possibilities for development of new kinds of river transport; placing contracts for the development of the most promising types; incorporating the new vessels into existing or newly organized transport systems; and providing information to interested groups on their performance.

2. Analysis and evaluation of current technological possibilities of multiple purpose development of the Amazon River Basin system to make the tributaries of the Amazon readily navigable, to reclaim and prevent future flooding of silted land along the rivers, and to provide electricity.

3. Analysis and evaluation of current experiments in land clearance, including detailed estimation of costs and returns of alternative techniques and types of machinery; placing of contracts for research and experimentation in new and promising techniques; provision of information on results to interested governments and private groups.

4. Analysis and evaluation of alternative techniques for logging and transporting Amazon woods, and encouraging research and developmental work in the use of forest products, including the manufacture of pulp and paper by combining many varieties of tropical woods.

5. Assistance to small-plane transportation, attempting to organize it into scheduled transport systems wherever feasible.

6. Evaluation of institutions in the basin concerned with research, development, credit and/or promotion, and helping to strengthen those with special promise.

An attractive possibility for organizing such a broad-based effort would be the establishment by the countries involved, with international technical and financial assistance, of an Amazon Basin Development Corporation. The agency would work with and through the individual nations. In the organization and operation of such an agency, careful consideration would have to be given to national sensitivities, including fears associated with military defense questions, with the possibilities of heavy immigration, and with the possibilities of economic domination by outside companies. Certainly the Alliance should be able to generate enough ingenuity to establish an effective international agency, capable of launching a powerful developmental effort, yet sensitive to the feelings of the individual nations of the basin.

Multinational Projects

The themes discussed above — transport, frontier development, and "opening up" the interior — have important common objectives:

1. They seek continent-wide development, that is, to push development to a broader, more effective and more dynamic level;

2. They seek to provide a sturdier physical basis for regional economic integration by removing barriers and by strengthening interconnections among the nations of Latin America; and

3. They encourage individual nations to cooperate with their neighbors in common activities with common objectives because more can be achieved if they work together.

These objectives can also be advanced by multinational projects in such areas as telecommunications, electric power, and development of international river basins other than the Amazon.[10]

The Central American nations, with technical and financial assistance from the international agencies and from the U.S. Government, have undertaken a number of such projects. They have carried out preinvestment studies for the creation of a regional telecommunications system, and studies are under way for the interconnection of the high-tension power systems of Honduras and El Salvador; Panama and Costa Rica; and Guatemala, El Salvador, and Honduras. The Central American Bank has created a $42 million fund to finance multilateral infrastructure projects.

The South American countries, with help and encouragement from the Inter-American Development Bank, have begun to review opportunities for joint projects. For example, a permanent committee for the study of multinational power projects has been established. Peru, Venezuela, Colombia, Ecuador, and Bolivia have completed feasibility studies for a 3,500-mile highway east of the Andes. Other multinational highway projects now under consideration would strengthen the links

---

[10] For a valuable discussion of some possibilities along these lines, see Inter-American Development Bank, *Multinational Investment Programs and Latin American Integration*, A Report Prepared by the Development and Resources Corporation, September 1966.

between Chile and Argentina, Paraguay, and Brazil, and link the Uruguay highway system with the systems of Argentina and Brazil.

A "Preinvestment Fund for Latin American Integration" has been established within the Inter-American Development Bank to encourage the study and design of multinational infrastructure projects.

This is potentially of great value. However, to enhance the probabilities of success in such international efforts, a number of measures would seem to be in order.

Possibly the most important of these is the working out of a scheme of continent-wide developmental planning. Resources are limited, and there is a shortage of trained individuals to prepare and to carry out international projects. The careful establishment of a system of priorities is therefore of the greatest importance. Broad policies will have to be established. For example, a migration policy will be called for, in view of population scarcity in some fairly resource-rich areas and population pressures on limited resources in others. Similarly, a decision should probably be made to give highest priority to projects that are especially important for regional economic integration.

Such policies can be implemented most effectively within a broad regional planning scheme. In addition, investments, when viewed in isolation, can sometimes be more harmful than helpful. Thus, for example, a proposal for an international highway may provide a positive cost-benefit ratio when analyzed by itself, but actually turn out to be damaging. This could be the case where a railroad serving the same general area is forced out of business by the highway, the costs of moving certain kinds of goods are increased, and some previously serviced communities are left without transportation. Clearly, individual modes should be viewed in an over-all transportation context.

For the purposes discussed here, continent-wide planning would probably be made up of a limited number of major sector programs, such as transportation, telecommunications, electric power, and multipurpose river basin development, with only limited ties between the sectors. Also it should logically be closely tied to the operation of the regional economic integration program as well as to activities of the international banks; thus, it might be jointly sponsored by the Latin American Free Trade Association, the Economic Commission for Latin America, the Latin American Institute for Economic and Social Planning, the Central American Common Market, the Inter-American Development Bank, and the World Bank, or some combination of these.

Another consideration in multinational projects is the importance and difficulty of arriving at a fair division of the benefits and costs. Countries are likely to hesitate to undertake joint schemes unless they have confidence in the equity of the division. Possibly a method well established in labor negotiations might be applied here; that is, the appointment to an adjudicating committee of representatives from the contending parties as well as so-called "public representatives." The latter could be chosen by agreement among the nations involved from a panel of experts in the fields of cost-benefit analysis and in the analysis of "joint costs." These are areas in which substantial progress has been made in recent years, and there are experts throughout the world qualified to be included on such a panel.

There is yet another consideration. Most of the Latin American countries already have difficulties in planning and carrying out their own large national projects. Joint programs, involving more than one nation, will compound these difficulties. In the case of the border programs now projected, an additional difficulty stems from the fact that they cover regions that are particularly backward, so that substantial progress is hard to come by. All this suggests that international projects should be approached in a realistic fashion. The planning and priority arrangements should be such that in the earlier stages the number of separate projects are limited, and that the earlier projects should be relatively short-term with visible impact. They should not be undertaken until the countries involved are ready to cooperate fully, and to make the necessary administrative arrangements so that the development projects do not drown in red tape. Also, the Alliance agencies should be prepared to provide an unusual amount of technical and personnel assistance as well as substantial financial assistance.

While reasonable caution is very much in order, the main point should not be lost sight of: there is an inherent logic in sponsoring international projects that can advance the development of the whole continent and tie the individual nations closer together. In addition, there are few matters as important as having the Latin American countries learn to work together on difficult and concrete development programs. Thus, programs such as described above might well command a substantial share of all resources — financial and human — made available by the Alliance for Progress.

Chapter 10

PREFERENCES, INDUSTRIAL PROMOTION, AND THE LATIN AMERICAN COMMON MARKET

FEW economic developments are likely to contribute as much to the region's long-run economic growth as the establishment of a Latin American common market. The Alliance recognized this from the beginning. But, while the lending agencies have found many ways to help advance the objectives of the Central American Common Market, they have not yet found a way of hastening the evolution of the Latin American Free Trade Association (LAFTA) into a genuine common market. The Latin American presidents, at the 1967 "summit" meeting, while agreeing that a common market should be achieved by 1985, showed much more interest in world trade and in trade preferences by the industrialized countries than in regional economic integration.

The Latin American Free Trade Association, conceived as an essential way-station to a genuine common market, has made relatively little progress in this direction, plodding along in painful product-by-product negotiations for the reduction of national tariffs. There are some formidable forces standing in the way of progress. As Miguel S· Wionczek, the Mexican expert on integration, has pointed out: "Each government believes it has a right to demand an immediate *quid pro quo* for any trade or other concession granted. No government seems ready to forego small benefits at present for larger gains in the future. In addition, there is no relationship between national industrialization policies and regional development goals: experts working on national plans and those dedicated to matters of integration coexist in happy isolation."[1]

There are some powerful anti-LAFTA groups which influence governmental attitudes and actions, mostly made up of older industrial firms in the consumer goods field living comfortably behind high walls of protective tariffs, many of them inefficient small entrepreneurs who

[1] Miguel S. Wionczek and Enrique Angulo, *Latin American Free Trade Association: The First Four Years* (New York: Carnegie Endowment for International Peace, January 1965), p. 59.

fear they would be extinguished by the outside competition. Equally important is the fact that few groups see significant advantages to be derived from pressing for a Latin American common market. This is due in no small part to the economic disharmonies in the Latin American situation. It is extraordinarily difficult to stimulate trade among countries that are in the throes of inflation and that tend to have very fragile foreign exchange situations. For example, Brazilian manufacturers with excess capacity find that poor internal credit, coupled with very unstable price patterns and recurrent devaluations, makes it almost impossible to produce for export. It is hard to imagine much political steam building up behind regional integration if the potential manufacturer-beneficiaries in the Latin American countries cannot see immediate short-run benefits in the elaboration of country agreements.

In Latin America, most of the support for regional integration comes from modern, sophisticated politicians or from experts and technicians (*tecnicos*) who are much more conscious of the limitations and difficulties of *national* development than the general public or most business groups. Supports for integration by U.S. and other lending agencies has been emerging stage by stage since the beginning of the Alliance for Progress.

Jockeying at the Presidents' Summit: The Issue of Trade Preferences

The summit meeting of April 1967 was remarkably revealing both of the differences in Latin American and U.S. positions and of the difficulties involved in making progress through joint action within the Alliance. At the meeting of the presidents, as well as at the meeting of the foreign ministers that preceded it, the Latin Americans disagreed with the U.S. representatives on the relative importance of the issues to be discussed at the summit. The United States wanted to put economic integration at the top of the agenda, together with the role that U.S. financial assistance and foreign investment might play in the development of integration. The great majority of the Latin Americans, by contrast, wanted to focus attention on the need for increasing Latin American export earnings and on international trade policies, particularly the granting of preferences by the United States and other industrialized countries to exports from the less developed nations. This was understandable. Almost all of them were experiencing increasing difficulties with their efforts at industrialization. Alliance financial assistance, while extremely helpful with regard to balance-of-payments shortfalls, did not seem to be adequate to generate a genuine forward move economically. Consequently, interest once again was shifting to international trade. In the near term — and for most political leaders the four-to-six year horizon is the critical one — this was far more important than the possibilities of regional trade.[2]

The summit meeting served to sharpen a critical point with regard to the creation of a Latin American common market: given conditions in underdeveloped regions where most national production, particularly in manufacturing, is carried out behind the protection of high tariffs and other barriers, the creation of a common market is possible only as part of a much larger set of arrangements favorable to such national production. The granting of trade preferences by the United States and other industrialized nations could be a part of such a set of larger arrangements.

The connection between trade preferences and regional economic integration, however, extends beyond the question of a *quid pro quo* for nations that are frightened of the readjustment problems involved in moving toward freer trade. The encouragement of production for sale to the industrialized countries, through preference, could be a force for more efficient production in Latin America. A common market that substituted regional monopolies and regional inefficiency for national inefficiency would not be a major gain from the developmental standpoint, and might even be a hindrance. An increase in efficiency and modernization is, therefore, critical. As Isaiah Frank has pointed out:

> The argument for preferences is in some respects an extension into the export sector of the infant-industry argument for protection of the home market. It rests on the need to overcome the initial disadvantages faced by a newcomer in manufacturing, including the high cost of gaining a market foothold. But unlike infant industry tariffs which can totally insulate inefficient domestic industries from outside competition, preferences extended to all developing countries provide built-in limitations on inefficiency. The exporter in the developing country would have to compete on equal terms with suppliers from other less developed countries, and with domestic producers in the advanced countries to which he seeks to export. He would also continue to compete, although not on equal terms, with exporters of the same product from other advanced countries, who might still be in a position to overcome their tariff disadvantage.[3]

[2] Joseph Grunwald, Martin Carnoy, Miguel Wionczek, "The United States and a Latin American Common Market," unpublished.

[3] Isaiah Frank, "New Perspectives on Trade and Development," *Foreign Affairs*, vol. 45 (April 1967), p. 535.

Although trade preferences for the developing countries have been much discussed in recent years, there are many unanswered questions about the subject. It is highly probable that the developing countries, in pressing so strongly for preferences, overestimate the short-term effect of such preferences on their own development, while the rich countries overestimate the economic and political damage that the granting of preferences would impose. It is extremely hard, given all the unknowns, to have any assurance about projections and simulation exercises. Under the circumstances, consideration might well be given to the possibility of the United States and Canada granting trade preferences for Latin American goods over a specified period of time as a test for relaxing trade barriers on a worldwide basis. One feature that may well emerge is a demonstration of the significant role that firms from the United States could play in Latin America's development, because of their knowledge of, and contacts in, the United States market. In fact, given the resistance to foreign private capital in the Latin American countries, preference may well emerge as a critical link in the chain of activities that will have to be carried out to make credible and viable both regional economic integration in Latin America and freer world trade in general.

Buffer Fund

Another key issue in the establishment of a Latin American common market, which was not fully faced in the summit meeting, was that of the problems faced by the medium-sized and smaller and less-developed countries in exposing themselves to trade from the industrially more advanced nations of Latin America — the big three. While these less-developed countries are given somewhat privileged status under present LAFTA arrangements, involving some unilateral tariff concessions, they are concerned about the impact on their producers of a genuine common market. It is here that the proposal of the United States for a "buffer fund" to help offset losses of integration might make some impact. If it were large enough, such a fund might be an inducement for the smaller countries to join a common market arrangement. Attention is normally focused on the possible displacement of industries in the smaller countries, but in this case such displacement would probably be limited, partly because tariffs in a common market arrangement are reduced gradually. More serious difficulties are likely to stem from the loss of customs duties, which are very important to some of the smaller countries, and from balance-of-payments pressure and displacement of labor. Of more importance than the difficulties, however, is the positive help that a flexible buffer fund can give to the smaller countries.

Promoting Industrial Expansion

It seems evident that *protection* and *compensation* are essential components of a common market. But, unless the common market can help generate growth in industry, there is not likely to be the necessary backing for it. (The word "industry" is used here in its broad sense to cover not only manufacturing but agricultural, mining, and service activities as well.)

Industrial promotion has always been an item of interest in discussions on Latin American economic integration,[4] but it has been a background item listed along with many others as playing some vague role in the development of a common market. The fact is that from the beginning, thinking about Latin American integration has, quite naturally, been greatly influenced by the success of European economic integration. Thus, the main focus has been on lowering national tariffs to promote intraregional trade. There has been an appreciation of the great differences between the European situation and that of Latin America, but, nevertheless, the greatest attention has been devoted to intraregional trade and on measures to encourage and expand it. However, under the special circumstances of an underdeveloped region it may be much more effective to focus on the promotion of large-scale manufacturing and agricultural activities, and think of trade as a tool to encourage such activities. This is not merely a matter of semantics, since the two are so interrelated. It is a question of where the main emphasis is to be put and the types of instrumentalities that are needed to achieve the end sought.

The less developed regions cannot follow the same path as the Europeans in generating economic expansion. In Europe before the establishment of the Common Market, the productive plant was already tremendous; entrepreneurship was well established and primed to conquer new markets. But it is well to remember that, even under these

---

[4] For a thoughtful treatment of the relation between investment and regional economic integration, see Paul N. Rosenstein-Rodan, "Multinational Investment in the Framework of Latin American Integration," Inter-American Development Bank, Round Table on Multinational Investment, 9th meeting of Board of Governors, Bogotá, April 1968.

remarkably favorable circumstances, it was promotion of a basic sector of the economy through the Coal and Steel Community that led the way, and a special promotional credit facility, a European Development Bank, was deemed necessary. Obviously these types of special-sector and promotional-facilities arrangements would be even more important as the lead factors in expansionary efforts in less developed regions. Business firms in such regions are not tooled up to be able to expand rapidly to take advantage of new market opportunities, nor are most entrepreneurs in a position to try out new productive fields without substantial assistance.

This suggests that industrial expansion has to be nourished not only through freer trade but through direct financial, technical, and marketing assistance, so that new national, regional, and overseas markets can be opened up. It then should be possible to move ahead much more surely and quickly with tariff reductions, if such reductions are tied to specifically promoted arrangements for regional industrial expansion.

Given all the difficulties involved, it is likely that to speed regional economic integration a new kind of instrumentality is needed to lead the way in creating an expansionary atmosphere in Latin America. An attractive approach would be to establish a Regional Development Corporation — a Latin American *fomento* agency — to carry out a wide range of activities and much more extensive regional trade.[5]

A *fomento* (development) corporation with a broad mandate and substantial resources — human and financial — would be in a position to assist Latin American firms to establish transnational operations and sales as well as to attract to Latin America large modern firms from the economically more advanced countries to produce advanced goods (such as machinery, and electrical and chemical products) for sale to the whole region. Once such firms are ready to set up important transnational operations, the removal of tariffs and other restrictions for the products of this industry could then be negotiated through LAFTA and the Central American Common Market. The location of the new plants, it is assumed, would be based essentially on productivity considerations, but without neglecting the proper balancing of industrial growing points in the various parts of the region.

Once several such specific industrial arrangements were evolved,

[5] This proposal was presented in an earlier paper. Harvey S. Perloff and Romulo Almeida, "Regional Economic Integration in the Development of Latin America," *Economica Latinoamérica*, vol. 2 (November 1963). This chapter draws heavily on that paper.

the need for a customs union would become more evident and the basis for true regional economic integration established.

Private Enterprise and Overseas Firms

The future of the Alliance for Progress will depend in no small part on its success in solving the dilemma faced by Latin America with regard to private enterprise and overseas private investments.[6] Simply stated, the dilemma is that a very broad spectrum of Latin American public opinion is not convinced that the expansion of private enterprise is in the public interest, but the functioning of public and cooperative enterprise in Latin America has not been successful enough to generate a strong push for public sector control. Even the members of the intellectual Left in most countries do not press for socialized industry. Their position tends to be essentially negative: they are against "capitalistic" enterprise.

The problems are compounded in the case of foreign investments made by the industrialized countries. Here the very strong forces of nationalism, joined with the practical interest of domestic business to keep out foreign competition, serves to create an atmosphere in most of the countries that encourages restrictive legislation and discourages positive inducements to outside firms in many of the industrial categories. Yet Latin America needs the technical and market know-how, as well as the other resources, that international capital can provide.

Lecturing the Latin Americans about the virtues of private enterprise and of foreign investment is hardly likely to be effective. It is much more useful to promote responsible, progressive competitive businesses, which can sell themselves. (The high regard in which Sears Roebuck is generally held, because of its efforts to use locally produced manufactured goods, is a case in point.)

The proposed Latin American *fomento* organization can make a major contribution if it is properly organized. The experience of Mexico provides a particularly pertinent model to use. Modern manufacturing industry in Mexico has flourished in recent years and a significant part of the growth has been due to the great volume of outside investment in Mexican industry. Two factors have played a particularly important role: the promoting activities of its *Nacional Financiera*, a development

[6] See Peter Nehemkis, *Latin America: Myth and Reality* (New York: Alfred A. Knopf, 1964), chapters 10–13.

corporation with an extremely broad mandate, and the "Mexicanization" program. *Nacional Financiera* has helped establish a variety of
business enterprises by assisting businesses and businessmen in many
ways. It is willing and able to provide a substantial share of the equity
capital. It will help a prospective business get the necessary roads,
power, and other infrastructure needs when these are inadequate and
the proposed industry is an important one for Mexico. It will "go to bat"
for the firm to get changes in government regulations when these stand
in the way.

The "Mexicanization" program is helpful in a different way. It is
a practical embodiment of the strong nationalistic feelings in Mexico.
Foreigners are discouraged by heavy taxes from owning more than
small minority interests in the sensitive extractive industries, while
strong inducements are offered to businesses in which the majority
holdings are in Mexican hands — that is, those in which Mexicans own
at least 51 per cent of the equity. This requirement has made it easier
to accept the great volume of overseas, mostly U.S., investment and to
bring an ever-increasing number of Mexicans into productive fields.

Business firms from the advanced countries, and especially from
the United States, normally prefer to maintain total ownership in their
own hands. Yet the large volume of U.S. investment in Mexico shows
not only that forced joint ownership is not a serious hindrance to investment, but that businessmen can be more concerned with the atmosphere
in which they do business and with adequate control over operations
than with the proportion of equity holdings they retain.

The "Latinization" of business in Latin America is probably more
important to economic expansion on a regional basis than Mexicanization has been in Mexico. Latin American businessmen worry about the
possible effect of economic integration on their operations — about
the competition from U.S. and European and Japanese investors who
are on the lookout for big markets and who have the capital and know-
how to take advantage of them. Latin American businessmen ask: How
can we compete against firms that do not have to worry about foreign
exchange reserves, who can count on help from home when it comes
to arranging credit terms, and who have better promotion, production,
and distribution techniques? How can this "unfair competition" be
overcome? The answer is to involve Latin American capital and Latin
American businessmen in the new enterprises, and to help them modernize and enlarge their present businesses. However, potential competition is not the only worry. The outsiders may *not* come in an appre-

ciable number, and economic integration may be slow in generating modernization and growth. On both counts, vigorous *promotion* of joint foreign-Latin American ventures would seem to be a critical ingredient.

The conclusion is that the proposed *fomento* organization should not only seek out firms and groups of firms ready to start region-wide industries in new fields where profitable operations are likely, but should be in a position to furnish risk capital and thus acquire equity holdings in the new firms. These holdings could then be sold to Latin American investors, thus encouraging more savings and investment in the region, and also more diffuse ownership of business firms. One or more possible formulas might be feasible and appropriate. If the Mexicanization pattern were followed, 51 per cent of the equity in each firm would have to be in Latin American hands. But there might not be enough Latin American private capital to buy up the 51 per cent if the expansionary push was really successful. The *fomento* corporation — backed by Alliance funds — might have to retain ownership of a significant share of equity in many of the new enterprises for a rather long period of time, in order to assure an eventual majority of Latin American ownership. The corporation would be in a position to combine its equity holdings into various kinds of mutual funds, so that Latin American investors could readily diversify their portfolios. It could be expected to make a major effort to develop a region-wide stock market, and to encourage Latin American savings and investment through a variety of means.

Additional means might well be employed to encourage private foreign investment under the special conditions and inhibitions existing in Latin America. Foreign firms might be permitted rather complete freedom of operations if they gradually increase their export sales to a specified percentage of production, following a pattern similar to that which has been applied in the case of the auto industry with regard to local "inputs." Foreign firms might also be required to make public offerings of their shares within a specified period of time, and to allocate specified percentages of their earnings and profits to R&D. Specific arrangements might be worked out with the firms to ensure that taxes on their earnings and profits are light in the early years of operations so that they can recover their investment in a relatively short period of time. This is important because most foreign firms are reluctant to make major investments unless their recovery period is quite brief. Such clear rules of the game could help satisfy the major parties concerned, and take the unnecessary guesswork out of activities that are risky enough under the best of circumstances.

A Regional Fomento Corporation

If a regional *fomento* corporation is set up, it could be expected to start with a few manageable activities and expand its program as it gains staff and experience. The following are the kinds of activities that ultimately might be appropriate for a well-established regional organization:

1. Publicizing opportunities for the establishment of industries on a regional basis — first to Latin American investors, and afterwards to outside capital;

2. Helping to organize Latin American multinational corporations to exploit opportunities involving unusually large economies of scale and requiring unusually large capital resources;

3. Strengthening national *fomento* organizations and helping establish new ones when needed;

4. Providing various types of financial aid to proposed regionwide industries when their feasibility, as well as their need for financial assistance, has been established. The *fomento* organization should not only be in a position to make loans, but also to acquire equity holdings in new firms;

5. Providing regional firms with technical assistance ranging from help in organization (including help in design of plant and product and in management arrangements) to assistance in marketing and transportation of products;

6. Promoting, where appropriate, uniform, high-level industrial and agricultural standards for export products;

7. Encouraging the study of the natural resources of Latin America to build a firmer base for industrial and agricultural development;

8. Encouraging national industrial programming on an increasingly uniform basis so that region-wide industrial programming becomes possible;

9. Promoting Latin American tourism, through means such as the development of low-cost systems of travel to and from Latin America and within the region, including "packaged" trips, encouragement of hotel and related construction, encouragement of high standards in the

maintenance of features of the national heritage which have cultural, historical, artistic, or natural value;

10. Assisting LAFTA, or its successor, to promote trade among the Latin American countries;

11. Encouraging, most of all, national interest and activities within these major categories, because the regional effort can flourish only to the extent that it encourages national expansionary efforts and sound national developmental policy.

Various groups and organizations already have responsibilities for some of the regional activities outlined above. The reason for suggesting a new regional organization with such a full range of interrelated activities is that it might well achieve on a regional basis the kind of success that *fomento* agencies with a very broad mandate have had in Mexico, Venezuela, and Puerto Rico.

The U.S. and international lending agencies can make a major contribution to the establishment of a common market by the declaration of willingness to provide an initial fund, of fairly substantial proportions, to promote the activities of a regional *fomento* organization. Such a fund should be administered by the Inter-American Development Bank, which is well suited to become a bank for Latin American integration. The Bank, working closely with LAFTA, would be in a position to establish a regional *fomento* agency to carry out the various types of activities described above as appropriate for such an agency. The Inter-American Development Bank has built up enough trust among Latin Americans that its management of a *fomento* fund is likely to be fully accepted. Of course, it is to be expected that the establishment of the *fomento* organization would be undertaken by the Bank only if it receives full support from the political leaders of Latin America.

In summary, a dynamic regional *fomento* organization, having available detailed information on industry prospects, armed with the capacity to channel bank funds and to attract capital from both Latin America and overseas, backed by the possibility of applying Alliance funds to overcome bottlenecks and to help finance regional infrastructure projects, could set the stage for a rapid increase in investment in existing and new industries and linked industrial complexes. It could be expected to promote tariff cuts on the products of such "promoted" industries. This, in turn, could provide the platform for agreements on scheduled across-the-board tariff cuts and removal of other restrictions on trade, as well as the harmonization of economic and financial policy.

It should also make evident that a region-wide planning framework is needed to help the individual countries to program their development, in keeping with the requirements of an evolving regional economic integration.[7]

At every stage, difficulties and problems are certain to arise, but once it is apparent that genuine regional economic integration is under way, practical solutions will surely be forthcoming. The problem now is to demonstrate the reality of the potential advantages.

[7] On this point, see Harvey S. Perloff and Raúl Saez, "National Planning and Multi-National Planning, under the Alliance for Progress," *Organization, Planning and Programming for Economic Development*, vol. 8 of *Science, Technology and Development — United States Papers Prepared for the United Nations Conference on the Application of Science and Technology for the Benefit of the Less Developed Areas* (Washington: U.S. Government Printing Office, 1962), pp. 47–54.

Chapter 11

STRENGTHENING MULTILATERALISM
AND FOREIGN ASSISTANCE

IN earlier chapters an attempt has been made to demonstrate that the concepts and mechanisms for assistance to the Latin American nations need a major overhaul. The purpose of this chapter is to suggest ways such reshaping might be accomplished.

The major international and U.S. assistance agencies have developed considerable sophistication in project analysis and in design and implementation techniques. They have made available to Latin America an impressive array of technical assistance and substantial financial resources. For the most part, the various agencies appear to be making valuable and often brilliantly conceived contributions through their separate project and program activities. However, their separate efforts have not been integrated into the coherent whole that the complex and multifaceted Alliance objectives require. Various crucial priority objectives and activities are essentially unattended.

The international reviewing and coordinating mechanisms, as organized, had neither the stature nor the control over resources to enable them to be an effective force in shaping the lending policies of the stronger international lending agencies. The United States had large technical staffs and in-country missions and had no need to rely upon the coordinating groups. And, finally, while recognizing the symbolic importance of multilateral Alliance agencies such as CIAP, the United States and many of the Latin American countries have preferred a bilateral approach in matters of major economic consequence.

One of the problems on the United States side is that the AID program, as an integral instrument of U.S. policy, is subject to the varied pressures and vagaries growing out of the complex U.S. policy interests in the hemisphere. AID is always susceptible to being used for advancing U.S. interests other than the development of its client countries. One such instance was the virtual elimination of assistance to Peru for several years in an attempt to use this as a lever in resolving a controversy between the Government of Peru and a U.S. petroleum company; another was the hurried loan to the Frondizi Government in

Argentina in a vain effort to keep it in power. Even where restraint and caution are used to prevent such perversions of the AID program, Latin American countries are suspicious of the motives behind U.S. assistance.

The problems on the multilateral side are equally serious. While Alliance founders recognized the symbolic and political significance of the partnership concept, and the need for multilateral mechanisms, the specific content of the multilateral concept was left quite vague.

One of the highest priority tasks before the Alliance is to untangle symbolism from function in multilateral matters, and to proceed with a careful assessment of the functions that can be best met by following the multilateral route. The assignment of functions, and the consequent design of institutional structures and roles, must carefully correspond to the political realities. Multilateralism can succeed only where the participating countries believe a particular multilateral approach will serve specific national or organizational interests. In the case of the United States, Congressional insistence on exercising control over appropriated funds and the vital importance of hemispheric development to U.S. national interests make it unlikely that the United States will delegate complete control of its aid funds to a non-U.S. agency. At the same time, however, to the extent that confidence in a multilateral effort is strengthened, this restraint will diminish. U.S. support of multilateral efforts is likely in cases where bilateral assistance appears to be far less effective for achieving specific U.S. development objectives in Latin America, or where a multilateral approach is the only feasible approach to these objectives, for example, in the case of political and most social development.

Some Suggestions for Changes in U.S. Mechanisms

Apart from the funds that it may make available, the United States possesses an immense reservoir of talent, skills, and administrative capabilities that the Latin American countries will need to draw on for some time to come. There is real question, however, whether AID, operating as a government agency, enjoys the flexibility, or status, to recruit and retain the high-caliber talent required for foreign technical assistance and research. This is not to say that the caliber of AID personnel is not high, nor that the AID technicians are not competent. However, there is a very rapid turnover of people, and the agency finds it increasingly difficult to compete with private industry and universities for skilled personnel, and no doubt the difficulty will increase.

Among the first organizational changes that should be considered is the separation of the AID agency from the Department of State and its establishment as a separate entity.[1] With this step, great effort must be made to provide AID funding on a multi-year basis. This will be difficult, of course, because Congress is extremely jealous of its prerogatives to review and control programs through the annual appropriation process. But if a separate organization, with clearly defined long-term purposes and goals, appeared to offer the most effective means of serving foreign policy objectives, it might be possible to win Congressional support for a more stable financing arrangement.[2]

Another innovation would be to establish a publicly funded Development Foundation, which would (1) study the technical needs of the Latin American countries and availability of expertise, (2) carry out applied research on developmental strategy, and (3) serve as a broker between universities and other sources of technical and intellectual talent and the Latin American countries. Unlike AID, the foundation would not be essentially operational. It would straddle the empty middle ground that now separates the universities and the U.S. research community from AID and the assistance agencies.

While it is probably easiest to see a foundation of this description as a U.S. public corporation, there would be much merit in establishing it as a multilateral agency, servicing the entire foreign-assistance community.

Suggestions for Change in Multilateral Arrangements

If multilateralization is to succeed, new institutions will be needed. Two such institutions would be particularly important to multilateralization of the Alliance, one to bring coherence to the decisions and activities of the donor agencies and the other, at last, to provide a powerful "executive" arm for the Alliance.

[1] Adolph Berle had proposed "upgrading" the Latin American effort within the Department of State before the Alliance was organized. A similar proposal — the establishment of an Under Secretary post for Latin American affairs within the State Department — was made in 1964 by the then Senator Hubert H. Humphrey, "U.S. Policy in Latin America," *Foreign Affairs* (July 1964), p. 587. The present proposal goes further.

[2] Also, there would be difficult legal and policy issues, but these do not appear to be insurmountable. There are such issues, for example, as the relationship of country ambassadors to the assistance missions. In this case, to the extent that AID came to be identified in Latin America as part of a larger multilateral effort, and an instrument somewhat apart from the overall prosecution of U.S. strategic and diplomatic policies, many of the political sensitivities in assistance operations which normally

A COUNCIL FOR LATIN AMERICA

A mechanism for achieving the coherence the Alliance now lacks can be created without serious disruption of present mechanisms. What is suggested here is the creation of a Council, comprised of high-level representatives of the major Washington-based assistance institutions, with effective staff support. One purpose of the Council would be to assure that the diverse "inputs" of various agencies are consistent with well-planned, long-term national and multinational assistance strategies. A second would be to assure that key priorities are identified, both in national and regional activities, and that the international agency response is appropriate.

In broad outline, what is required is a firm undertaking by the Washington-based international agencies to work out clear agreements on the diagnosis of country and regional problems — normally following the lead of national and regional planning and development agencies, as well as of CIAP — and decide on the types of lending arrangements that they are prepared to undertake consistent with the overall strategy emerging from this diagnosis. The technical base for the preparation of this strategy need not require a large new staff but can be built on existing agency staff.

The creation of the proposed Council would provide a good opportunity for upgrading CIAP. CIAP's review and evaluation of country situations could take on operational importance, serving both as a basis for the preparation of overall strategy guidelines by the lending agencies and for noting results obtained from the implementation of the guidelines. CIAP would then be in a key transmission-line position, able to keep the lending agencies informed of region-wide and individual country viewpoints, and to keep the recipient countries informed of those of the agencies. The impact of the latter could be substantial. It is unlikely that the aid-recipient countries could afford for long to deprecate the CIAP role, if it were in the position of mediating between them and the agencies. The political advantages to the United States and to the international agencies of a buffer between them and the aid-recipient countries cannot be overestimated.

If CIAP is to do this, it will need considerable staff and organiza-

---

preoccupy ambassadors in the recipient countries would eventually be reduced. If this were the case, aid operations would pose fewer reasons for ambassadorial concern, and the need for day-to-day ambassadorial direction of the aid program as part of the U.S. policy apparatus would be correspondingly reduced.

tional strength. Perhaps at the outset, in order that interagency confidence in CIAP is assured, the international agencies themselves might temporarily make staff available to it.

The Council also would serve as a focal point for assuring that international efforts are undertaken, and for recommending action to the assistance institutions. For example, were the Council to adopt a proposal for intensive work on region-wide transportation and communications planning, it might suggest that responsibility for these efforts be lodged in the World Bank which has already developed a substantial capability in these fields. The Council might subsequently recommend that financial support be provided by AID, the World Bank, IDB, or other sources, as appropriate. The Council might take the lead for the international agencies in encouraging and mobilizing lending agency support for such multilateral regional undertakings as the Andean or Plate River groupings. Of course, the participating countries must themselves work out the difficult political accommodations and the structure of these agreements. Yet, there will be technical assistance and major financing roles for the international agencies which the Council can coordinate.

The Human Resources Commission. As suggested earlier, the purpose of the Human Resources Commission would be to assure that far greater, concerted Alliance effort is given to the role of people in development. This commission should be within the interagency Council for Latin America and perhaps its director should be a permanent member of that Council because of the importance and complexity of this undertaking. (Other considerations suggest that the commission should also be associated with the existing OAS Cultural Council.)

Probably the most urgent task to be performed by this proposed Human Resources Commission will be the elaboration of country analyses and strategies for human resources development. Again, great care will have to be given to the selection of staff, and the shaping of this particularly important entity. Because of acute national sensitivity to foreign participation in this sector, multinational rather than bilateral activities appear to be most appropriate. What is suggested here is a mechanism whose primary function would be to assure that the human resource priority needs are given concentrated and concerted attention by international agencies and recipient countries. A commission of this sort need not be institutionally elaborate, but rather might be structured as a small, joint Latin American and interagency unit (IDB, AID, IBRD, CIAP).

AN INTER-AMERICAN DEVELOPMENT ORGANIZATION

One of the most attractive possibilities for the future would be an Inter-American Development Organization, centering on the Inter-American Development Bank. Such a move would provide the occasion for a reorganization of the whole donor approach to Latin American development, moving from banking to a broader concept of external assistance.

Such an Inter-American Development Organization should have a governing board with broad developmental interests and knowledge extending beyond international banking. Its component units might be:

1. The existing IDB, strengthened as a lending agency with adequate funds and an increase in top-level personnel.

2. A regional *Fomento* Corporation, such as suggested in the preceding chapter, to help promote common-market industries and region-wide productive activities in general.

3. A Social Progress Trust Fund to focus on the critically important objectives of agrarian reform and urban infrastructure for low-income groups, assisted by U.S. AID and other agencies.

4. A "Social Foundation" for making grants and soft loans (at zero or low interest rates) to help promote the "rationalization" of the Alliance through improved information, research, and planning, as well as the intellectual and social development of the region in cooperation with the various OAS bodies. Such a foundation might absorb the present Fund for Special Operations which is geared in large part to helping finance so-called social projects. A flexible, essentially non-banking agency of this type would be in a position to work closely with the proposed Human Resources Commission to help finance, through soft loans and grants, activities designed to improve the human resources situation. The foundation would also manage the proposed Social Progress Trust Fund.

Such an Inter-American Development Organization would be in a good position to serve as the major operational arm of the proposed Council for Latin America. The relationship would combine policy coherence with much greater capability than currently exists to carry out the high-priority measures identified in previous chapters as critical to the future success of the Alliance.

A variety of alternative ways could be used to try to achieve the objectives which have motivated the organizational proposals above. As

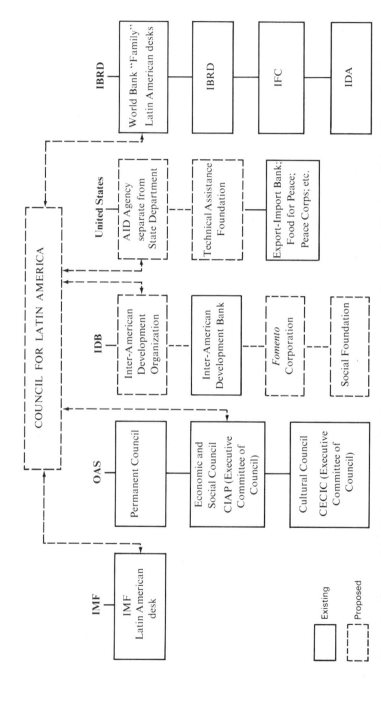

Figure 2. *Suggested institutions and coordinating arrangements to advance the objectives of the Alliance for Progress.*

outlined here, proposals are set down mainly to give some content to the broad purposes considered to be critical for the success of the Alliance. Since a relatively large number of existing as well as proposed institutions have been referred to, the key agencies are set down in Figure 2 to help clarify the presentation. In the case of the organizations with worldwide responsibilities, representation, it is assumed, would be through the Latin American "desks" of the agencies. The placing of the proposed Council for Latin America at the head of all the agencies is not meant to suggest direction from a central body, but rather a "federated" coordination of agency activities touching directly on Alliance objectives and activities. What the chart cannot do, considering the number of agencies involved, is give the sense of what is behind the proposals set down here: to bring greater coherence to the inherently variable and complex operations involved in the Alliance for Progress.

Increasing Financial Assistance to Latin America

Few of the steps suggested here as necessary to make the Alliance for Progress a thoroughgoing success can be carried out unless financial assistance to Latin America can be substantially increased.

During the first eight years of the Alliance, as we have seen, total new aid commitments, from the United States, Europe, and the international lending agencies, have averaged about $1.75 billion a year. Disbursements of long-term aid have increased over time and are now running at an average of $1.2–$1.4 billion. With a large reverse flow, however, due to repayment of debt, actual net official transfers to Latin America are about $1 billion a year.

Projections for the future (by Hollis Chenery and by the staff of CIAP), while admittedly based on some arbitrary assumptions and involving many uncertainties, suggest that in the early 1970's, Latin America as a whole will need some $2.5 billion in net official financial transfers (compared with the present $1 billion) to meet the 2.5 per cent growth target and close to $3 billion to meet the hoped-for 3 per cent per capita increase in GNP.

Amounts such as these, no matter how carefully developed the projections may be, have an unreal air about them in the face of the increasingly negative reaction of the U.S. Congress to foreign aid bills. The 90th Congress in 1968 cut the President's relatively modest request of $627 million for the Alliance to $336.5 million.

Diminution of official U.S. assistance has coincided with a tightening of the international money market, making it difficult for the under-developed countries to get either directly or through the multilateral financial institutions the required resources under interest and repayment terms that would not overburden their future foreign exchange availabilities and put them on a debt treadmill.

Because of the extreme difficulties associated with traditional approaches to foreign aid, some new solutions are badly needed. An approach that deserves the most careful consideration is the use of a major part of U.S. aid funds to *subsidize* interest rates paid by Latin American borrowers, rather than in the form of direct lending by U.S. AID, thus providing a powerful multiplier for whatever financial assistance can be made available. This would amount to a testing within the Western Hemisphere of the proposal submitted to the 1964 United Nations Conference on Trade and Development by D. Horowitz, Governor of the Bank of Israel. His proposal was for a subsidy by all the richer countries of the world to the World Bank's soft-loan agency, the International Development Association (IDA). Under this scheme, the IDA, the World Bank, or some other international institution would borrow on commercial terms from private investors (with the private market operations facilitated by a special system of government guarantees); the IDA would lend on extremely soft terms (1 per cent interest); and the difference between the market cost of borrowing and the IDA charges would be met out of an "interest equalization fund" maintained through annual appropriations by the industrialized countries.

This proposal has been thoroughly analyzed by the staff of the World Bank.[3] Possible difficulties have been noted, most of them centering on the problems of getting the appropriate backing from a substantial number of industrialized countries and of borrowing on a relatively large scale for purposes of IDA lending in the commercial markets. The scheme, however, seems ideally suited for management under Alliance for Progress auspices; it would make very good sense to apply it first on a limited scale both to help overcome some of the Alliance's financial problems and to test its feasibility for possible extension on a worldwide basis.

The advantages of using this plan for Alliance financing are that it would provide a way to increase the total amount of development loans and grants available to Latin America without increasing sub-

[3] International Bank for Reconstruction and Development, *The Horowitz Proposal*, A Staff Report, February 1965.

stantially the U.S. budgetary allocations for that purpose, and at the same time it would enlarge the scope for multilateral operations. Its application might take the following form:

1. Funds appropriated for U.S. development assistance to Latin American countries would, in the main, be used to increase the U.S. contribution to the Inter-American Development Bank. Direct assistance by U.S. AID would be limited to program and sector lending to a limited number of countries according to U.S. political and strategic considerations.

2. The IDB would extend its operations to cover program and sector loans as well as project loans, making hard loans at, say, a 4 per cent interest rate and soft loans at rates varying between zero and 1 per cent.

3. IDB would borrow within the U.S. commercial market up to a prearranged limit at commercial interest rates with a U.S. government guarantee.

4. The U.S. contribution to the Alliance for Progress would be used by IDB to subsidize loans to the Latin American countries, covering the difference between the commercial rate and the 4 per cent rate in the case of hard loans or the 0–1 per cent rate in the case of soft loans.

5. The annual requirements of IDB and its related institutions would be determined on the basis of the CIAP annual country reviews. CIAP, U.S. AID, and IDB (or the representatives of the Council for Latin America, if such a council were established) would agree on a system of priorities for the IDB lending program, as well as on various classes of loans with repayment terms and interest rates compatible with the developmental and balance-of-payments situation of the potential borrowers. The Council for Latin America would organize financial consultative groups (for each country so desiring) to extend the assistance operations to include not only the World Bank and IMF, but also the European countries, Canada, and Japan. IDB would become the "lender of last resort." The amount it would lend to each country would be determined by the needs, priorities, and performance of the country, as evaluated in CIAP's country reviews, and by the funds made available by other institutions and governments, the "residual" being covered by IDB funds to the extent possible.

The multiplier effect of employing aid funds as an interest subsidy, as against direct use, is substantial. For example, assuming: (a) IDB would raise money in the private capital market at 6.5 per cent, and IDB's service charge would amount to 1 per cent, so that IDB would make loans to Latin American countries at about 7.5 per cent (actually, just about the rate charged by IDB under its Fund for Ordinary Operations at the end of 1967), and (b) the desired lending terms for those operations would be 4 per cent (with a five-year grace period and twenty-five-year amortization), then a "subsidy" of $150 million would permit IDB to make loans of $500 million at the indicated 4 per cent.[4] Other examples under the same assumptions are as follows:

Total loans	Required subsidy
$ 333 million	$100 million
500 million	150 million
1,000 million	300 million
2,000 million	600 million

Clearly, funds used for subsidy purposes can be stretched a long way.

This proposal not only has the merit of removing much of the U.S. aid program in Latin America from the pressures of day-to-day political considerations, but of strengthening and vitalizing the multilateralization of the Alliance for Progress. At the same time, the legitimate and more permanent interests of the United States could be adequately protected by a vigilant and vigorous participation of the U.S. delegations in the IDB, in CIAP, and in other OAS bodies. Above all, given the critical importance of adequate funds to carry out the ambitious objectives of the Alliance for Progress, the proposed method would open the door for mobilization of the required amounts of external resources without creating a large burden on the U.S. budget.

The AID function would be less burdened by day-to-day administrative operations and could concentrate on the more important policy issues. Small field staffs in each country, together with headquarters technicians, would be able to provide the information needed for effective U.S. participation in the Alliance, and to implement U.S. program and sector loans as well as technical assistance operations.

A Final Note. The basic concepts of the Alliance for Progress — coupling self-help and reform with external assistance, and encouraging

---

[4] The amount of the subsidy in this example has been calculated as the difference between the total amounts of the loans ($500 million) and the present value, at the moment the loans are authorized, of the future flows of amortization and interest payments discounted at the market interest rate, including commission charges (7.5 per cent).

regional arrangements that can help overcome national limitations in the process of rapid development — are both sound and imaginative. Substantial experience has now been gained in efforts to implement these concepts, and, in the process, many weaknesses have become evident, and exciting potentialities for the future have presented themselves. A major restructuring of the Alliance is thus in order. New ways must be found to move this great social invention in the making to a higher plane of excellence and effectiveness. This book has sought to provide some guidelines for the search.

DEVELOPMENT OF THE ALLIANCE
FOR PROGRESS: A CHRONOLOGY

1958
April: Tour of South America by Vice President Richard Nixon that resulted in U.S. review of Latin American policy.

June: Central American Common Market Treaty signed.

August: Brazilian *aide-mémoire* sent to all OAS members outlining President Kubitschek's Operation Panamerica: a proposed multilateral program to stimulate Latin American economic development.

               Under Secretary of State Douglas Dillon announces U.S. support for an Inter-American Bank, reversing long-held U.S. policy.

September: Informal meeting of Foreign Ministers in Washington that established a "Committee of Twenty-one" that was to discuss the Kubitschek recommendations of economic cooperation.

1959
January: Fidel Castro assumes power in Cuba after flight of Fulgencio Batista.

April: Meeting of Committee of Twenty-one, during which the United States expressed support for a Latin American common market and a willingness to discuss commodity problems; provision is drafted for an Inter-American Development Bank, to be established December 30, 1959.

1960
February: Montevideo Treaty signed by seven South American nations creating the Latin American Free Trade Association.

               A new agency of the World Bank, the International Development Association (IDA), created to extend "soft" loans.

July: President Eisenhower's Newport Statement announcing U.S. support for Latin American social reform measures.

September: Act of Bogotá signed, calling for social reforms and social development of Latin America; United States promises to provide a special fund for these purposes.

October: John F. Kennedy, in campaign speech at Tampa, Florida, asks for an "alliance for progress" to help development of Latin America.

1961
January: Report of Task Force, chaired by Adolph Berle, urging need for a joint economic-social-military approach to Latin America, and aid on the basis of a long-range economic plan for the whole hemisphere.

March: President Kennedy, in speech to Latin American ambassadors, outlines proposal for an Alliance for Progress.

April: Abortive invasion attempt of U.S.-supported Cuban exiles at the Bay of Pigs, Cuba.

May: U.S. Senate passes by voice vote $500 million for aid to Latin American countries, but Senate leaders warn implementation can only follow Latin American reforms.

June: Signing of agreement making the Inter-American Development Bank administrator of a Social Progress Trust Fund of $394 million to contribute to social development and institutional progress of Latin America.

August: Signing by OAS members (except Cuba) of Punta del Este Declaration and Charter outlining Alliance program.

                Resignation of President Quadros initiating a three-year long political crisis in Brazil.

November: Teodoro Moscoso appointed Assistant Administrator for Latin America of AID and U.S. Coordinator of the Alliance for Progress.

                IA-ECOSOC reformed and upgraded by OAS Council.

                IA-ECOSOC establishes panel of experts (later Committee of Nine) to review long-term plans for Latin American economic development and reform.

1962
January: Cuba placed outside the inter-American system by vote of Foreign Ministers at Punta del Este meeting.

July: Military coup in Peru; the United States suspends diplomatic relations and economic assistance.

November: Alberto Lleras Camargo, ex-President of Colombia, and Juscelino Kubitschek, ex-President of Brazil, chosen by OAS to review Alliance and to suggest reorganization.

1963
June: Lleras and Kubitschek submit reports on the Alliance; both propose a new multilateral and independent agency to manage Alliance activities and allocation of funds.

Senator Wayne Morse, chairman of the subcommittee on Latin American affairs, criticizes Kennedy Administration's failure to require reforms before funding projects.

July: Military coup in Ecuador; relations resumed by the United States three weeks later.

Founding of the Association for Economic Development of Latin America (ADELA) composed of private corporations in Europe, Japan, and the U.S. to encourage business investment in Latin America.

September: Military coup in the Dominican Republic: U.S. relations and aid suspended.

November: Second IA-ECOSOC meeting approves suggestion of two Presidents and creates Inter-American Committee for the Alliance for Progress (CIAP).

Hickenlooper Amendment, attached to foreign aid bill, providing for suspension of U.S. aid in countries where government abrogates contracts with U.S. nationals.

President Kennedy assassinated and President Johnson takes office.

December: Dominican government reorganized and aid resumed (in January).

U.S. Alliance administration reorganized with Assistant Secretary of State Thomas Mann made coordinator of all activities relating to Latin America.

1964
March: CIAP members installed with Carlos Sanz de Santamaría, Colombia's former finance minister, as chairman.

April: "Revolution" in Brazil sweeping out Goulart government and installing military government.

July: CIAP begins to review each country's development achievements and programs annually.

Venezuelan charges of Cuban aggression and OAS Foreign Ministers vote to break all diplomatic and trade ties with Castro regime.

November: Announcement of U.S. cooperation with Latin America on birth control programs.

1965
March: U.S. Congress passes Latin American aid bill with amendment prohibiting loans to countries that expropriate U.S. property without compensation.

May: Dominican revolution and subsequent U.S. action initiate far-ranging debate on need for changes in OAS Charter.

August: First inter-American conference on birth control held in Cali, Colombia. Latin American church hierarchy refrains from comment.

November: President Johnson pledges U.S. aid to Alliance will go beyond 1971 terminal date.

Spain pledges $1 billion to Latin America over decade (mostly producers' credits) but will not place funds within Alliance framework.

1966
January: Havana Tri-Continental Conference resolutions calling for increased revolutionary activity in Latin America.

March: The United States at Panama Meeting refuses to sign draft revision of OAS Charter guaranteeing long-term aid to Latin America.

IA-ECOSOC, at meeting in Buenos Aires, changes structure, functions, and size of the panel of experts and its relations with CIAP; Committee of Nine to be replaced by Committee of Five under CIAP auspices.

April: Chilean Congress passes legislation allowing government to purchase interest in foreign-owned copper mines.

Fulbright amendment to Foreign Aid Bill gives CIAP veto power over Alliance loans.

May: Collective resignation of Committee of Nine members.

June: At IA-ECOSOC meeting in Washington, Latin American countries drop demand for U.S. pledges of aid embedded in OAS Charter.

August: "Little Summit" meeting to discuss subregional integration by Presidents of Colombia, Venezuela, Chile; initiation of efforts to develop Andean subregional grouping including Ecuador and Peru.

1967
February: Reorganization of OAS structure through a protocol to the OAS Charter, with CIAP made permanent executive committee of upgraded Inter-American Economic and Social Council.

Trinidad-Tobago becomes a member of the OAS.

April: Meeting of Presidents with agreement to establish a complete common market in Latin America by 1985.

June: Colombia, Ecuador, Chile, Peru, and Venezuela agree to establish a subregional common market for the five countries.

September: First full-dress conference on population policies in Latin America held in Caracas, Venezuela.

October: Barbados joins the OAS.

1968
February: Creation of Andean Development Corporation by Bolivia, Chile, Ecuador, Peru, and Venezuela to promote subregional development.

Meeting of Inter-American Cultural Council at Maracay, Venezuela, establishes a special development fund ($25 million) to finance multinational projects in fields of education and science and technology, and an executive committee (parallel to CIAP) to direct programs of the Cultural Council.

March: United Nations Conference on Trade and Development ends without concrete results.

April: Population Reference Bureau reports that Latin American population growth reached an all-time high of 3 per cent per year in 1967, and is still on the rise.

May: Galo Plaza inaugurated as Secretary General of OAS.

July: President Johnson meets with Central American Presidents to discuss problems and future of the Central American Common Market.

October: U.S. Congress passes Appropriations Bill cutting assistance to the Alliance from a recommended $627 million to $336.5 million. Military juntas overthrow the governments of Peru and Panama.

1969
January: President Richard Nixon takes office.

TWO CASE STUDIES: COLOMBIA AND CHILE

THE effectiveness of the present mix of national effort and international cooperation in Latin America can be seen most sharply in the context of specific national situations. The cases of Colombia and Chile illustrate the kinds of problems the Alliance has to face. Colombia and Chile are no more "representative" than any other pair of countries, but they are interesting and important countries and the Alliance has been deeply involved with them from the very beginning. They have received more and broader types of assistance than any other Latin American country except Brazil, and in this sense, at least, provide a fairer test of the aid approach than would countries that have had only limited contact with the kind of effort envisaged in the Alliance for Progress.

Some understanding of the problems of these countries and of the way in which the Alliance for Progress fits in can be obtained from their development plans and programs and from the evaluation studies of the Committee of Nine and CIAP, which analyze these plans and the situations behind them. The evaluation studies are particularly useful for our purposes because they look at the plans and the national problems specifically in terms of the Alliance objectives as well as of the national goals.

Colombia

Colombia, at the northwestern tip of South America with a population of some 19 million (1967), is a middle-sized country in Latin American terms, standing between giant Brazil, with its 86 million people, at one extreme, and small countries like Nicaragua, Panama, and Costa Rica, with populations under 2 million, at the other.

It has been said of Colombia that geography has been both kind and cruel to her. Because of topography there are a variety of climatic zones, which permits broad diversity in agricultural products, ranging from bananas and sugar to wheat and potatoes. But the mountainous terrain makes transportation difficult and expensive, and limits internal communication. The country is crisscrossed by three Andes ranges that separate the country into regions quite different from each other. The capitals of the major regions — Bogotá, Medellín, Cartagena, Barranquilla, and Cali — have been continuously in competition for position. All this has been favorable to decentralized development.

The Colombian social structure is hierarchical, keeping to a remarkable degree the colonial customs of the Spanish upper classes. While there has been a tendency towards racial blending, leadership still is held by descendants of Europeans. There are extremes of wealth and poverty, although probably no more than in most other Latin American countries. There are millions of individuals scratching out a miserable living in the countryside. Their counter-

212

parts in the cities, many in the so-called marginal population, reside in vast slums at the edges of the cities, with little work or income-producing opportunity. The annual per capita income is less than $300. As elsewhere in Latin America, there are significant political and social forces for modernization and powerful pressures for changes, but these tend to be overbalanced by a pervasive national conservatism, which finds its most distinct expression in the ruling classes.

Since the late 1930's Colombia has been a violent and troubled land. The remorseless and destructive conflict in the countryside has its root in the old hatreds and jealousies between Colombia's two traditional parties, Liberals and Conservatives. The assassination of a Liberal leader on April 9, 1948, was blamed on the Conservatives, and the killing led to civil war. Thousands died in the rioting that swept the capital. In the countryside, guerilla bands were organized, and year after year the slaughter went on. In some instances, entire villages were wiped out.

By 1957, the nation was exhausted and weary of bloodshed. It was also disenchanted with the repressive dictatorship of General Gustavo Rojas Pinilla, who had come to power four years earlier on the promise of restoring order and stability. The Liberals and Conservatives joined forces in his overthrow and agreed to form a coalition to last sixteen years. This delicate political truce has provided the ground rules for national politics since. According to this armistice agreement, the parties would alternate the presidency and divide evenly all government offices down to the level of municipal councils. The arrangement, unwieldy as it was, at least helped to reduce the mass slaughter. However, by 1957 social unrest and violence had become so ingrained that lawlessness continued to dominate some of the rural areas. Following energetic efforts by the army to suppress the outlaws, the violence was largely brought under control within a decade. There still exists a small rural guerrilla movement, seemingly supported by Castroite and other Left groups.

In 1958, Alberto Lleras Camargo became the first president under the Liberal-Conservative coalition arrangement. Lleras, a capable and farsighted statesman, had been not only an outstanding leader in his own country but one of the moving spirits of the inter-American system. He had served as the Secretary General of the Organization of American States and, long before the initiation of the Alliance for Progress, had strongly urged the United States to support Latin American economic and social development. When President Kennedy held out an offer of U.S. aid, he was one of the few leaders of international reputation in Latin America who openly embraced the Alliance and spoke warmly of its great potential.

Devoted to the economic development of his own country, and convinced of the need for the government to take a positive and carefully planned role in such development, Lleras had invited experts from the United Nations Economic Commission for Latin America to help establish a planning office in Colombia and to prepare a national economic plan. As a result, shortly after the Charter of Punta del Este was agreed to, Colombia was able to present a ten-year development plan to the Committee of Nine for evaluation. It was the first such plan to be submitted. Called the *Plan General de Desarrollo Económico y Social*, it was a giant document of some 830 pages. It reviewed in detail Colombian economic experience during the previous decade, underlined the economic problems that had to be overcome, pinpointed goals and targets for development, and outlined a ten-year investment program. A more detailed four-year investment program was also included for the period from 1962 to 1965, based on a "rollover," four-year planning system.

In keeping with the arrangements established under the Charter of Punta del Este, an Ad Hoc Committee on Colombia was organized by the end of March 1962. The Committee presented a report with its recommendations to the government of Colombia in July of that year, and this report was then made available to the U.S. Agency for International Development and international financial agencies.[1] The report reviewed the strengths and weaknesses of the plan and suggested improvements. The report also said that Colombia had met the Alliance requirements, and urged the provision of a substantial amount of external assistance. Consistent with the plan, the report recommended a total of external financing of some $200 million annually over the four-year period of the detailed program. This amounted to roughly 15 per cent of the projected new investment for each year of the period.[2]

A major plan goal was achievement of an average annual rate of growth in the gross domestic product of 5.6 per cent over the period from 1960 to 1970. During the first five years of the 1950's, largely because of good coffee prices, the gross domestic product had grown annually at the rate of 5.3 per cent; during the second half the rate of growth slowed. This reversal reflected unfavorable developments in the coffee market as well as unsound fiscal and economic policies. The cumulative annual rate of growth was 4.3 per cent for the decade as a whole, but by 1960 was only 4.1 per cent. It was evident that a concerted effort would be required to achieve the plan growth target, and that a number of extremely difficult problems would have to be overcome. Of these, the coffee issue was central.

COFFEE: A MIXED BLESSING

Colombia is second only to Brazil as a world coffee producer, and receives the major portion of its export earnings from coffee. At their peak in 1954, coffee exports amounted to 82 per cent of the total export earnings; in 1960 they amounted to 66.5 per cent.

Actually, Colombia is capable of producing a wide variety of agricultural products, but it has not exploited the opportunities for diversification. Coffee production dominates the economy and, to some extent, the politics of the country. Coffee does have certain advantages: it can be grown on hillsides that are often not useful for other crops, and it generally provides a higher average income to farmers than any other major crop. However, coffee trees take a long time to mature. Everyone plants when prices are high. Five years later, when the trees begin to bear commercial quantities, the world has too much coffee. Prices drop, growers are discouraged, and few trees are planted. Seven to ten years later the twelve-to-fifteen-year-old trees reach their commercial peak, and before long there will again be a shortage.

---

[1] The Committee was made up of four experts from Latin America, including one from Colombia itself, a French economist who had played a large role in development of the European Common Market, and the author, who was serving as the U.S. representative on the Committee of Nine.

[2] Actually, shortly after the development program was launched, the turn of events and the pace of implementation made it evident that Colombia would not be able to meet its plan targets and in the years that followed continual revisions were made in all the estimates.

During World War II, the Latin American coffee producers lost a sizable market in Europe, and the United States established price controls and set country quotas on its imports, including coffee.[3] Production fell to low levels. After the war, prices rose from the war-controlled 13.6 cents a pound to more than 27 cents in 1948. Demand from the partially recovered European market began to be felt. While new plantings were encouraged, demand outstripped supply. The average price of Manizales coffee rose sharply. In 1950 the price was 53 cents a pound; by July, 1954, with prices pushed along by speculation, it reached a peak of 88.3 cents a pound.

In response to the high prices, consumption in the United States fell from some 19 million bags in 1953–54 to less than 15 million in 1954–55. Prices fell, but not precipitously. Frosts in the coffee-producing countries delayed the day of reckoning. Meanwhile, new plantings were now bearing and world output of exportable coffee rose from 34.6 million bags in 1956 to 46.2 million bags in 1957, 51.3 million bags in 1958, and 58.6 million bags in 1959. Prices plunged. Average prices of Manizales fell from the peak of 88 cents a pound in 1954 to 52 cents in 1958, 45 cents in 1959 and 1960, 43.6 cents in 1961, to a trough of 39.5 cents in 1963.

It is easy to grasp what these erratic price movements meant for Colombia. In the middle 1950's Colombia earned an average of over $500 million yearly from coffee sales (a peak of $589 million in 1954), but, coffee exports earnings then declined to $363 million in 1959 and to $308 million in 1961. With non-coffee exports improving only slightly, total export earnings declined from some $705 million in 1954 to $474 million in 1959 and $434 million in 1961. The inevitable restrictions on imports that followed had an unfortunate impact on Colombia's economic development.[4]

Against this background, it is little wonder that coffee producers and the countries for whom coffee is of primary importance, including Colombia, pressed strenuously for an effective price stablization system that would include the consumer as well as the producer nations. The United States was at first resistant to such schemes, the obvious intent of which was to hold prices at abnormally high levels. But it soon became evident that the objectives of the Alliance could not be achieved for several countries unless something was done to preserve coffee export earnings. After protracted negotiations, an international coffee agreement was signed in 1962. It provided export quotas for each of the coffee-producing nations, with the understanding that governments would take measures to control coffee production.

While it was essential for Colombia's economy to put some sort of floor under export earnings, the limitations on coffee production and exports also meant that the major base of Colombia's economic growth and prosperity in the past had been undermined. In a real sense, the International Coffee Agreement signaled the end of an era and placed in sharp focus the economic problem facing Colombia.

---

[3] John P. Powelson records the ups and downs of coffee in recent decades in *Latin America: Today's Economic and Social Revolution* (New York: McGraw-Hill, 1964).

[4] As the report of the Ad Hoc Committee on Colombia pointed out, under the then existing circumstances, "For Colombia every cent of variation in the New York price of coffee means an increase or decrease of $7.5 million dollars in annual income. This is equal to 50 cents for every man, woman and child in the country."

THE SEARCH FOR NEW GROWTH ELEMENTS

It was evident that the economy had to find new growth engines. Fortunately, the country was in a relatively favorable position to achieve the economic diversification called for. Various studies had demonstrated that Colombia could increase output of cotton, sugar, bananas, oilseeds, and livestock. Cotton had already experienced sturdy growth. Conditions for developing the livestock industry were unusually favorable.

The ten-year plan set out specific production and export targets for each of the major crops. In addition, the plan targeted substantial increases in industrial production. The manufacturing industry, which in 1959 represented only 17.5 per cent of the gross domestic product, was to contribute over 20 per cent of the projected increase in GDP during the first part of the 1960's.

THE INVESTMENT PROGRAM

The public investment program was to total a little over a billion dollars over the four-year period, 1962–65, or roughly $250 million a year. Of the four-year total, some $485 million was to be directed at encouraging the expansion of directly productive investment, some $470 million into economic infrastructure, and some $235 million into social development.

With the assistance of the World Bank, Colombia made a significant beginning in the 1950's in extending its transportation and communication networks. During this period, some 30 per cent of total public investment was allocated to these fields. For the 1960's the plan envisioned eliminating the more serious development bottlenecks resulting from the deficient transportation system. The highways were to be greatly improved and extended, the railroad system expanded to interconnect key economic centers, and a much greater role given to river transportation.

The question of human resources development was not overlooked. According to the latest census, that of 1951, 42.5 per cent of Colombia's total population was illiterate. Only 13 out of every 100 pupils finished five grades of primary education and only 2 per cent of the population had completed high school. The plan outlined an ambitious program to construct 22,000 new elementary school classrooms by 1965, to train a corresponding number of teachers, and to give some additional training to many of the present teachers whose qualifications were deemed deficient.

OTHER ELEMENTS OF THE PLAN

An atmosphere for development was also to be created by pushing ahead with land and tax reform programs, and through a host of improvements in the organizational and administrative government. Specific targets were provided for land distribution and settlement and for increases in governmental revenues.

As Albert Hirschman points out,[5] land reform has been a long-standing issue in Colombia. Reforms had been unfolding at an extremely slow pace for at least thirty years. Even before the organization of the Alliance, Colombia passed an agrarian reform law and established an Agrarian Reform Institute

[5] *Journeys Toward Progress: Studies of Economic Policy-Making in Latin America* (New York: Twentieth Century Fund, 1963).

(INCORA) to carry out its provisions, following the ground broken by the earlier *Instituto de Colonización y Asentamento.*

Also, Colombia had developed a new tax program in 1960 aimed at increasing the yield of taxes and achieving a greater equity in tax incidence, mainly by increasing the importance of direct taxes and through new measures to tighten tax administration. (The tax effort — as measured by the ratio of governmental revenues to GDP — was one of the lowest in Latin America, and still is.)

FINANCING THE INVESTMENT PROGRAM

The Colombia plan gave estimates of government revenues and expenditures, and of the emerging balance-of-payments situation, and it was possible to arrive at a meaningful estimate of external financial needs. The case for external assistance rested on the fact that, even with a maximum effort to increase exports and internal savings, there would be a financing gap for essential sector investments which could only be filled by external assistance.

The plan projected external capital needs rising from some $200 million in 1962 to $300 million in 1965, with foreign credits for the public sector of roughly $150 million annually during this period.

EVALUATION OF THE PLAN

The Ad Hoc Committee made a generally favorable evaluation of the plan in spite of shortcomings in the government's proposals. Its report recommended Alliance for Progress financial assistance to help cover Colombia's external financing needs. A visit to the country by the Committee had convinced its members of the determination of the governmental leadership to press for the development program. Also business and labor leaders, in interviews, voiced general approval of the plan's strategy — even though they had not had any part in developing it — and seemed willing to cooperate with the government in carrying out the plan. An important element of uncertainty, however, was that the Administration that submitted the development plan was soon to go out of office.

Not unexpectedly, there were many weaknesses and uncertainties. For example, in few instances were plan objectives supported by detailed production and marketing studies to indicate real expansion possibilities. Also, while willingness to carry out the necessary measures seemed to permeate the governmental ministries, it was obvious that many were not equipped to implement concerted development programs. This was especially so in respect to agriculture, which was viewed as occupying a key role. Not only was planning for this sector quite sketchy, but the agriculture ministry was administratively and technically ill-equipped to carry out ambitious programs. Furthermore, as is so often the case in underdeveloped countries, there were few "bankable" projects ready to be submitted for external financing.

Some other public sector programs were on relatively firm ground. This was particularly true in the case of transportation and electric power. In these areas, the World Bank over a long period of time had sponsored detailed studies and had provided a series of loans, so that these sectors seemed to be moving ahead in an orderly way.

In sectors that had not received this type of assistance, the situation was quite different, particularly in the field of education. Here, projected programs had serious shortcomings. While the plan proposed a relatively well-conceived primary school program, it made very little reference to secondary, university, and technical education. It gave no attention to the pressures that mass instruction in reading and writing would inevitably exert on the higher levels of education, nor to the many new skill requirements that would grow out of the development program itself, including the training of professionals, technicians, and others at the university level.

The Ad Hoc Committee agreed with the general proposed strategy of development, but suggested the injection of more realism in plan particulars. It pointed out that a number of the targets for farm production were too ambitious. It also pointed out that it would be extremely difficult to achieve the ambitious goals set for industry. The delays which had been experienced in expanding oil refinery output and output of the steel industry were indicative of the kinds of problems to be encountered. The committee suggested that the greatest opportunity in the near future might lie in the more traditional industries, rather than in the newer industries.

The committee also noted that, although taxes were increasing under the tax reform of 1960, the plan projections of public revenues were overestimated, and public expenditures were running substantially above the projected totals for such outlays. (For example, governmental expenditures in 1961 exceeded the program estimates for that year by 18 per cent.) The effort to increase taxes would have to be intensified considerably if the targets set in the plan were to be achieved.

None of these problems seemed unsolvable. Nor were the difficulties unanticipated. Colombia had very little experience in planning. It was facing great economic difficulties and undergoing a basic change in its economic structure. The governmental organization could not be expected to be at a desired level of proficiency, as it had traditionally been geared to provide only limited public services.

Parallel to the evaluation of the Colombian plan by the Ad Hoc Committee, the AID and the IDB carried out detailed evaluations of their own and began to work out specific arrangements for speeding up the flow of external assistance to Colombia.[6] At the same time, the World Bank, which had also carried out a parallel study on Colombia's investment program, could substantially increase its loans for a series of specific projects. The World Bank also organized a "Consultive Group" on Colombia to encourage loans from a number of the more developed countries and to get some coordination among the lenders.

From 1961 to 1967, more than $1 billion was committed to Colombia by all the lending agencies — excluding the IMF and the U.S. Treasury (see Table A-1). The commitment peaks were in 1962 ($179 million) and 1967 ($186 million), with U.S. funds providing more than half of the total. Disbursements, of course, lagged behind commitments, and the amortization of loans reduced the net transfers of funds to Colombia to still more modest

[6] Since there were no significant differences in approach and analyses among these various evaluating groups, it is not possible to say whether the report of the Ad Hoc Committee had any particular impact on the donor agencies. The conclusions of the Committee probably did have some small impact on the Colombian government through the personal contacts of members of the Committee with top officials of the government.

Table A–1. Long-Term Loan Commitments to Colombia from the United States and International Agencies

(million dollars)

Agency	1961	1962	1963	1964	1965	1966	1967	Total
IBRD	41.5	50.0	73.8	45.0	–	41.7	25.0	277.0
IDA	19.5	–	–	–	–	–	–	19.5
IDB:								
Social Progress Trust Fund	–	31.4	–	8.1	10.5	–	–	50.0
Ordinary and special operations	12.4	4.2	24.9	–	27.2	27.4	35.6	131.7
Eximbank	54.4	3.4	2.5	22.0	3.9	3.4	25.5	115.1
AID	20.0	89.9	26.2	65.9	65.0	16.5	100.0	383.5
Food for Peace[a]	–	–	6.9	13.4	–	16.9	–	37.2
Total	147.8	178.9	134.3	154.4	106.6	105.9	186.1	1,014.0

Source: Estimates prepared by staff of IBRD.

a Includes all Food for Peace operations under Titles I and IV of P.L. 480.

Table A-2. External Financial Assistance to Colombia from the United States and International Agencies

(million dollars)

Item	1961	1962	1963	1964	1965	1966	1967
Disbursements:							
IBRD	23.9	27.6	41.2	52.7	29.3	31.8	32.8
IDA	–	3.9	2.5	2.0	2.3	2.5	4.8
IDB:	0.1	7.0	13.2	21.2	10.0	19.0	22.9
Social Progress Trust Fund	–	(3.8)	(9.5)	(6.8)	(5.1)	(7.2)	(8.2)
Special operations	–	(0.1)	(0.3)	(0.1)	(0.5)	(0.5)	(5.1)
Ordinary operations	(0.1)	(3.1)	(3.4)	(14.3)	(4.4)	(11.3)	(9.6)
AID:	1.5	37.8	59.7	38.1	40.7	58.2	58.6
Projects	(1.5)	(7.8)	(9.1)	(6.5)	(12.8)	(14.5)	(33.4)
Programs	–	(30.0)	(50.6)	(31.6)	(27.9)	(43.7)	(25.2)
Eximbank	57.1	3.2	5.1	0.6	10.7	10.4	15.7
Food for Peace[a]	10.0	5.2	4.7	1.2	2.4	1.6	3.6
U.S. Treasury	–	–	–	–	–	10.8	–
IMF	65.0	7.5	48.5	7.5	–	37.8	71.4
Total disbursements	157.6	92.2	174.9	123.3	95.4	172.1	209.8
Amortizations:							
IBRD	7.4	5.6	6.9	5.2	6.2	10.2	11.4
IDB:	–	–	0.2	0.8	0.7	2.0	3.4
Social Progress Trust Fund	–	–	(0.2)	(0.3)	(0.4)	(0.5)	(n.a.)
Special operations	–	–	–	–	–	–	(n.a.)
Ordinary operations	–	–	–	(0.5)	(0.3)	(1.5)	(n.a.)
AID	–	–	0.1	0.1	0.2	0.2	3.1
Eximbank	31.9	20.2	25.5	23.5	36.8	28.8	13.8
U.S. Treasury	–	–	–	20.0	24.0	33.5	5.2
IMF	–	–	–	–	–	–	37.5
Total amortizations	39.3	25.8	32.7	49.6	67.9	74.7	74.4
Net inflow	118.3	66.4	142.2	73.7	27.5	97.4	135.4

n.a.—Not available.

a Includes all Food for Peace operations under Titles I and IV of P.L.

Source: Pan American Union.

sums (Table A–2), but even the net totals put Colombia among the top recipients of Alliance loans.

The results can best be analyzed in terms of the periods covering the two administrations that followed the administration of Alberto Lleras Camargo during which the initial development plan was prepared.

RESULTS OBTAINED

During 1962–65, the gross domestic product in Colombia increased at an annual rate of about 4.4 per cent. The plan's goal was 5.6 per cent. This meant that, with an annual increase of over 3 per cent in population, instead of achieving the Alliance goal of an annual per capita increase of 2.5 per cent in GDP, the per capita increases over the period were somewhat less than 1.5 per cent per year. Given the unequal distribution of income, large sectors of the population were probably no better off at the end of the period than at the beginning.

The goal of 5.6 per cent was to be achieved by increasing coffee exports slightly each year in accord with the anticipated growth of population in the consuming countries, and by increasing the production of the more promising crops. However, during the first part of this plan period, export earnings hit new low levels, reflecting the lowest coffee prices in well over a decade. Unfortunately, even in the second half of the period, when coffee prices had bounced back to higher levels (for example, they averaged 48.8 cents in 1964 compared to 39.5 cents in 1963), the stimulus to the economy was not enough to produce a strong forward movement.

The government responded to the drop in export earnings by tightening import controls. The cutbacks on intermediate and capital goods imports limited industrial expansion and kept industrial employment relatively stagnant.

While the plan called for sizable increases in tax revenues and public sector savings, taxes increased only modestly. The group in power was clearly not prepared to increase the tax burden. At the same time, governmental expenditures rose sharply, and large deficits were incurred. This created inflationary pressures, and these, in turn, credit restrictions, further restricting private sector expansion.

Consequently, public and private investment fell far short of plan targets. During the four-year period, government investment was some 85 per cent of the target overall, while private investment was only 75 per cent of the target which had been set in the plan.

Most disappointing of all was the relatively small amount by which non-coffee exports increased. There are explanations, of course. It is extremely hard to go from a one crop economy — with all the institutions geared to the production, financing, and marketing of that crop — to a modern, diversified, highly productive type of agriculture. To compound the difficulties, Colombia did not have a realistic exchange policy geared to promoting the nation's exports, and the peso continued to be overvalued in spite of a devaluation in 1963.

Overall, it would seem that during the 1962–65 period Colombia made relatively little progress in bringing about the major economic changes called for by its ambitious plan or in pushing the country's development forward.[7]

---

[7] However, during this period two developments with importance for the future took place: (1) the pacification of most of the countryside, and (2) the creation of the

DEFICIENCIES IN GOVERNMENT POLICY

The lack of progress was due in large part to governmental policies that fell short of what the circumstances required. In early 1962, when Colombia first submitted its plan and applied for international assistance, most observers associated with the Alliance saw Colombia as a potential showcase of the Alliance. All the ingredients necessary for moving ahead rapidly seemed to be present. With Lleras Camargo as President, the country was ably led. A sensible development program had been devised. Needed instrumentalities for carrying programs forward were taking shape. There was a widespread, if low-keyed, enthusiasm for moving ahead.

But no sooner had the plan been evaluated and arrangements made for substantially increasing international financial assistance than a new government came into office. Even before the changeover in government, however, serious doubts began to arise, particularly with regard to fiscal policy and inability to retain confidence in the peso. It was, of course, politically difficult to raise taxes and undertake a devaluation just before an election.

The new President, Guillermo Leon Valencia, a charming man from a prominent family of the Colombian landed aristocracy, quickly demonstrated that he had little taste for running a complicated and ambitious development program, and even less for enforcing a disciplined monetary and fiscal policy. Shortly after the new government took over, economic pressures resulting from the sharp fall in coffee prices created many short-run fiscal and monetary problems.

The Ad Hoc Committee and the various international agencies urged the Colombian government to devalue the peso. The new Finance Minister, Carlos Sanz de Santamaría, presented the Colombian Congress with a package plan calling for devaluation and a wide variety of new taxes designed to provide revenues of more than 400 million pesos. At about the same time, Colombia got a standby agreement from the International Monetary Fund for $57.5 million and a little later a "program loan" (essentially, a balance-of-payments loan) of $60 million from the United States.

The Congress agreed to the devaluation, but unfortunately it delayed increasing taxes and it authorized a 40 per cent increase in the minimum wage accompanied by wage increases of 25 per cent in the private sector and 30 per cent in the public sector. The inflationary effect was aggravated by a provision requiring that wages be reviewed at the end of each six-month period in which the cost of living increased by more than 5 per cent. Because wages and salaries represent a very high percentage of government expenditures, this Congressional action jeopardized the budget surplus in the current account. Colombian technicians had expected an increase in prices of about 7 per cent after devaluation, but the cost-of-living index, which had been relatively stable until the end of 1962, rose 30 per cent in 1963. Meanwhile, because of inaction on tax increases, the government was nearly bankrupt. It was as much as a year behind in paying some of its bills.

Thus, any potential usefulness of devaluation was quickly dissipated by the wage and fiscal policies. The continued deficit in Colombia's international trade, inflation and resulting speculation, as well as increasingly severe import

Monetary Board to have a governmental institution running Colombia's monetary policy, which, until early 1964, was the responsibility of the Banco de la República, an institution owned and managed by the private banks.

restrictions, all combined to throw the development program entirely out of kilter. Foreign trade credit dried up, and the economy stagnated.

In an effort to prevent further economic and monetary deterioration, during the latter part of 1964 and in 1965 the various international agencies and AID joined forces in bringing very strong pressures to bear on the Colombian government to proceed with devaluation and to undertake policies aimed at reducing inflationary pressures. As part of the pressure on the government to undertake at least a minimum program of economic rationality, the U.S. government, the IMF, and the World Bank withheld loans to Colombia for nearly eighteen months after July 1964. The Colombian government responded to the pressures by undertaking a limited type of devaluation (the introduction of a second foreign exchange rate for imports in addition to the existing official rate), by cutting back on import licensing, and by increasing taxes. These measures seemed to have a favorable impact on the economy, and economic conditions began to improve.[8]

How is the Alliance performance in Colombia during 1962–65 to be evaluated? It seems evident that external financial assistance played a key role not only in meeting the large balance-of-payments deficits but in bolstering the economy. Balance of payments deficits on current account reached high levels in each of the plan years except the last: $165 million in 1962, $132 million in 1963, $150 million in 1964, and some $20 million in 1965. During the same years, net external financing from the United States and the Washington-based international agencies amounted to $66 million, $142 million, $74 million, and $27.5 million. Without such transfers of capital, the economy would have gone into a tailspin.

It is not easy to determine whether "holding the line" is an adequate rationale for substantial external loans. It seems entirely possible that without Alliance assistance, the economy could have fallen into chaos. Given the tradition of violence, this could, in turn, have degenerated into very destructive social and civil strife.

Actually, various useful basic measures were taken during the four-year period. Roads and electric power and other infrastructure were expanded. A broad new plan for education was prepared so that a more substantial base for improvements in human resources could be anticipated. Production increased in several important agricultural crops and in several of the manufacturing industries. Thus, there were elements of progress that could be usefully built upon should a serious developmental effort be undertaken.

THE GOVERNMENT OF LLERAS RESTREPO

By the time that the new Liberal government headed by Carlos Lleras Restrepo, a distinguished economist and long-time leader of the Liberal Party, came into office in August, 1966, the economic policies of the previous administration had begun to achieve some monetary stability to restore business confidence. The Lleras government immediately strengthened efforts to wipe out inflationary financing of the budget and to extend the trade liberalization program. It undertook to re-establish a meaningful planning effort, with a

[8] During 1964, the cost-of-living index rose only about 8.5 per cent over the level of 1963; however, a buildup of inflationary pressures continued, and in 1965 and 1966 prices rose again, registering increases of 14 per cent and 13 per cent.

strengthened planning office, and to carry out a vigorous program to achieve domestic austerity, diversification of exports from coffee into other foreign-exchange earners like cattle, petrochemicals and other processed products, and strong support for the regional economic integration effort.

Hardly had the new administration come into office than coffee prices dropped sharply (5 cents a pound in six months). The result was a 10 per cent drop in foreign exchange earnings and an immediate foreign exchange crisis. Imports continued to increase as a result of the freer exchange and trade policies that had been instituted.

A mission of the International Monetary Fund in November 1966 recommended a substantial devaluation to stimulate exports, by raising the peso income of exporters, and to restrict imports, by increasing their cost in domestic currency. The President refused to accept the Fund's recommendation, which was presented as a precondition to the granting of an IMF loan, and instead imposed strict exchange controls, froze foreign exchange holdings in Colombia, and postponed some commercial payments. The government argued that a devaluation without careful controls on capital movements would only raise internal prices rapidly and break the wage line that the President had been able to maintain in personal negotiations with unions.

The United States government, which had earmarked $100 million for Colombia, largely for a "program loan," now declared that no U.S. loans would be extended until an exchange policy agreement had been worked out between the IMF and the Colombian government. At the same time, the World Bank said that loans would be withheld until such an agreement had been reached. While in a way this seemed to be a repeat performance on the part of the international lending agencies, paralleling the pressures brought on the previous Colombian government to achieve a disciplined fiscal and monetary policy, in substance the situation was different. It was not a question of a lack of fiscal discipline as earlier, but of the lending agencies adopting a strategy for solving immediate economic problems that the President considered not in keeping with political realities.

After several months, a compromise solution was agreed on, and new loans were negotiated. By the end of 1966, the Colombian planners had worked out a substantial development program, involving gross external financing of some $240 million, with the major emphasis on investment in agriculture (including ten "agrarian-reform" irrigation districts), in highways, in low-cost housing, and in schools and hospitals. The plans were in tune with the Alliance emphasis on social reforms and self-help.

ECONOMIC PERFORMANCE IN 1966 AND 1967

The overall performance of the Colombian economy has improved since the end of 1965. Gross domestic product increased by about 5.3 per cent during 1966, and by 4.5 per cent in 1967, when a major stabilization effort was under way and another drop in coffee prices caused exchange difficulties. In response to the stabilization program, price increases were kept to 8 per cent in 1967, a substantial improvement over the preceding years.

In the two years after it came to power the government of Lleras Restrepo in the main followed policies to accelerate the rate of economic and social development within a framework of financial stability. In general, the government's fiscal, wage, and monetary policies were designed to reduce the rate of inflation, and a flexible exchange rate policy tended to move the rate gradually to a more realistic level. Progress was also made in preparing development projects for external financing. In response to these achievements, financial aid from the international lending agencies increased substantially. Gross disbursements from official loans increased from about $95 million in 1965 to about $172 million in 1966 and $210 million in 1967 (see Table A–2).

At the same time, domestic resources were mobilized in greater amounts to match the inflow of foreign aid. Current revenues increased at a fairly rapid rate after the introduction of new taxes and administrative measures designed to avoid evasion.[9] Simultaneously, the government imposed strict controls on current expenditures. These fiscal policies resulted in substantial increases in public savings during 1966 and 1967, a particularly impressive accomplishment when compared with the chronic deficit situation of the previous decade.

The government also improved the management of public enterprises. In addition, the Planning Department was reorganized, and sector planning made considerable progress. The improvement in project preparation and the seriousness of the development drive resulted in substantial increases in public investments. During 1967 public investments accounted for about 45 per cent of total fixed investments, compared with about 36 per cent for the period 1962–66.

Production of crops other than coffee was the principal recipient of resources from the government. In addition, many steps were taken to stimulate increased exports. These included: the establishment of an export development fund financed by a 1.5 per cent tax on all imports, the establishment of a new tax credit of 15 per cent for "minor" exports (other than coffee and petroleum), the extension of the "Plan Vallejo" system which allows duty-free imports of materials to be used in producing exports, the offer of improved credit terms to exporters, and encouragement of regional economic integration to increase intraregional trade. If these incentives and efforts prove effective, Colombia could be on its way to a solution of some of its most troublesome economic problems.

There was some, although limited, progress in the area of social development. Financial and legal measures were taken to speed up land redistribution, especially through irrigation and colonization schemes. The government's financial contribution to INCORA, the land reform agency, in 1967 was 42 per cent above the 1966 level, the previous high. During 1963–67, some 63,000 farmers were settled, most of them during the latter part of the period.[10] On the other hand, efforts to revitalize rural self-help measures had limited success. The community development programs (*Acción Communal*) operated effectively in some rural areas, but in other areas they were taken over or suppressed by the local political bosses and proved ineffective. Colombia's governmental structure is decentralized to an unusual degree. There are more than 800 local governments, usually lacking adequate financial or administrative resources and frequently dominated by local political leaders who are uninterested in or hostile to social and economic development. The task of developing democratic attitudes and institutions in the rural areas of Colombia is a long and arduous one. The Lleras government has shown an awareness of the problem, but has not yet developed new approaches to it.

[9] Tax revenues increased from 10.6 per cent of GDP in 1965 to 12.6 per cent in 1966. While still a low level even by Latin American standards, this was an important achievement.

[10] INCORA, *Informe de Actividades*, January 1968.

Progress in population control is complicated by the opposition of the Catholic hierarchy. In July, 1967, a declaration by the Colombian bishops specifically condemned intra-uterine devices and birth control pills, and criticized the activities of the Colombian Association of Medical Faculties and the Colombian Family Planning Association. Nevertheless, the government continued its family planning activities. It contributed funds to the Medical Faculties for instruction courses in family planning, but the opposition forced it to move cautiously.

The government also gave high priority to expanding and improving the education system. The education program includes expanded basic training and advanced study for teachers, continuing review of curricula, the use of modern communications media such as radio and television, and emphasis on medium-level technical education to provide training for 80,000 skilled workers each year during the four years of its duration. Illustrative of the magnitude of the education program is the fact that in 1967, largely through double-shifting, facilities for the enrollment of 300,000 additional pupils were provided. In addition, the school construction program made room for an additional 100,000 pupils.

To sum up, the economic policies initiated by the government during 1966 and 1967 were generally well suited to the developmental needs of the country. The overall economic development effort was strengthened by a far-reaching administrative reform (approved in July 1968) and a stabilization effort that promised to lay the foundation for achieving higher rates of economic growth in the near future.

In the main, Colombia has had a developmental-minded leadership, dedicated to carrying through basic social and economic reforms in the face of some of the most vigorous internal opposition in Latin America. It is evident that if a government of the present caliber cannot make progress, the future for Latin America may be bleak indeed. The loans that have been granted by the donor agencies have helped to hold back serious decline of Colombia's economy and helped to sustain a moderate rate of growth in 1966 and 1967.

Chile

The capacity of the Alliance to adapt to changes in governments and governmental policies, as well as to respond effectively where political rigidities block reform-minded governments, has been tested as severely in Chile as in Colombia. The extraordinary difficulties of carrying out reform programs in Latin America are highlighted by the experience of the Christian Democratic government of President Eduardo Frei Montalva, which came into office in November, 1964, with goals closely paralleling those of the Alliance.

BACKGROUND AND UNDERLYING DIFFICULTIES

Chile ranges from about 45 miles to 225 miles in width and stretches 2,600 miles from the parched nitrate sands of the Atacama Desert bordering Peru in the North to the desolate point of Cape Horn in the South. In 1967 it had a population of about 9 million. Chile has a relatively high level of industrialization compared with most of Latin America and fairly advanced systems of education and social security that were achieved within a framework of political democracy and stability.

But Chile's past has not been tranquil, and the past is reflected in the problems that beset the country today: a succession of periods of rapid economic expansion alternating with periods of relative stagnation; prices and wages that have chased each other in an inflationary round dance; an agricultural sector that is far less advanced than other major economic sectors; and an inequitable distribution of wealth and income.

For many years, Chile's main export and principal industry was sodium nitrate. But German chemists developed a synthetic nitrate during World War I, and by the mid-1920's Chile's nitrate industry went into a serious decline.

Fortunately, the mining and export of copper, of which Chile has an estimated 22 per cent of the world indicated and measured reserves,[11] provided a strong substitute for nitrates and essentially played the same vital role in furthering the country's economic growth. Copper exports already had some importance during the nineteenth century, but it was not until the 1920's that they became the prime mover of the Chilean economy. For the past forty years copper has brought Chile more than half of its foreign exchange. But earnings from copper have been subject to violent ups and downs. A sharp drop in the demand and a precipitous price decline in the early 1930's reduced Chile's export earnings to only 30 per cent of their previous levels. The reduction paralyzed the Chilean economy.

This situation led to an attempt to diversify domestic production by establishing a development corporation, Corporación de Fomento de la Producción (CORFO), which, under outstanding leadership, was successful in setting up new and sizable industries such as steel and petroleum. The enterprises created for petroleum production and electric power have remained government-owned, but many other enterprises were either sold to private interests, or established by the private sector with the backing of CORFO.

But Chile was not able to maintain the momentum of this industrialization effort, largely designed for import substitution. Opportunities for import substitution were limited by the small size of the Chilean market and skewed income. Many of the new industries had to be protected by extremely high tariffs. Also, while import substitution policies caused a significant change in the composition of imports, as elsewhere in Latin America, they did not reduce imports either in absolute amounts or in relation to gross domestic product. Imports increased at the rate of almost 6 per cent per year during the decade that preceded the establishment of the Alliance for Progress. With exports growing at a relatively much slower rate (around 2 per cent per year), serious balance-of-payment difficulties followed.

Chilean development was also retarded by the extremely low level of savings throughout the fifties. Gross national saving actually declined in relation to GDP, and in 1960 amounted to only 13.5 per cent. This was mainly a result of the disincentive effects of inflation, as well as the heavy burden on the economy of an extensive social security system and of fringe benefits granted to workers over the years. Demands for more consumer goods by all sectors of the population became political imperatives and, in the absence of a substantial growth of production, only a small proportion of gross national product was devoted to investment.

Generations of reliance on a rich mineral resources base had contributed to relative neglect of farming by the government. In the twenties Chile had

---

[11] Computed from data in U.S. Department of the Interior, Bureau of Mines, *Mineral Facts and Problems, 1965 Edition*, p. 283.

been a food exporter, but a generation later as a result of neglect and mis-management of agriculture the country had to rely on food imports. Agricul-tural products were purchased from abroad at an annual cost in foreign ex-change of some $125 to $150 million. One-fourth of Chile's work force was engaged in agriculture, which accounted for only one-eighth of the gross domestic product. In the fifteen years before 1960, while population increased by roughly 2.7 per cent per annum, agricultural production (including live-stock, timber, and fishing) rose at a yearly rate of only 2.4 per cent, resulting in a noticeable drop in the per capita domestic supply of food and agricul-tural raw materials.

During the 1950's, all these factors combined — limitation of import substitution opportunities in the manufacturing sector, insufficient growth of exports, stagnation of agriculture, and a low rate of savings — produced a decline in the rate of growth of the Chilean economy. In 1960 the gross domestic product per capita was lower than it had been in 1953, 1957, and 1958. The same factors, together with a large government deficit financed largely by the Central Bank, induced a revival of secular inflationary trends: during the 1950–60 period consumer prices increased 21-fold and money supply 26-fold.

In the early 1960's, the traditional economic problems were aggravated by a series of natural disasters, including the most severe earthquake in recent history. The conservative government then in power, burdened by these emer-gencies and the additional expenditures they entailed, found it increasingly difficult to make any serious efforts toward economic development or to fight inflation. An ever-growing proportion of the politically conscious public felt an urgent need for reform. As a result, Chile took a sharp turn to the Left. In a sense, this was similar to developments in the 1930's when, under the pressure of great economic difficulties, a Popular Front government (including com-munists and socialists) had been formed. The 1964 presidential election was for all practical purposes a contest between two political parties, both advo-cating radical reform programs and both with unusually strong popular backing — the FRAP, a socialist-communist coalition having the support of the most powerful labor unions including the highly paid copper workers, and the Christian Democrats, who were able to bring together a coalition of middle-class groups and a large proportion of the almost forgotten urban and rural lower-income workers. The former's candidate was Salvador Allende and the latter's Eduardo Frei. In the election, Frei also had the unofficial backing of the traditional rightist and middle-of-the-road parties which, with no chance of their own victory, considered him the lesser of two evils.

Eduardo Frei became president of Chile under the banner of a reform movement, advocating far-reaching economic, social, and political change. His basic planks — agrarian reform, tax reform, an anti-inflation program, "Chileanization" of the copper mines, and major progress in education, health, and community development — were, in essence, a specific embodi-ment of the broad Alliance for Progress principles. The fact that the Christian Democratic victory is probably the only example of a group reaching power with the central purpose of converting into reality the aspirations underlying the Alliance concept is a measure of the difficulty of bringing about the "peaceful revolution" President Kennedy hoped would transform Latin America.

PRE-FREI ALLIANCE ASSISTANCE

The conservative government that preceded Frei's had not been particularly keen on planning, but nevertheless it had encouraged CORFO to complete the ten-year development plan on which it had been working for some
period of time. In 1961 the Chilean government officially "adopted" the plan
which called for annual investments of more than $600 million for the period
1963–65, to rise gradually to almost $1 billion from 1966 to 1970 when invest-
ment would reach 21 per cent of GDP. It was estimated that about $250
million of external financing would be required annually during 1963–65, and
about $200 million annually for the period 1966–70. The government re-
quested the World Bank to examine its program as background for projected
loan applications, and early in 1962 asked the Committee of Nine for an
evaluation by an ad hoc group in order to make Chile eligible for Alliance
funds.

Both the World Bank and the Ad Hoc Committee found the overall goals
of the Chilean plan to be reasonable, and most of the public investment program to be soundly based. However, both evaluating groups also found
serious shortcomings: agricultural development had not received sufficient
attention; the plan lacked an adequate program of land reform; its social development program was weak, and the projected tax reform fell short of
what was needed.

With 9 per cent of the farms occupying 70 per cent of the arable land and
a large proportion of all farms producing far below their potential, there was
obviously an urgent need for thorough land reform. It was equally evident that
the government in power was not likely to carry through such reform. However, the government was determined to achieve the financial stability it considered a prerequisite to growth. This was something to build on, and the
U.S. government committed substantial sums to Chile's development program, $166 million in 1961, $148 million in 1962, $98 million in 1963, and
$260 million in 1964. During the same period, the World Bank and the IDB
provided a series of loans for specific projects, and the IMF standby agreements also contributed to the solution of balance-of-payments problems (see
Table A–3).

But even these generous funds, among the highest Alliance outlays per
capita in Latin America, could not produce a vigorous move forward when
economic and social policies were timid and conservative.

THE FREI PROGRAM AND ALLIANCE ASSISTANCE

The developmental program proposed by the Frei government and the
difficulties the government has had in implementing it provide valuable
insights into the Latin American condition, and tell us a good bit about the
problems and potential of the Alliance. The elements of the program, while
obviously geared specifically to the Chilean situation, delineate more sharply
than any general commentary how modern, progressive Latin Americans
view their problems.

The main objectives of the Frei program were: (1) increasing copper
production to 1.2 million metric tons a year by 1970, a proportionate increase
in exports, and the "Chileanization" — meaning a greater national participation — of the copper holdings; (2) diversification of export industries; (3) an

Table A-3. External Financial Assistance to Chile from the United States and International Agencies

(million dollars)

	1961	1962	1963	1964	1965	1966	1967
Commitments:							
U.S. AID	111.9	42.4	51.1	152.5	16.4	93.2	50.5
U.S. Eximbank	12.0	46.4	17.0	19.6	3.6	2.6	279.3ª
Food for Peace	8.6	24.3	8.1	30.6	25.8	8.1	20.7
U.S. Treasury	33.8	34.7	21.5	57.7	46.7	10.9	–
IDB	18.6	20.6	17.4	12.9	27.7	45.5	36.5
IBRD	25.0	–	24.0	–	7.2	60.0	–
IMF	75.0	–	40.0	25.0	36.0	40.0	–
Total	284.9	168.4	179.1	298.3	163.4	260.3	387.0
Disbursements:							
U.S. AID	49.3	67.2	75.4	76.9	55.7	66.0	55.5
U.S. Eximbank	59.7	21.4	34.6	16.0	26.6	9.5	13.8
Food for Peace	27.2	12.3	19.2	21.2	16.4	11.2	7.4
U.S. Treasury	27.4	14.2	33.5	43.6	44.9	17.1	4.6
IDB	0.4	3.5	9.8	22.3	16.0	16.6	14.9
IBRD group	6.2	10.1	12.6	6.3	15.1	18.4	17.4
IMF	76.0	–	40.0	20.0	36.0	30.0	10.0
Total	246.2	128.7	225.1	206.3	210.7	168.8	123.6
Amortizations:							
U.S. AID	–	1.9	2.2	1.7	1.1	1.2	2.9
U.S. Eximbank	13.5	17.0	20.5	22.7	24.8	25.6	25.4
U.S. Treasury	–	–	0.1	4.2	12.6	22.2	–
IDB	–	–	0.2	0.5	1.3	3.4	4.5
IBRD group	3.2	3.5	5.3	5.1	5.2	5.2	5.6
IMF	16.7	12.7	–	10.0	37.0	44.8	25.2
Total	33.4	35.1	28.3	44.2	82.0	102.4	63.6
Net inflow (disbursements minus amortizations)	212.8	93.6	196.8	162.1	128.7	66.4	60.0

ª The major part consists of Eximbank financing of the mixed copper

Sources: Official agencies for 1961–66 and preliminary estimates of the

increase in agricultural production, and agrarian reform; (4) an increase in national consumption combined with an income redistribution policy; (5) the curbing of inflation; (6) the organizing of local groups through a community development, popular promotion program; and (7) an increase in social expenditures, mainly for education, health, and housing.

The program called for an annual increase in GDP of 5 per cent during 1965–67 and 6 per cent during 1968–70 and for a sharp increase in savings and investment. Balance-of-payments projections indicated a need for external financing of $200 million in 1965, $285 million in 1966, and $350 million in 1967.

1. *The Copper Agreements.* The government's program recognized that copper would continue to be the mainstay of the economy for a long time to come. While only the extreme Left political groups had advocated outright nationalization of the copper mines, there had always been a widespread sentiment for a larger national participation in the copper industry, even though many realized that a large amount of outside investment was needed to achieve a high level of production and that the production and marketing know-how of the foreign firms was an asset to the nation.

The Frei government proposed a specific solution, the "Chileanization of copper." The government would buy into the various mine holdings to increase investments in copper production. Thus, Chile would be acquiring a sizable proportion of future assets rather than merely taking over existing assets. The people would acquire a vested interest in high production and high efficiency and, in a sense, share in the returns from the production and marketing know-how of the foreign firms.

The Frei government undertook negotiations with the three major U.S. firms immediately after coming into office and announced agreements shortly thereafter. Psychologically, it was a good moment to negotiate with the copper companies because they had been worried by the relatively good election showing of the leftist coalition dedicated to the total nationalization of the copper companies.

Preliminary agreements were signed with the companies in December, 1964. The goal was to increase the production of the mines by about 70 per cent by 1972, and to refine most of the copper in Chile, with a participation of the government in the ownership of the copper concerns, and a closer connection between government policies and the production and sales practices of the companies.

Approval of the new copper policy by the Chilean Congress was needed before the final agreements with the companies could be signed and put into effect. The Frei Administration ran into trouble with the Senate, in which the opposition parties held the majority, largely because of the way the terms of the agreements became known. Before the details of the agreements could be announced in Chile, the terms worked out by the companies and Chilean government officials had to be approved by the corporate shareholders in the United States. To get such approval, company officials described the terms as highly favorable. At the same time, the State Department, to ward off possible anti-Frei sentiment because of "nationalization" of American-owned mines, also described the agreements as essentially favorable to the companies. Reports of the statements by the U.S. government and company officials made headlines in the Chilean newspapers. The political opposition, claiming a "sell out," held out against the new copper law.

After almost a year and a half of political maneuvering, the new copper law was finally approved in April, 1966. The delay made it impossible to achieve the original goals by 1970, and postponed the planned increase in production by two years. The situation in 1966, as seen in that year's CIAP Country Review, is summarized in Table A-4.

By early 1967, the Government Copper Corporation had signed the final agreements with the Kennecott Copper Company, the Anaconda Copper Company, and the Cerro de Pasco Copper Corporation. The agreement signed with Kennecott provided for government participation of 51 per cent in a new joint company, Sociedad Minera El Teniente, to replace the Kennecott subsidiary, the Braden Copper Company. The initial value of the government share would amount to $80 million, which would be financed with a loan from Kennecott. The $216 million required for the planned expansion — an increase in installed capacity from 180,000 metric tons to 290,000 within five years (see Table A-4) — was to be covered by $20 million of Chilean government loans to the new company and by loans from Kennecott and external

Table A-4.   Chile: Copper Expansion under Frei Government Plans, 1966–72

Mining concerns	Productive capacity			Invest-ment required (million US dollars)	Govern-ment share in ownership
	1966	Expansion	1972		
	(thousand metric tons)				*(per cent)*
Large concerns:					
Anaconda	384	163	547	151	–
Chuquicamata	(293)	(61)	(354)[a]	(80)	–
El Salvador	(91)	(–)	(91)[a]	(20)	–
Exotica	(–)	(102)	(102)	(51)	25
New exploratory company	–	–	–	n.a.	49
Braden-El Teniente	181	109	290	216[b]	51
Cerro-Rio Blanco	–	61	61	89[b]	25
Total, large concerns	565	333	898	456[c]	
Small- and medium-sized concerns	135	65	200	115[c,d]	n.a.
Total mining productive capacity	690	408	1,098	571[c]	
Total refinery capacity	410	140[e]	650[e]		

n.a.—Not available.

[a] Later information placed the estimate for Chuquicamata at 510,000 tons and El Salvador at 110,000 tons.

[b] Later estimates placed the figures at $230 million and $91 million respectively.

[c] Includes the cost of expansion in refinery capacity.

[d] Preliminary estimate of the Chilean authorities.

[e] CIAP Secretariat projections.

Source: Pan American Union, *El Esfuerzo Interno y las Necesidades de Financiamiento Externo para el Desarrollo de Chile*, Doc. CIAP/46, mimeographed (Washington, D.C., 1966).

financial institutions. Later estimates raised the total costs of the project to $230 million, financed by loans from the Chilean government ($27.5 million), Kennecott ($92.7 million) and the Export-Import Bank ($110.1 million). Under the terms of the agreement with Anaconda, the Chilean government acquired 25 per cent of the new Exotica mining plant, and 49 per cent of a new exploratory company. Anaconda was to raise the capacity of its Chuquicamata mine and also increase the total refinery capacity in Chuquicamata and El Salvador from 235,000 to 380,000 metric tons a year. The agreement with Cerro Corporation provided for a government share of 25 per cent in the ownership of the Rio Blanco mine.

All the agreements provided for a reduction of the tax burden on the copper companies, which had sharply increased over the last fifteen years. At the same time, the government plans also envisaged a substantial increase in the production of the small and medium-sized mining concerns and of the government-owned copper refinery.

The cost of the total expansion program was estimated at some $570 million, including expenditures on new houses for workers, hospitals, and other social projects.

Looked at from a distance, out of the heat of local politics, these arrangements appear as a significant advance both in an extremely sensitive area of U.S.-Latin American relations and in the management of the natural resources of less developed countries.

2. *Inflation and the Efforts to Curb It.* Chile has long suffered from inflation. The Frei government decided, on taking office, that stabilization was an essential ingredient in moving the economy forward. After a long and heated controversy, the government announced its intention to attempt to achieve stability over a four-year period. The cost-of-living index had shown an annual increase in prices of around 45 per cent in 1963 and 39 per cent in 1964. The announced plan was to try to limit price rises to 25 per cent in the first year (1965), 15 per cent in 1966, and 10 per cent in 1967, and to achieve stability in 1968.

The announced effort of the government brought the problems of inflation in a country like Chile into sharp focus. A host of institutional arrangements had evolved which tended to reinforce inflationary pressures in the economic system. For example, the government granted salary adjustments to public employees at the beginning of each year, generally increasing them in proportion to the loss of purchasing power caused by inflation in the preceding year, thus assuring an equal amount of inflation in the following year. Private wage rates followed the government's.

The Frei administration took a relatively bold approach to the inflation problem. It did not treat it in an isolated way as was customary in Latin America, but linked its stabilization policy to general economic development and to an effort to redistribute national income in favor of urban workers and the agricultural sector. This policy soon began to show positive results. However, the government was not able to get the Congress to pass the measures needed to *sustain* a successful anti-inflation drive.

In 1965, as the government had intended, agricultural prices rose at a substantially higher rate than the prices of industrial and imported goods.[12]

___

[12] The cost-of-living index (based mainly on the typical expenditure pattern of low-income urban workers) showed a rise of 26 per cent. The wholesale price index increased between 25 and 30 per cent (the exact figure depending on the relative

Table A-5.   Indicators of Progress in Chile, 1960–67

Indicator	1960	1964	1965	1966	1967[a]
Per-capita GDP annual rate of increase[b]	—[c]	1.4	3.5	3.4	1.0
Rate of increase of total GDP	—[c]	3.9	6.0	5.9	3.5
Minimum wages in real terms (1960 = 100)[d]	100.0	88.5	95.0	97.5	97.4
National savings (as percentage of GDP)	13.5	14.7	16.8	16.7	16.1
Tax revenues (as percentage of GDP)	14.7	13.5	17.2	20.6	21.4
Exports of goods and services (in millions of current dollars)	588.7	691.0	784.6	992.4	997.2
Agricultural production (1960 = 100)	100	100	97	104	107
Industrial production (1960 = 100)	100	137	150	164	168
Cost of living (annual increase in %)	–	38.4	25.9	17.0	21.9
Wage index (annual increase in %)	–	45.3	47.9	38.4	35.4
Public investment in housing (constant escudos of 1966)	376.6	420.2	586.5	665.8	649.8
Agricultural imports (in millions of current dollars)	n.a.	157.7	153.5	172.3	172.7
Total imports of goods (in millions of current dollars)	559.1	623.5	628.3	784.5	824.2

n.a.—Not available.

[a] Preliminary estimates.

[b] GDP figures have been thoroughly revised by the Chilean government since the 1967 Pan American Union report used here was released.

[c] Not given because of substantial changes in bases of calculation.

[d] Based on monthly figures in Santiago.

Source: Pan American Union reports, including *Evolución Reciente de la Economía de América Latina*, Doc. CIES/1138 (1967).

During that year the gross domestic product increased 6 per cent, and most of that increase was devoted to a rise in real wages. The workers' total real income increased some 10 per cent, while the growth of profits and other non-worker income was only 2 per cent. The cost of living, which had increased by 26 per cent in 1965, rose by 17 per cent in 1966. These increases exceeded the targets set by the government, but still represented a major holding operation under Chilean conditions.

The government's policy was helped by some favorable and largely unexpected developments, such as the rise of world copper prices, but performance in 1965 and 1966 was still noteworthy. Chile dampened inflation while at the same time maintaining a healthy overall economic growth rate (6 per cent rise in GDP in 1965 and 1966); reversed the irrational policy of holding down the relative prices of agriculture in a country that badly needed substantial improvements in farm and livestock production; and raised real wages and the share of the workers in national income.

The government's efforts to encourage a downward trend of inflation into 1967 foundered on a combination of developments: unusually high private sector wage increases (more than 30 per cent for organized workers), adverse

weights given to its different components) while agricultural wholesale prices increased about 36 per cent. Data from: Jorge Cauas, "Stabilization Policy: the Chilean Case," Paper presented at the Conference on Key Problems of Economic Policy in Latin America, University of Chicago, November, 1966.

weather conditions which resulted in severe crop shortages, and lower prices for copper. The cost-of-living index rose by 22 per cent in 1967 in comparison with 17 per cent in 1966. The Frei administration hoped to reconcile the diverse economic and social objectives of its policies through a program of forced savings that would be put into effect in January 1968. But political opposition killed the proposal. An alternative program to hold down inflationary pressure through certain wage increase controls and austerity measures was proposed early in 1968 by the able finance minister, Raúl Saez, formerly coordinator of the Alliance's Committee of Nine, but it was emasculated in the legislature. The Frei administration also has had difficulty in getting support for the desired tax increases, and will probably continue to have difficulty in achieving the high-priority objective of stabilization.

3. *Promoción Popular*. The Frei government, largely through the Christian Democratic party, has launched a concerted community development effort called *Promoción Popular*. The effort is focused on the organization of a variety of community groups, including neighborhood groups, centers for mothers, athletic clubs, cultural centers, organizations of artisans, and organizations of unorganized workers (not more than 10 per cent of the workers of Chile were organized when Frei took office).[13] The success of this effort and the manner in which it is used may have a great deal to do with the future of democratic development in Chile. It is a beginning of no small importance.

4. *Social Reform*. As could be expected of a progressive government, the Frei administration has placed major emphasis on social reforms. The government, immediately upon coming into office, vigorously pushed tax collections in the face of a long-standing tradition of tax avoidance by wealthy groups. A capital levy was imposed, applied to real estate, automobiles, stocks and assets held abroad. Based on a new assessment survey completed in 1965, property taxes in two years increased two or three times over what they were before Frei (although by modern standards they are still extremely low in relation to the low tax rates). Tax revenues rose from 13.5 per cent of GDP in 1964 to 17.2 per cent in 1965, 20.6 per cent in 1966, and about 21 per cent in 1967, making possible a surplus in the current fiscal account in 1965, 1966, and 1967.

The government also moved ahead vigorously in the realm of social development. In education a campaign was launched to register the children of school age who were out of school, and 186,000 were registered in 1965 against an average of 40,000 a year in recent years. As the government was unable to build schoolrooms quickly enough to provide for all the new needs, empty buildings of all kinds were turned into schoolhouses. While this expedient had its shortcomings, the government was able to keep its campaign promises and to make the whole nation conscious of the importance of an education for all schoolchildren.

The health program was expanded not only through existing hospitals and clinics but also by putting into service mobile units that could bring medical care to the "marginal and rural sectors." Free medical care was increased. The housing program similarly was speeded up. In two years, 87,000 permanent homes and 48,000 emergency dwellings were built.

---

[13] This situation is likely to have changed as a result of legislation permitting establishment of unions among farm workers.

Plans for a vigorous land reform program, however, got off to a very slow start. They were opposed by the Right as far too radical and by the Left as not going far enough. A complex agrarian reform bill, that provided for expropriation of poorly developed lands, to be paid for by long-term government bonds, and for taking productive land under special circumstances, immediately ran into political trouble.[14] To make progress it was essential to pass a constitutional amendment that would permit expropriation of private land without immediate cash settlement, and to pass the reform law. These measures were not passed until July 1967. Carrying out of the law is likely to meet strong opposition. For some time, probably, only a minority of landless rural labor will be helped. But the Frei government is committed politically to a far-reaching land reform, and is convinced that it is an essential element in modernizing the economy and the society.

POLITICAL PROBLEMS

In the legislature, the Right and Left have joined forces at various times to delay passage of critical elements of the Frei program, such as the bill implementing the copper agreements, the law to provide power to reorganize the administrative structure, the stabilization program, and agrarian reform. The Rightist group could force the President to yield points on the agrarian bill, which the socialist-communist faction supported, in return for the government yielding points on the copper law. A new Chilean President is usually granted broad reorganizational powers when he takes office, but President Frei was not. He has had to work each administrative reorganization through the Senate in a separate bill.

EXTERNAL ASSISTANCE

Even with the relatively vigorous internal effort made by the Frei administration to mobilize resources, the ambitious governmental program needed substantial financial assistance from outside. Governmental estimates, presented in 1965 to CIAP and the Committee of Nine, indicated that the government hoped to raise 11 per cent of the required resources from foreign sources. The gross requirements for foreign financial assistance for the years from 1966 to 1970 were estimated at some $637 million, with a greater concentration in the earlier years.

The United States government and the international lending agencies responded quickly to the call of the Chilean government for financial assistance, and both commitments and disbursements have been substantial in recent years. Commitments totaled about $163 million in 1965, $260 million in 1966, and $387 million in 1967 (see Table A–3). U.S. AID has provided a series of program loans to finance all aspects of the government's program without reference to specific projects. Certain problems associated with these loans have arisen for both the lender and the borrowing country. Frei has expressed dissatisfaction with the program loans on the grounds that the

[14] Major provisions are that privately owned irrigation land in excess of 200 acres may be subject to expropriation, as may be abandoned or "poorly exploited" land. The test of poor exploitation depends on such factors as the amount of land under cultivation, amount of fertilizer used, capital invested, and whether certain laws have been observed.

quarterly AID reviews were infringing on his government's right to make its own policy, and he turned down one proffered program loan on this ground. The U.S. reply has been that the conditions are merely the specification of the Chilean government's own policy positions. However, to achieve better coherence, in 1967 U.S. lending was divided between the program loans and separate sector loans in agriculture and education.

There is little doubt that the external financial support provided by the U.S. government and the international lending agencies was very important in permitting Chile to move ahead with some assurance in its large program of investments, its stabilization policy, and its efforts to promote social progress. Balance-of-payments figures are very dull and abstract when put against the picture of a vigorous social revolution under way. Yet it is hard to emerge from a close examination of the Chilean situation without concluding that the Chilean "revolution" would be in very bad trouble without substantial external assistance.

INDEX